HAUNTED
TOWN
HALLS

HAUNTED TOWN HALLS

FROM THE CASE FILES OF
THE SEARCHER GROUP

Peter J. Roe

QUAGMIRE PRESS

The Publisher: Quagmire Press Ltd.
Website: www.quagmirepress.com

Library and Archives Canada Cataloguing in Publication
Roe, Peter J., 1969-, author
    Haunted town halls / Peter J. Roe.

Issued in print and electronic formats.
ISBN 978-1-926695-44-0 (softcover).--ISBN 978-1-926695-45-7 (ePub)

    1. Haunted places--Ontario. 2. City halls--Ontario. 3. Ghosts--Ontario. I. Title.

BF1472.C3R64 2018   133.109713   C2018-904676-7
                                                C2018-904677-5

Project Director: Hank Boer
Project Editor: Sheila Cooke
Cover Image: Peter J. Roe; Goja1/Thinkstock; Roksana Bashyrova/Thinkstock
Photos: all photos are courtesy Peter J. Roe except: pp. 27, 68, 247 courtesy Toronto Public Library; p. 67 courtesy Shannon Ringrose; p. 92 courtesy Whitchurch-Stouffville Museum; p. 93 courtesy Ashley Chappell; pp. 192, 195, 200, 202 courtesy James McCulloch; pp. 210, 211a&b courtesy Richard Palmisano; p. 218 courtesy Barry Schneider; p. 240 courtesy John Lackey, Town of Orangeville; pp. 260, 262, 266 courtesy Kent B. Armstrong.

Produced with the assistance of the Government of Alberta.

Alberta Government

PC: 32

What are ghosts if not the hope that love continues beyond our ordinary senses? If ghosts are a delusion, then let me be deluded.

—Amy Tan

Dedication

~

To the spirits that linger within and who visit
the edifices described in the following pages,
I dedicate this book.

~

Table of Contents

Foreword

~

G hosts and history are synonymous. Academia would have you believe history by its very nature is dead—it has come and gone.

To most people, history is studied no differently than scientists might study a cadaver. They will tell you that history is 20/20 hindsight. But to a paranormal investigator, history is alive and well in the hearts and minds of the spirits who remain; these spirits still have stories to tell and can provide us valuable lessons and deep insights.

This is why we investigate spirits.

The social complexity of people—living or dead—is the same. We find it natural to do what we are used to doing, so when looking for spirits of the dead, there is no better avenue than going back to our grass roots: the town hall.

In their time, these magnificent buildings were the embodiment of community; they were (and still are) places where people gathered to attain news, discuss important matters or simply to celebrate. No wonder they had a powerful draw to people who worked there or relied on the social interaction that they provided. Spirits are social, and as such they wish to return to these places for many different reasons, as you will see demonstrated in this book.

As investigators looking for evidence of life after death, making contact is (to put it mildly) no easy task. The challenges are many. For one, we don't know why a spirit would manifest itself to an unsuspecting bystander and yet hide from an investigator.

We don't know why certain human brains (such as those belonging to legitimate psychic mediums) receive frequencies from the top end of the spectrum ten times clearer than the majority of us. Is there a way to create an unobstructed portal through which we may openly communicate with the human energies that have departed the physical from our side of the "veil"?

These are some of the questions we continually seek to answer as well as many more wherever we investigate, including the town halls you are about to explore with us. I hope you enjoy delving into history from this perspective as much as I do.

–Richard Palmisano, Paranormal Investigator,
Theorist, Author, Founder of The Searcher Group

Preface

The supernatural is the natural not yet understood.
                                    –Elbert (Green) Hubbard

E arth is haunted the world over. Ghosts do exist. We have heard them, we have seen them, we have been physically touched and we have been emotionally affected by them. This fact must be understood or nothing marvellous will come of the true-life encounters you are about to read.

Contrary to societal norms, these people are not dead. It is high time they are accepted as being very much alive, simply existing as a form of energy outside the physical that we who are still a part of the limited, five-sense realm are striving to understand (before we ourselves join them, someday).

The idea of returning from death in a form seemingly more freeing than a physical one appealed to me from a very early age. Most paranormal enthusiasts who dedicate themselves to pursue answers in this field attribute their own origins similarly; others decide to explore this subject after a supernatural encounter of their own.

It matters not whether someone believes in the existence of ghosts. There are many things in the universe that exist without the help of anyone's belief. The Searcher Group is not in business to convince people that ghosts exist, nor is our team out to upset people's personal beliefs or preconceptions. We are simply trying to understand what to expect after physical death before we experience it ourselves. What we do is share what we've learned with those who are truly interested.

When we investigate, we are privileged to meet history in the form of those who have gone before us. Our hope is that we will gain intelligence during our outings that will ultimately aid humankind in creating a means with which we can communicate freely and openly with the spirits of the deceased. Should we happen to expand, enlighten or even open a few minds, bring comfort to those seeking answers or even provide an ear for those with experiences of their own to share, then I believe there is definite worth to this line of work.

I am sincerely grateful to those people in spirit form who have shared pieces of their stories during our brief time as guests among them and those who have inadvertently given reason for a reader to shiver. I wish nothing but peace and contentment for all the souls out there, wandering through or comfortably residing within the spaces The Searcher Group has been invited to visit.

Acknowledgements

*Sometimes you will do good and not get an acknowledge-
ment for it. Don't let that dishearten you; the world is
a better place with your good deeds.*

–Gugu Mona

~

Any labour of love that produces work such as this is
rarely ever accomplished by one person alone, and
Haunted Town Halls is most certainly no exception.

A gigantic thank you to Hank Boer of Quagmire Press, and
to my exceptional editor, Sheila Cooke. Your input and support
has made shaping my first published book an education and an
absolute joy.

To my immediate family—wife Kim and daughter Libby—
I am grateful that you continue to endure the time this kind of
work requires me to be away from home with such understand-
ing. Thank you for allowing me to pursue this after-hours passion and for lending me your ears when I am bursting to share
the latest news of our ghost adventures.

To my parents, brothers, uncles, aunts, nieces, nephews, in-
laws and extended family, thank you too for your support for
me doing what I've been doing over the years—crazy and dan-
gerous as it often sounds, I'm sure.

An extra-special acknowledgement goes to John Roe for taking the time to wade through my information-heavy manuscript and apply his own professional journalistic skills with invaluable editing suggestions.

Thank you to the many guests and observers who accompanied us on our excursions all over southwestern Ontario. Your participation and input has been greatly appreciated. I thank you for bringing your sense of wonder, intrigue, open-mindedness and (especially) skepticism along for the ride. This work is not as glamorous as reality TV shows make it out to be, but nevertheless I hope you found your particular experiences with us in the field enlightening.

Heartfelt appreciation goes to Kathleen Dills (Halton Hills), Scott Wilson and John Lackey (Orangeville) for sharing your remembrances of key—and very personal—figures revealed throughout the course of our town hall visits.

I want to thank all the "heritage nuts" and passionate historians alike who have contributed their valuable time and resources researching those nuggets of information gleaned from the hundreds of cases The Searcher Group has had the privilege to take on, including: Pat Farley, Gerda Potzel, John Mark Rowe, Alicia K. (Halton Hills); Fred Robbins (Whitchurch-Stouffville); Fay McCrea, Judy Lewis, Jim Dodds, Kim Blacklock (Caledon); Wayne Townsend, Laura Camilleri (Orangeville); and Bruce Bell, Richard Fiennes-Clinton (Toronto).

An extra nod of serious appreciation goes to Cynthia Fisher and the super-helpful staff comprising the Toronto Reference Library's Humanities and Social Sciences Department. Our team cannot underscore enough the importance of libraries as sources of priceless information. Kids, put down the cell phone and game console—go explore a library today!

Speaking of libraries, thank you to the digital archives of the Toronto Public Library for the use of vintage photographs of the Acton Town Hall, Caledon Township Hall, City Hall No. 1 and the Waterford Old Town Hall. Similarly, thank you Ashley Chappell and the Whitchurch-Stouffville Museum for generously supplying the images of the former Stouffville Town Hall, Kent B. Armstrong for your phenomenal candids taken of the team in Toronto, Shannon Ringrose of the Norfolk Public Library (current Waterford Town Hall photo) and Barry Schneider for permission to reprint his postcard image of the Orangeville Town Hall exterior.

A special note of thanks goes to Barb Cole, Tony Harris and Michelle Sarson, formerly of Wellington County Paranormal Investigations (WCPI). Exploring this field is a huge undertaking, and your willingness to assist me in Orangeville underscores the importance of co-operation—not competition—between serious paranormal investigators.

A tremendous amount of thanks must go to every property owner, manager and steering committee maintaining each location we were permitted to investigate. Our team is continuously grateful to be trusted to explore your historic buildings safely and respectfully. Likewise it's a privilege to be entrusted with your personal experiences, especially the ones that began with, "This will sound crazy, but..." Ultimately, I hope the tales told within these pages do your townships service and your histories justice.

To the members and friends of The Searcher Group, past and present, I am truly indebted for all of your hard work going into the field and exploring new territory together before reliving it all over again while tirelessly transcribing hours and hours of recorded data. Then—buoyed by the results—you are inspired to return to the trenches to continue doing what we do. Thank you Joanna Buonopane for sharing your psychic talents, James McCulloch for your eagerness going into each assignment, David Roe for bringing professionalism when you were available to help, Victoria Jaime for your keen observational senses and enthusiasm, Michele Hewer for revealing things we otherwise would never know and John Mullan for turning theory and ideas into actual gadgets and equipment we use in the field.

A very special mention of appreciation goes to Paul Palmisano and the amazing discoveries he makes after dedicating himself to reviewing hundreds of hours of both video and audio surveillance data—sometimes for jobs he was unable to be on-site for. Between analysis and using humour to lighten even the scariest of situations, Paul's contribution to the team continues to prove invaluable as we move forward in our efforts to some-day bridge the gulf between planes of existence.

My largest debt of gratitude is reserved for Richard Palmisano, founder and director of The Searcher Group. Richard encouraged me to pursue the idea concerning a Searcher Group "Town Hall Tour" and suggested I be the one to write about it. As a seasoned author who has documented his studies and built ground-breaking theory regarding the nature of paranormal phenomena over many years, Richard's input throughout the formation of this book was inestimable. I hope this publication serves as a worthy addition to The Searcher Group atheneum.

～

Introduction

Why Town Halls?

What is history if we're not talking about the dead and past events?

–Richard Palmisano

～

ince 1979, The Searcher Group has endeavoured to estab-lish meaningful communication with people who have gone before us. By doing so, we not only unearth frag-ments of long-forgotten history and stories waiting to be told, but we also gain intelligence regarding the age-old mystery of life after death and how that plays into our experience as human beings—inside and outside of the physical.

What are commonly referred to as "ghosts" or "spirits" are people who, for whatever reason, choose to continue dwelling in private residences or public buildings after they have shed their corporeal bodies. From our observations, it appears that many of these entities are quite content going about their own affairs as if life (as we know and call it) never ended. Meanwhile, there are ghosts of people who have unfinished business they feel needs resolving and still others with information to share or a story they wish to tell. Some of these people continue to exist apparently without realizing or accepting that their physical selves have expired.

Those familiar with paranormal investigation will no doubt recognize that common locations for ghostly activity are typically focused within areas where profound human emotion have transpired en masse. Jails, courthouses, hospitals, sanatoriums, asylums and even theatres have proven to be reliable settings for intense investigations for good reason; these places have borne witness to the most heightened expressions of human emotion.

So why would a town hall be haunted? In order to answer that question, we must recall why town halls were erected in the first place. Town halls acted as beacons for the community; they were often visually discernible from neighbouring structures. To newcomers and denizens alike, town halls stood as proud, physical representations of the district, and many structures that were erected around them were architecturally complementary in design. A community with a town hall was likely one that was prosperous, and the elaborateness of the building tended to reflect that fact.

Throughout history, generations of people have converged on town halls. Inside those doors, untold numbers of meetings determined the fates and fortunes of their communities; visitors and locals alike stood up and made impassioned arguments and pleas for their politics, beliefs—even their lives. Many town halls housed council chambers, police stations, jail cells and courtrooms, and some even maintained gallows. Town halls are where scores of people went to register their businesses and land claims, file complaints, pay taxes and report births and deaths. Town halls also played host to weddings, memorials, dances, markets, cinemas, music concerts and live performance artists.

Emotion is a powerful source of energy. Over three decades of observation in the field, The Searcher Group has discovered that not only do we maintain emotion and memory after physical death, but also that emotion is the key to motivating spirit manifestation in the physical realm. There are as many different displays of spiritual manifestation as there are intensities and ranges of emotion. When we truly appreciate their significance coupled with the spectrum of emotions these buildings have witnessed, is it any wonder that former or present-day town halls continue to attract, welcome and house ghostly members of the community?

Town halls are among the few standing historical touchstones you can visit for free. If you are fortunate enough to steal a moment to yourself inside one, try to quiet your mind, ask to speak with someone in an otherwise empty room and truly listen. Based on the adventures you are about to read, I'm confident a representative of the past will do their best to introduce themselves to you. For your sake, I hope they're friendly.

Investigation Explanation

In a balanced organization, working towards a common objective, there is success.

–Arthur Helps

Unlike most teams that are content with exploring a location over the course of one night, The Searcher Group specializes in conducting investigations over several visits in order to maximize the potential for data gleaned in the field.

As briefly as I can summarize it, our standard investigation procedure looks like this:

1. Preliminary tour: select members tour the location during daylight hours to identify pitfalls, areas of possible safety concern and to record baseline readings of the atmosphere using thermometers and EMF meters. Drafts, creaks, heat sources and exterior traffic patterns native to the location are also noted.

2. First investigation: the team saturates the location with surveillance equipment, both audio and audio/visual, often leaving the equipment for long periods of time while the team waits outside the property. While on the property, respectful, experimental EVP sessions are conducted to evoke some type of response.

If data analysis reveals EVPs containing names, dates or historical information and/or visual media captures recognizable human-like forms, then permission is sought for...

3. Subsequent investigations: the team invites a pre-tested clairvoyant onto the property to tour the site with them. The medium is not made aware of the location, nor is fed any piece of information pertaining to the location prior to their arrival. In the course of their visit, should the clairvoyant make successful contact and provide the team with names, dates and/or messages to convey on behalf of a spirit, the team may arrange a subsequent investigation with another medium to attempt to gain identical (and possibly new) information.

4. Research: finally, the team turns its attention to history, researching archives, newspapers and phone directories, consulting historians and interviewing living witnesses. This research may result in the discovery of historical facts that corroborate both hard data and clairvoyant-gleaned information.

This painstaking, labour-intensive process often produces what The Searcher Group deems irrefutable evidence of life-after-death existence. For a closed-minded skeptic to dismiss three pieces of verification (two of which would be admitted in a court of law) should call into question the mindset of the skeptic, not the proof provided by the investigator.

In the case of this Town Hall Tour, because windows of opportunity proved scarce and time was of the essence, the team conducted its preliminary tour and employed the services of its clairvoyant beginning with the inaugural investigations. Because these were short-term visits, time and resources limited the depth and breadth of historical research that we are known for conducting on longer-term cases. Between individual results and efforts to work with (often little) information gleaned from each location, some cases include more intriguing results than others.

Glossary of Para-phernalia and Terms

Dana Barrett: What is that thing you're doing?
Dr. Peter Venkman: It's technical. It's one of our little toys.
—Ghostbusters (1984)

Throughout our Town Hall Tour you will encounter several references to various kinds of equipment The Searcher Group employs in the course of its adventures. The following are definitions of some of these instruments as well as terminology common to the field of paranormal investigation.

Devil's Toy Box: a cube consisting of six square mirrors assembled so that each of the interior surfaces reflects the others. Based on the Victorian belief that souls become trapped within the confines of a mirror after death of the physical body, this cube is designed to contain—and trap—spirit energy once it has entered it (theoretically).

Digital voice recorder: a compact, hand-held electronic audio recording device. The ability of these devices to capture audio frequencies emitted below the range of ordinary human perception makes this invaluable piece of equipment a staple.

Disembodied voices (DV): vocal remarks not uttered by anyone physically present that are heard in the moment, either through a parabolic microphone or by the unaided ear. Our team has found that these are very rare occurrences; rarer still is recording a DV simultaneously.

Electromagnetic field (EMF) detector (Gauss meter, KII meter): typically used in the construction trade to measure electromagnetic energy on job sites. Based on the theory that ghosts are composed of or emit electromagnetic energy, these meters are staples in the paranormal field as well.

Electromagnetic interference (EMI): a form of staccato static that is sometimes captured by our digital recorders; its pattern closely resembles the rhythm of someone speaking (at varying intensities). While we cannot rule out the possibility these may be incoming cell phone frequencies, we also cannot ignore the fact that they are only recorded in seeming response to an investigator's question or statement while in the field.

Electromagnetic (E) probe: a proximity meter developed and manufactured by Colorado Para-Tech designed to detect electromagnetic energy; flashing lights and/or loud beeping sounds alert the investigators to the fact that an anomalous source of electromagnetic energy has interacted with this device.

Electromagnetic (EM) pump: a box that emits a strong field of electromagnetic energy. In theory, the EM pump provides energy an entity may absorb or draw from in order to manifest and be heard, felt or seen by the investigators. This device is especially useful as an alternate source of power to "feed" spirit people at locations where unexplainable battery drainage in cameras and recorders occurs at extraordinarily rapid rates.

Electronic voice phenomena (EVP): unexplainable voices that are captured on audio-recording devices (analog, digital hand-held or cameras). The Searcher Group has been fortunate to capture voices ranging from whispers to shouts, single words to whole sentences—even vocal expressions of dogs, cats and horses. *See also* EVP session.

EVP session: a formal period during an investigation when the team remains stationary and quiet, asking questions of the spirits aloud, leaving 10–20 seconds of silence between questions or statements in hopes of capturing a disembodied response either in the moment or on a recording device running in tandem.

Full spectrum (FS) camera: a digital camera designed to capture images using the full light spectrum.

Gauss meter: *see* Electromagnetic field (EMF) detector.

Infrared (IR) camera: a digital camera designed to capture still or moving images using the infrared light spectrum.

KII meter: *see* Electromagnetic field (EMF) detector.

Motion detector: an "electronic eye" that emits sound and/or lights up when movement within range is recognized. These are especially handy when deployed in view of surveillance cameras or digital recorders in instances when investigators are absent from the immediate vicinity.

Natural tri-field meter: a particularly sensitive EMF-detecting device designed to ignore human-made sources of electromagnetic radiation (i.e., lights, computers, power boxes) and instead detect subtle energy emitted by the living and even from within rocks and crystals.

Ovilus III: affectionately dubbed the "Paranormal Speak 'n' Spell" by The Searcher Group, the Ovilus III operates as a portable dictionary from which it is believed spirits can choose words they wish to use and "say" them electronically through a built-in speaker. Field experiments using the Ovilus have proven interesting but largely inconclusive.

Parabolic microphone: a large parabolic dish focuses sound waves into a sensitive microphone, significantly enhancing ordinary environmental acoustics. Several disembodied voices have been heard through headphones connected to this device during our investigations.

Pendulum: a centuries-old instrument (a small weight hanging plumb from a chain) used in ghost investigations as a means of real-time communication with spirit energies.

Powder trap: first implemented by original "ghost hunter" Harry Price (1881–1948), this inexpensive and low-tech experiment involves leaving an even layer of flour or baby powder in a controlled area of suspected paranormal traffic.

P-SB7: *see* Spirit Box.

Real-time EVP (RT-EVP) recorder: a digital recorder designed specifically for paranormal investigation to capture sound emitted at 15 Hz, far below ordinary human hearing range.

Spirit Box/P-SB7: sometimes referred to as a "Ghost Box," these experimental instruments are used for direct communication during an investigation. Essentially modified digital radios, these devices have the ability to sweep through every available local AM or FM band of radio frequencies anywhere from 100–350 milliseconds a pass. Sensible words or phrases coming from the speaker ought to be impossible, but The Searcher Group has recorded many words—sometimes whole phrases—that are often in direct response to questions being asked by the investigators. Although far from perfect, the Spirit Box is considered by many in the investigative field to be the closest means of communicating with spirits of the deceased in real time by electronic means.

Spirit Communications Device No. 1 (SCD-1): an application created by Steve Huff of Huff Paranormal for use in conjunction with a computer program/mobile device to mimic the function of a Spirit Box or P-SB7. *See also* Spirit Box/P-SB7.

Surveillance camera: the workhorse of the team's gear. Deploying standard and infrared video cameras at every investigation has garnered several instances of not only visual evidence, but audible as well. The camera's extremely sensitive microphone system is capable of capturing EVP sometimes missed by our digital recorders. All data is recorded directly onto a DVD for easy (digital) storage and analysis.

Tagging: the act of distinguishing sound or physical events that occur during an investigation as having no paranormal basis for the benefit of data analysis.

Trigger object: a physical item placed in an allegedly haunted environment, designed to provoke a disembodied response (audible or physical) while being monitored by a surveillance camera or digital recorder. For example, a Pop-O-Matic die roller or wind chimes.

Chapter 1

Acton Town Hall Centre: First Investigation

Where we live makes an impression on us. Perhaps psychically it also influences us. So there is a natural desire to learn the history of one's home.

—Frank Touby

~

Team: Richard, Paul, Joanna, James, Peter
Guest: Alicia

Standing, key in hand, shivering in the brisk wind of a particularly cold March evening before the towering, red brick edifice at Willow and Bower streets, it was difficult to contain my excitement for the night ahead. As a resident of nearby Georgetown, I'd marvelled at several references in the local press to "Jimmy," the ghostly caretaker of the Acton Town Hall Centre. The idea that several people who had worked inside the building reported multiple incidences of phantom footfalls and anonymous doorbell-ringing was intriguing enough, but the fact that the administrators of the former town hall publicly admitted to these occurrences surprised and impressed me even more.

Acton Town Hall, present day

The decision to erect a town hall in Acton was born in 1881 out of a need for a building to host both the local council and community events. After much political debate and a couple of major construction setbacks, the town hall opened its doors to welcome the council and public in March 1883. According to the Acton Town Hall Centre website, the spacious auditorium on the second floor hosted high school performances, meetings, dances, minstrel shows and amateur dramatics while the first floor "housed the police station, council chamber [for 91 years], library and practice room for the Acton Citizens' band."

In 1974, the regional government moved to Georgetown; three years later, the building was deemed unfit to remain standing. Fortunately, grassroots organizations formed to save the former town hall from demolition and undertook years of painstaking renovations and restorations, beginning in 1982. Four years later, social service agencies moved into office spaces on the first floor, and in 1988, the Acton Town Hall Centre became the first designated historic building in Halton Hills. Today the space is once again hosting business and social events as it did over a century ago.

But it is the earlier years that are of immediate interest, in particular regarding a gentleman named James Robertson. Jimmy was a local son who fought in World War I with the 4th Battalion, 1st Infantry Brigade. After the war, he returned to Acton and took up lodging in one of the jail cells, becoming a self-appointed watchman of the Acton Town Hall for several years. In late 1945 he was credited with saving the town hall from burning down by running several buckets of water from the ground floor up to the auditorium to douse the flames erupting from a heating unit before the local fire brigade arrived on the scene.

It wasn't long after Jimmy's death in 1960 that reports of ghostly activity began. At least two paranormal investigation teams and a news reporter have tried their luck at capturing evidence of Jimmy for themselves—the latter with high hopes of producing a sensational news article to coincide with Hallowe'en. Collectively, the various participants claimed to have felt presences and heard unexplainable creaks, bangs and indecipherable whispering, yet none of the perceived phenomena could be definitively attributed to the ghost of Jimmy.

Acton Town Hall, early days

Now, in March 2014, it was The Searcher Group's turn to try.

Because James, our newest investigator, had displayed signs of psychic sensitivity over the course of his first year with the team, I intentionally withheld all mention of Jimmy the ghost and the history of this location from both he and Joanna, our team medium. It was important to observe—uninfluenced by suggestion—how each person would react as they explored this reputedly paranormally active site for the first time.

Rounding out this evening's crew was a young, aspiring local writer. Alicia had answered a recruitment advertisement weeks before and expressed her proclivity for historical research. This night marked her introduction to the team and was in effect a test to gauge her interest in becoming a full-fledged member.

~

We let ourselves into the Citizens' Hall, erected in 2013 abutting the south side of the original town hall structure, and hurriedly transported our equipment inside. The hall was well-lit and open-aired. Several staircases and an elevator near the centre of the room made the auditorium on the second floor easily accessible. Deciding to make Citizens' Hall our base camp, we placed our things on several small tables.

Once warmed, the team began to tour the property, paying close attention to Joanna and the psychic sensations she was picking up on. We began with Willow Hall on the second floor, accessed by twin stairwells rising in opposite directions, east and west.

Inside the beautifully restored auditorium, the team spread out and gravitated toward the open stage and the spacious Bower Room beyond. We were quick to note the echoing nature of the acoustics—a good thing for a performer or orator on the stage, but a challenge for investigators listening for subtle changes in sound frequencies.

We walked past the stage, explored the concession stand and entered the Mill Meeting Room—a large coat-check area that doubled as a green room for stage performers, as evidenced by several full-length mirrors lining two of the walls. As we moved about carefully, Joanna said she was picking up the residual energy of a person who had only just been in each room ahead of us and had disappeared, leaving behind a trail of energy. I likened this idea to that of a psychic jet stream.

"Most of the activity is going to be below," said Joanna. "That's where they are right now."

The team continued the walkabout downstairs, where—opposite the main entrance doors of the town hall—we found a pair of jail cells with their original cumbersome, barred doors intact. The first cell was seemingly empty, save for a metal bed frame dangling from one wall and a small window sill opposite, close to the floor. The second cell had been converted into a kitchenette to accommodate the staff of a nearby office, which was locked and inaccessible to the team.

When asked about the presence she had sensed from upstairs, Joanna declared that a male figure was actively eluding the team as we explored the premises.

It was time to break out the gear.

Leaving an activated digital recorder behind in Citizens' Hall, Richard, Paul and I moved the surveillance cameras into the old town hall and proceeded to deploy three of them. Camera 1, on the main floor, faced both jail cells from the main entrance/foyer. Camera 2, in Willow Hall, covered the auditorium, the stage, a podium and a piano in the northeast corner. We positioned Camera 3 to shoot the entire length of the Mill Meeting Room at the east side of the building.

Seconds after Richard and Paul left the first surveillance system monitoring the jail cells, the camera microphone picked up the first electronic voice phenomenon (EVP) of the evening...

EVP: [Male] Get back!

...followed by a heavy bang close to the camera and rattling of dishes in the cell kitchenette before all went quiet.

⌒

While the surveillance cameras were being deployed, James followed Joanna with his digital recorder, prepared to log her psychic impressions as she sensed them. Almost immediately their attention turned to the northwest corner of Willow Hall, where an upturned table and several stacks of chairs were stored.

It was behind this table that Joanna sensed a frightened young male, cowering. "A tween," Joanna shared. "About twelve [years old]. Tall and slim, dark pants, a white shirt and suspenders, so I'm thinking that puts him way back [in time]."

Joanna continued, speaking to the entity. "Can you give us your name?" she asked, pausing to listen for a reply. "I feel it starts with a J. Don't be afraid; you are safe with us. Can you tell me why you're still here? He's looking down; he's not making eye contact; he's scared. He doesn't trust people."

Remarkably, without any foreknowledge of the name of Acton Town Hall's alleged spirit, James asked, "So you think his name is Jim or Jimmy?"

"Something like that," acknowledged Joanna. "I feel like he has been on his own for a long time, even when he was alive. I feel like he used to work around here."

"Jimmy, did you help take care of the building?" inquired James.

"He nodded to say that he did help with the building," Joanna acknowledged. "He assisted. There was an adult here that kind of took him in."

James continued to press for information. "Have you been here a long time as a custodian?" he asked.

"I'm just getting nods. I'm not getting any words. He's just not comfortable."

"Can you tell me how long you worked here?"

"Until he passed away. I think he passed away as a child."

"Jimmy, were you an orphan here?"

Joanna paused. "I get a nod, yes. I don't think he lived here, but this is where he spent most of his time."

James suddenly felt a brief wave of nausea. At the same time, his digital recorder captured an EVP.

EVP: [Male; faint] Hey.

James wondered if he had bumped into somebody other than Jimmy, causing the temporary nausea. If there was a second spirit present, was this person the reason Jimmy wasn't comfortable conversing freely with Joanna?

~

While Richard and Paul finished deploying Camera 3 in the Mill Meeting Room, back inside the auditorium, Camera 2 captured another disembodied voice.

EVP: [Male] Harry!

After a short pause and no response came another call.

EVP: [Same male] Deanna!

Again, no response was recorded.

~

Alicia and I stepped onto the second-floor mezzanine of Citizens' Hall, where I had placed two equipment cases. I retrieved an EMF meter as we conversed and moved toward the railing overlooking our base camp below.

Alicia glanced downward and then quickly looked back a second time. "Is someone there?" she asked, startled.

I followed her gaze down toward the building entrance; I saw no sign of anyone in the area.

Alicia then described seeing a dark, male figure on the ground floor looking up at us in the brief moment she had turned her glance away from me.

Recalling I had left one of my digital recorders activated in the vicinity, I encouraged whoever was present to speak into it and convey a message. If that person attempted to oblige, the recorder did not pick it up.

~

James and Joanna walked toward the back of the stage where an original councillor's chair stood, resembling an imposing throne. Joanna sensed that Jimmy liked both the chair and performing on stage.

Moving toward the concession stand, Joanna shared that Jimmy enjoyed this area the most; that he was behind the bar at that moment and even claimed to have served drinks to patrons of the hall. Inside the Mill Meeting Room, Joanna sensed Jimmy liked to use the mirrors to watch himself perform.

Continuing to the top-most mezzanine just inside Citizens' Hall, James and Joanna were joined by Alicia, who informed them of her possible sighting of a male figure below. Just then, Joanna remarked that Jimmy was fascinated by the equipment inside the nearby cases while simultaneously, James began to feel pressure on the fingers of his right hand followed by a slight pull, as if someone was urging him closer to the equipment cases.

Although Joanna was sure Jimmy was nowhere near James, she did not discount the possibility that Jimmy was attempting physical contact from elsewhere. Almost immediately James felt pressure midway along his right forearm, strong enough that he could feel a throbbing sensation. Slowly his right arm began to rise above one of the open equipment cases as if directed. Joanna reported that the equipment was definitely piquing Jimmy's interest.

James used this opportunity to describe the gear in order to gain Jimmy's trust. Extracting the Pop-O-Matic bubble from one of the cases, James demonstrated how to roll the die inside it. "All you do is push down on it," said James, depressing then releasing the clear plastic bubble with a pop, "and it pops up and it shows the number one. So you can yell out, 'One!'"

James pressed the plastic dome again. As the small cube settled, an excited response was captured on James' recorder.

EVP: [Female or child] Two!

The die did not land as the unseen watcher had anticipated. "Now it shows the number four and you can yell out, 'Four!'" James said animatedly.

Before any further responses could be recorded, the demonstration came to a halt as Richard stepped onto the mezzanine to speak to the trio gathered there.

⁓

With the surveillance cameras in full operation, the team assembled to tour the building together, beginning with the second-floor auditorium. As everyone moved about Willow Hall, some climbed the stage and took turns sitting in the councillor's chair.

As the unblinking eye of Camera 2 monitored the team, its sensitive microphone captured a male's voice addressing someone unseen.

EVP: [Male; firm] You have to put that away.

There was no response.

EVP: [Same male] Will you listen to me?

Again, no response was recorded.

EVP: [Same male; frustrated] Patrick!

Unaware of the disembodied voice behind us, the team pressed onward touring the Bower Room behind the stage. We disappeared from Camera 2's sight as we made our way past the concession area toward the Mill Meeting Room. Once everyone was out of view, the camera captured the sound of wood creaking underfoot as someone unseen crossed the auditorium floor, their purpose and direction unknown.

Meanwhile, in the jail cells below, a digital recorder left inside the first cell picked up various wooden knocking sounds, ticks, taps and a loud thump that resembled a footfall in the immediate vicinity. Someone seemed to be restless, which became more evident as the team made its way down the twin set of staircases leading from the auditorium.

EVP: [Male; frantic] Carol! Get down, now!

The male in the jail cell area needn't have panicked. The group did not approach but instead turned back into Citizens' Hall for a much-needed break. Paul had brought some food to munch on while we discussed our initial impressions of the investigation.

Following the break, the team set off again, this time beginning at the east side of Citizens' Hall where a framed oil portrait of a young woman named Dorothy Moore was displayed. We gathered before the painting to begin an EVP session. Although Joanna did not pick up on anything having to do with the portrait itself, Richard claimed to hear a disembodied voice and stepped away momentarily to investigate its source. Unable to find one, he rejoined the group.

As Alicia shared the impression she had of the figure she had spotted in her periphery earlier, everyone present heard a disembodied moan with a reverberating, echo-like tone; it was recorded by James. Minutes later, Paul claimed to hear a male voice but also noted that he sensed the presence of a woman's spirit, which was the first mention of a female thus far in the investigation. Little did any of us realize at the time that Paul's intuition would prove to be accurate.

From his place among us on the ground floor of Citizens' Hall, James encouraged Jimmy to perform onstage upstairs. Several wooden-sounding footfalls emanated from the second floor of the old town hall and were recorded over the course of 90 seconds in seeming response.

We returned to the jail cells on the main floor. Just outside the cells, Paul asked, "What year is it?"

The microphone of Camera 1 captured a promising response.

EVP: [Male] O-seven.

While most of the team tried communicating from inside the cells, Paul and I took a seat on a pair of benches facing each other across the front entrance landing, asking our own questions aloud to the empty air.

I noted a long rope inside the west wall leading to the old bell tower high above and recalled reports of people hearing the modern-day doorbell being rung by invisible fingers. "Can you ring the doorbell, please?" I asked.

Camera 1 caught a direct reply.

EVP: [Male] I can't ring the doorbell.

～

Before we broke for dinner, I placed a digital recorder on the apron of the Willow Hall stage and activated a proximity detector nearby. Paul elected to remain behind on the property while the rest of us left to get takeout food.

Over the next 22 minutes, the recorder on the stage caught multiple knocking sounds, a noise like a cabinet or cupboard door closing, someone inhaling then exhaling, a wooden creak, a stack of chairs rattling, and a subtle tap as if someone were taking a cautious step and trying their best to be quiet about it.

Downstairs, the digital recorder inside the jail cell captured the distant sound of a rhythmic knocking pattern of two knocks, a pause then another two knocks. One more pair of wooden knocks closer to the cell area was recorded mere seconds before Paul arrived to ask questions of the empty air. He did not hear these same knocks, nor were they recorded by the camera trained on the cells.

Paul moved to the second floor. As he made his way into the auditorium, he asked, "Anyone here want to talk to us?"

The recorder on the stage caught a response.

EVP: [Unknown gender; high-pitched whispering] Hello!...Hi!

Paul continued to encourage communication, but no further EVPs were recorded. Soon after, Paul went downstairs to join the team for dinner in Citizens' Hall.

⌒

After dinner, the team took up positions between both sets of stairs leading up to Willow Hall. A CD of Hit Parade songs from the 1940s was left to play softly from the stage while the team listened for disembodied reactions to the music. Before long, we heard subtle sounds of movement coming from the auditorium floor, and Camera 2 captured several intriguing voices.

EVP: [Male] Seven.

The music changed to a more upbeat tune.

EVP: [Male] Dancing.

Bing Crosby's voice crooned "White Christmas."

EVP: [Male] Peter, you can do better than that.

A long pause followed, then…

EVP: [Same male; shouting] Annie! Get back!

Paul, James and Joanna began another tour of the second floor. As they moved past the stage and closer to the concession room, Joanna sensed the presence of a female.

They stopped so she could concentrate. "She has more pain associated with her—sadness, more emotion," said Joanna. "Jim was content."

EVP: [Female] Pity.

Joanna continued, trying to focus on the flashes of information coming to her. "I feel like there's an S-H in her name," she said, exhaling and squinting. "I can't tell."

At that moment, the digital recorder inside the jail cell captured a loud impact sound. None of the investigators was anywhere near that area of the building, above or below the cell.

With the prospect of a long drive home, Joanna and Alicia prepared to leave for the night. As the team left the jail cell area headed for Citizens' Hall, Camera 1 captured yet another exchange of disembodied voices.

EVP: [Male] Carol.
EVP: [Female] Here.

Then came the sound of a heavy impact on wood.

EVP: [Same male] Carol!

Camera 1 then captured Paul returning alone from Citizens' Hall, having said goodbye to the ladies, to turn off the lights in the jail cells on his way to the restroom. As he disappeared inside the men's room…

EVP: [Male] He will come back.

The camera did not record the reaction of the male when Paul exited the washroom and did *not* return the same way he arrived but instead chose the opposite direction and re-entered Citizens' Hall through an alternate door.

~

Following Alicia and Joanna's departure, the four remaining team members took a short break. James and Paul stepped outside for some fresh air while Richard replaced the DVD-R disc of Camera 1. I stepped inside the jail cell to check the batteries of the digital recorder and begin a new recording. I placed it on the metal bed frame hanging from the south wall of the narrow room, then went to join Richard in the front entrance of the town hall.

As we conversed, the recorder in the cell picked up two footfalls, likely originating from the auditorium above (where the 1940s music continued to play softly). Simultaneously, a second digital recorder in my hand caught a voice that we also heard in the moment.

DV/EVP: [Male; faint] Hey.

Both Richard and I stopped talking to listen for any more anomalous sounds, but none came.

I began to wonder if there was a particular song that was upsetting the female, so on Richard's suggestion I returned to the auditorium and stopped the CD player. Two seconds later, the recorder I was holding picked up a possible reaction.

EVP: [Female; distant, calling] Hello?

~

Back in Citizens' Hall, Paul suggested we try a P-SB7 session. We settled around the portrait of Dorothy Moore, where Richard activated the P-SB7. The room was immediately filled with pure white noise static. Standing absolutely still, the four of us proceeded to ask questions.

James went first. "Is there a woman here named Shannon? Or with an S-H in her name?" The hiss of white noise continued for five seconds before someone spoke to us.

P-SB7: [Female; cheerful] Hello!

"What is your name, please?" I asked. Within seconds, all of us heard a distant, echoing sound we couldn't identify. We looked to Richard, who raised his knuckles to his eyes and mimed he had just heard the sound of someone crying.

We all took turns asking for an explanation for this woman's sorrow. The P-SB7 continued spewing an uninterrupted stream of static.

"What year is it, ma'am?" I asked, trying to sound respectful. "Please help us out." The incessant hiss continued for nine seconds, then another voice came through.

P-SB7: [Male; quiet] Hey.

"Who are you, sir?" I asked, hoping to maintain a steady momentum of communication. "We think we can hear you through this device. Can you speak up, please?" At that moment, a pair of distinct footfalls echoed on the concrete floor of the hall, seeming to retreat behind Richard.

"Did you hear that?" I asked, excitedly.

Richard nodded. "Yeah, I did."

"Whoever's here, can you please speak with us using this device?" I called out. The uniform white noise broke once again.

P-SB7: [Unknown gender; friendly] Hello.

"Hello!" we all called back.

"Who are you?" I asked.

"What's your name, sir?" asked James after a pause.

With still no response, Richard asked, "Can you tell us why the woman is so sad?" An answer came through nine seconds later.

P-SB7: [Male; casual] I don't know.

More questions were asked, but no further voices responded via the P-SB7.

～

We re-entered the original part of the building and settled at the base of the twin staircases below Willow Hall to begin another session. I took the lead with the questions.

Peter: Did you like the music?

P-SB7: [Male; friendly] Yup!

P-SB7: [Female A] Yeah.

P-SB7: [Female] Yup!

Peter: Yeah?

P-SB7: [Female A; quiet] Yeah.

Peter: Are you the woman we've been hearing?

P-SB7: [Female; quiet] Uh-huh.

Peter: What is your name, please? [White noise for nine seconds] Jimmy, are you here?

P-SB7: [Male A; whispering] Henry!

P-SB7: [Male] What do you want?

P-SB7: [Male A] You're here!

Peter: Jimmy, what's your last name?

P-SB7: [Male] Bart!

P-SB7: [Female] Shut up.

P-SB7: [Young female] Hannah.

Peter: Are you the same Jimmy who saved the building from burning down?

P-SB7: [Older male] Uh-huh.

Peter: Yeah? What year was that?

P-SB7: [Male; thoughtful] Erm...

The rest of the session garnered nothing but stray radio signals full of beeps, grunts and words that suggested a conversation we were overhearing but were not a part of. Richard turned the P-SB7 off.

We all stepped back onto the first-floor mezzanine of Citizens' Hall, standing stock still as we asked questions.

Addressing the sobbing woman, Paul asked, "Can you tell us why you're sad?" A sharp snap sound erupted, though no one on the team had moved.

"Miss? Is somebody holding you here?" Paul continued. We heard and recorded footfalls and sounds of movement receding away from Citizens' Hall over the course of five seconds, followed by silence.

Moving back to the twin staircases, the team tried in vain to evoke responses for another 15 minutes but received nothing substantial. James, Richard and Paul stepped outside for a short break.

Bringing my own Spirit Box upstairs, I activated it in the Bower Room behind the stage. I had not begun to speak yet when voices erupted from the device in greeting.

Spirit Box: [Older male; friendly] Hello!

Spirit Box: [Male] Watch, Jeff.

Spirit Box: [Female; distant] Hello!

Peter: Hello? Who's this?

Spirit Box: [Male] Who are you?

Spirit Box: [Unknown gender; friendly] Hello!

Spirit Box: [Male; distant] Hello!

Spirit Box: [Female] Matthew...really?

Spirit Box: [Male] Stephie...

Peter: How are you?

Spirit Box: [Older male] We're okay.

Spirit Box: [Young male; clear] Great!

Spirit Box: [Older female] Uh-huh.

Peter: Yeah, I can hear you.

Spirit Box: [Female] You can?

Peter: What's your name, please?

Spirit Box: [Unknown gender; impatient] Hurry up!

Spirit Box: [Young male] Ji-im!

Peter: Has anybody died in the Acton Town Hall?

Spirit Box: [Female] Uh…

Spirit Box: [Male; stern] Enough!

No other sensible replies came through the Spirit Box after this exchange.

I turned the device off just as Richard, Paul and James wandered onto the stage. They all appeared weary, so it came as no surprise when Richard suggested we call it a night and begin packing up the equipment.

Wandering alone toward my equipment cases on the second-floor mezzanine of Citizens' Hall, I stopped to address the female whose sobs we had all heard emanating from this very area. I let her know that the team had heard her lament, but we were unable to assist her without more information. "If you need our help, now's the time," I offered, pausing to listen between each statement. "Let us know before we go, all right?"

It was one week later as I finished analyzing my recordings that I heard the soft whine of a female, seemingly responding to my parting words.

Afterthoughts

It took James and I a week to transcribe our audio recordings and Paul about three weeks to analyze the audio and video data from all three surveillance cameras (18 hours' worth). We now had several names of people we could attempt to address directly on our next visit. We may even have obtained a year (1907), so that too was a possible lead to research.

James Robertson's Spirit?

Although he is still blamed for the disembodied footfalls, sounds of floor-sweeping and prank doorbell-ringing, one lingering question remains: does the spirit of James Robertson actually reside at the Acton Town Hall?

There is very little periodical information available on long-time Acton Town Hall fixture James Robertson; he preferred to live alone and rarely spoke to anyone. Given his overseas experiences in World War I—he was among 18,000 fellow Canadians who withstood the first German gas attacks at Saint-Julien, Belgium—he likely suffered from post-traumatic stress disorder, but people did not openly discuss personal problems back then.

So how does a researcher find clues to a ghost when the person was a social phantom to begin with? There are no photographs of Jimmy, and scant newspaper mentions refer to a James Robertson being paid $1.50 for fulfilling an unspecified duty at Hallowe'en in 1941 and $2.00 for labour in 1943 by the town council. Perhaps Jimmy's largest claim to (unwanted) local fame was that he saved the Acton Town Hall from a fire that erupted from an auditorium heating stove in the wee hours of December 20, 1945.

Robertson left the town hall to live and work as a caretaker at the local Baxter Labs building in 1957 before leaving that job (apparently too many people made too much noise for his comfort) and moving into the Station Hotel (now the Red Harp pub). A brief obituary tells us he passed away at Toronto's Sunnybrook Hospital on October 23, 1960, and that his remains were interred at Acton's Fairview Cemetery among fellow war veterans. Interestingly, when Robertson enlisted in 1914 he gave his age as 21 years old, which would make him 67 at death— yet his headstone claims he was 70. We may never know the reason for the discrepancy.

The grave of James Robertson. Is this the same Jimmy who haunts the Acton Town Hall?

Given Jimmy's propensity to avoid people while alive, why should we expect he would interact with anyone in spirit form? If he is present—even in occasional visitation—it's doubtful he would make himself known, preferring instead to avoid social interaction at all costs. So if this is the case, who was the young male Joanna and James met in the auditorium? Had we inadvertently debunked one claim of a Jimmy and replaced it with another?

~

Whoever he was, we can only imagine what a sight it may have been when James, Joanna and Alicia left the second floor of the town hall and stepped out onto the Citizens' Hall mezzanine beyond, for in his physical lifetime there was nothing occupying that space but open air. Perhaps the reason Joanna did not feel the young spirit's presence directly interacting with James' arm over the equipment cases was that he decided it was safer for him to remain inside the original town hall boundaries, lest he were to find himself falling two storeys if he attempted to join the trio on the modern-day mezzanine.

The same theory might account for the extraordinarily faint female whimper that was caught in the same area near the conclusion of this investigation. Although recorded voices of spirits are often soft and whispered, perhaps the recorder picked up the tail-end of a woman's moan as heard through a window from outside the original building.

There were also a couple of instances where one spirit seemed to have some semblance of control over others that desired to communicate. We've encountered this phenomenon many times before; not only are spirits social, but also, even after physical death, hierarchies continue to be observed.

The team was eager to return.

~

Chapter 2

Acton Town Hall Centre: Second Investigation

When they talk of ghosts of the dead who wander in the night with things still undone in life, they approximate my subjective experience of this life.

–Jack Henry Abbott

Team: Joanna, Victoria, David, Peter
Guests: Alicia, Nicole, Stephanie, Tim

If it was possible to be any more thrilled to return to investigate the old Acton Town Hall later that year (2014), I certainly was feeling it when we did. Thanks to the promising results accrued during our initial visit, we now had a series of names for some of the building's ghosts to try addressing directly, and I was keen to see or hear what—if any—kind of responses doing so might provoke.

The downside of life interfering with best-laid plans was evident prior to this visit. Mere days before, I received word that neither Richard nor Paul was able to participate. And although James had forewarned me of his own unavailability a month previous, his absence was particularly disappointing because he seemed to have made some headway communicating with the spirit named Jimmy the first time out.

However, buoyed by the presence of Victoria, Joanna and Alicia, I decided we should press on with my brother David, who was no stranger to investigating with us in the past. Since determining the Acton Town Hall Centre was not likely a dangerously haunted location, I suggested David ask his wife Nicole along to help; she had expressed interest in participating in a formal investigation. Then I received two more guest requests from Joanna and Alicia: Joanna's cousin Stephanie was a "sensitive" seeking an opportunity to hone her skills, while Alicia's brother Tim was a natural skeptic who was curious to experience a Searcher Group investigation firsthand.

Acton Town Hall Centre and Citizens' Hall, 2018

I welcomed our rookie guests, grateful for their help. I was now interested to see if somehow the dynamic of a group comprised of more women than men would affect the data outcome.

I arrived earlier than everyone else to set up the surveillance systems. On this occasion, Camera 1 was set up to film from the same corner of Willow Hall where young Jimmy was first encountered by Joanna and James. From this angle, most of the auditorium floor, the stage, the twin stairwell exits to the main level, a pair of doorways leading to the second-floor mezzanine of Citizens' Hall to the south and even some of the concession stand behind the stage were in full view.

Camera 2 was deployed on the main floor, facing the jail cells again but this time even closer than before. I wanted to ensure that not only would disembodied whispers be captured originating near or from within the cells, but I also needed assurance that the wind chimes I was going to place in the short passage between the cells were in sharp focus in case they were touched when no one on the team was present.

Alicia and Tim arrived, followed by Victoria, David and Nicole. After introductions we established base camp in Citizens' Hall, and I began to review the game plan for the evening. Partway through my spiel on safety protocols, we all heard a loud crash; the noise seemed to have originated from deep inside the adjacent town hall building. Amazingly, this sound was not captured by the digital recorder I had with me, nor by either camera.

Leaving one of my digital recorders behind in Citizens' Hall, I activated a second recorder to take with us as I led the group on their first tour of the premises. Victoria brought her recorder too. Within three minutes of the group leaving Citizens' Hall, the recorder I left behind captured the sounds of something moving about nearby, followed by a light scraping noise similar to a solid object being dragged across a table surface.

We settled at the bar of the concession stand upstairs to deploy the first of the evening's experiments: a glass of rum. Hoping to attract one of the resident spirits with a trigger object of an alcoholic nature, rum was poured to a level marked on the side of a shot glass and left on the bar.

We moved into the mirrored Mill Meeting Room, where I demonstrated how to interact with the Pop-O-Matic die shaker for the benefit of any invisible observers. I placed a second digital recorder near the plastic toy, hoping to capture signs of movement around it culminating in the familiar sound of the die inside the bubble being flipped.

Satisfied that everyone was familiar with the layout of the second floor, we moved downstairs to visit the jail cells on the main floor of the old town hall when Joanna and Stephanie arrived.

~

It was time to begin the investigation in earnest. I asked Joanna to take the lead, following any odd energy fields she might pick up along the way. The group started up the stairs toward the auditorium, at which point Joanna stopped on the first landing and brought everyone up to speed with a brief recap of her previous findings, including the female spirit we had all heard at various times that night.

"She didn't really interact that much; I didn't really connect with her," Joanna shared. "But I did feel angst or suffering and sorrow, so I was going to try to make a point of connecting with her today. It's almost like when [Jimmy]'s energy dissipated, then her energy came in. It's like they don't overlap much. They may not even know each other," she postulated.

Joanna's statement inspired a brief comparison to the film *The Others* (2001), during which time Alicia heard two loud, drawn-out exhales. She asked if anyone else had heard them as well, but no one had. My digital recorder, resting a few metres away, did not capture anything, but fortunately, Victoria's recorder—clutched in her hand—caught both exhales clearly, suggesting that the male doing the breathing was very close by and likely standing among us.

~

We ascended to the upper-level mezzanine of Citizens' Hall and entered the auditorium, approaching the stage.

Joanna turned to Victoria. "I'm getting an intense sadness. I don't know if you're getting that?"

"No, I'm just finding something like...heavy," Victoria replied.

Everyone settled around the south and west edges of the stage.

"Hello?" I began. "Is there a woman here? Do you remember us from the last time we were here?" I looked to Joanna after a moment of silence. "Nothing yet?"

She shook her head, concentrating. "Not that I hear, no."

"What's your first name, please?" I asked.

"I thought I heard a hum," Victoria said, glancing around, searching for a source.

Just then, a sharp tap echoing from Citizens' Hall caught David's attention. "That was behind me," he reported calmly.

Inside Citizens' Hall, my digital recorder also captured the sound. Upon later analysis, the recorder revealed the sounds of someone tripping and stumbling on the concrete floor, creating a loud, reverberating tap noise as if they were attempting to recover their footing.

"She's here," Joanna shared from beside the stage on the second floor.

Alicia spoke up next, claiming to have heard sounds of movement coming from the Bower Room behind the stage. I heard it as well and could best describe it as shifting.

"I have a response from my feet all the way up," Stephanie murmured to Joanna, who acknowledged and confirmed the sensation.

"Ma'am?" I said. "Could you please talk to Joanna here? Let us know who you are?"

"I'm getting imagery," Joanna responded. "I see her with a handkerchief in one hand." Joanna paused to focus for a few moments. "And she's distraught," she continued. "She's crying. She's standing, and I see her all in black; a slender-fitting top and a long skirt. Something devastating has happened to her."

"Madam, or ma'am? Is there something we can try to help you with?" I asked.

"'Nobody can help me,'" Joanna replied on behalf of the female spirit. She then raised her face and looked to the team. "I feel such a loss, as if she lost a child."

"Is this true?" I asked, turning to speak to the empty air above the stage.

"I'm getting a 'Yes,'" Joanna said.

"How old was your child?"

"He's a baby."

"We're sorry for your loss. Do you work here at the town hall?"

"No," shared Joanna. "What I'm getting is that it wasn't a good marriage and he had extra-marital affairs, so the child was all she had. She's just inconsolable."

"Is anybody else feeling really heavy?" Victoria asked. "I keep feeling a pressure on my head."

"Well, her energy is so depressed here, you'd be getting it in waves," offered Joanna.

"Ma'am, could you tell us your last name, please?" I asked, fishing for historical data.

"Again, names aren't the best for me," Joanna cautioned, "but I felt like she said, 'Duncan.'"

Another loud crack issued from Citizens' Hall, behind us. Was this noise simply an indication of clumsy movement, or was it perhaps a purposeful distraction from our focus on Mrs. Duncan?

"Come on in," I called. "We're just here visiting. Is the young man here? Do you remember us? Jimmy, are you here?"

Silence fell over the auditorium as we listened for a reply.

Suddenly, Victoria reacted. "I thought I saw something over there—a light by the ceiling," she pointed.

"I saw it, too," agreed Tim, "close to the speakers."

"When you saw that, I was sensing her going to an empty crib," Joanna shared. "But it wasn't a crib that we have [today]; it is more like a…"

"A bassinet?" I asked hesitantly, hoping I wasn't influencing the image Joanna was sharing.

"Yeah," she acknowledged.

Alicia frowned. "Why would she be here with a bassinet, though?"

"She may be illustrating a memory," I suggested. "The baby's death may not have occurred here, but it may have been registered here at the town hall, in her day."

I didn't wish to waste time worrying about the "why" while Joanna seemed to be sharing a fruitful connection with Mrs. Duncan, so I pressed for more verifiable information. "I just want to confirm your last name, Duncan. Is that your married name?"

"Yes," Joanna conveyed.

"How old are you, ma'am?" I asked.

"Again, I'm not confident with this, but I get 37."

"What year is it, please?"

"She said, '1871'?"

"Why do you choose to stay here and grieve for your infant?"

"I don't find her interested in communicating while she's attending to her child," Joanna said.

Her words made my heart sink. My experience with this kind of telephonic communication has always been short-lived—often shut down by the spirit when a seemingly ordinary question has somehow offended it. In this line of work, spirits hold all the cards.

"Well thank you for communicating so far," I countered, hopeful my sincerity might encourage further discussion. "We're going to walk around a little more; you're welcome to follow us, and if you change your mind about us helping you somehow, please let us know, okay?"

Joanna chuckled. "She's ignoring you."

~

Continuing onward, everyone gathered in the Bower Room directly behind the stage and spread about the wide open space.

Victoria began to profess what she was feeling with some trepidation. "Now in here I'm feeling the heaviness is gone, but I'm feeling cramping...lower. [The environment] feels like it's changed, but it's not heavy, just more like a cramping."

None of the other women related feeling anything similar to Victoria, and three minutes passed during which everyone listened quietly.

Again Victoria broke the silence. "Okay, there's music going on, right?" she said, her eyes darting from person to person, seeking verification.

Everyone stood stock-still, listening harder. "Nope," said Joanna.

"Nothing?!" Victoria said, incredulous. "I'm hearing music!"

We all strained to listen again, remaining absolutely still. Suddenly, Stephanie's eyes widened in realization and Victoria met her gaze smiling, relieved she wasn't going crazy.

"Where do you hear it coming from?" I asked.

"This way, behind me," Stephanie said, indicating Citizens' Hall.

"What kind of music?" I asked.

"It's waltz music! Waltzing!" Stephanie blurted.

"It reminds me of an old record," Victoria shared.

"It's one-two-three..." said Stephanie, trying to recreate the rhythm vocally.

Alicia shifted closer to Stephanie, listening intently before reacting with a gasp. I settled between Victoria and Stephanie, hoping to hear this mysterious music for myself. A motorcycle roaring past the building at that moment made it difficult to concentrate.

As the rumbling of its engine faded, Victoria spoke up. "I'm not hearing it now." She listened again, then shook her head. "I don't hear it. It's like they stopped to say, 'Why are they listening to me?'"

After a few more moments of silence, the group moved south through the concession area and gathered in the Mill Meeting Room, opposite. Upon entering, Victoria let us know her abdominal cramping had disappeared.

"It's clear in here," Joanna nodded. "It's mostly pressure differences; that's how I feel it."

Suddenly, Alicia started with a gasp.

Victoria nodded in acknowledgement. "I heard it," she said.

"You heard something, too?" asked David. "I heard a moan."

The team moved northward along a corridor that led to the back of the stage. Joanna, Stephanie and Victoria held back from the rest of us to converse.

"I still feel her here," Joanna said for the benefit of Victoria's recorder. "She's not moving from the stage; she's lingering like it's her room and the baby's in there and she's just reliving…" Her voice trailed off as she concentrated on the mental image she was observing.

"This room's thick," agreed Stephanie before turning to Victoria. "Did you have ovary pain in here?"

"Yes, that's why I said 'cramping.' I didn't know how to explain it!" Victoria giggled as she indicated the digital recorder in her hand. "I guess Peter's going to hear that, now!"

Joanna and Stephanie laughed, the awkwardness of the ovarian subject now divulged.

The light-hearted reprieve was short-lived. Joanna encouraged anyone with a camera to start taking pictures in the direction of the stage, where she continued to visualize Mrs. Duncan.

"Mrs. Duncan," I called, hopeful we might continue to converse. "Can you hear me?"

"She's here, but she's faint and her back is toward us," Joanna said. "She's in her own world right now, not acknowledging that we're here anymore."

I urged the women of our group to begin asking questions as a last-ditch attempt to woo Mrs. Duncan back to communicating, but according to Joanna, it was in vain.

Within seconds, both Victoria and David reported hearing more noises coming from the direction of Citizens' Hall. It would seem someone was feeling very brave while they were at a safe distance, far from the team.

"There's something weird on my camera," said Tim, who approached me with a puzzled look. "Do you know how the iPhone does a facial recognition and it'll [focus] on a person? It did that, just over here," he gestured, indicating the empty stage. "There's nothing over there."

"Did you take a picture?" I asked.

"I did; I took a few," Tim replied, "but there's nothing in the photos."

~

After such an intense start to our evening and with no further answers from Mrs. Duncan, we needed to remove ourselves from the environment and let our equipment take over. Victoria left her digital recorder on a stack of chairs in the Bower Room before following everyone else to the ground floor of Citizens' Hall. Meanwhile, inside the auditorium, Camera 1 continued to roll.

Analysis later revealed that 65 seconds after the team had left Willow Hall, Victoria's recorder caught sounds of movement nearby, beginning with subtle flicking and progressing to wooden knocks, soft clicks and an echoing slap resembling a bare footfall. Eighteen minutes after the team's departure, the steady drone of the building's air system was punctuated by a female or young male's voice humming at an extremely high frequency, barely perceptible to the human ear. This subtle but undeniable humming was captured at varying intensities and intervals a total of 10 times.

Between the short periods of humming activity, evidence of movement in the vicinity of the recorder continued, including wooden-sounding knocking, loud metallic bangs, a female or young male sighing and hollow thumps resembling objects being moved inside a cupboard or cabinet—possibly from inside the kitchen behind the concession stand.

~

Following a short break, our next stop was a visit to the portrait of Dorothy Moore at the east side of Citizens' Hall. The cold stare depicted in the portrait unsettled the women of the group. Joanna did not connect Dorothy's visage with that of the female spirit in the auditorium.

We retraced our steps and entered the old town hall again, this time headed for the jail cells to conduct an EVP session. Confident I would continue to catch more activity in Citizens' Hall while we were away from it, I left one of my digital recorders on the 1874 Steinway piano, hoping a note or even a tune might be heard during analysis.

Within five minutes, a snapping sound resounded through Citizens' Hall; within 11 minutes, a wooden knock; within 12 minutes, another snap sound, followed by silence. Then, as this same recorder captured me asking, "Who was waltzing tonight?" from the adjacent town hall, an indistinguishable male voice cut in and overlapped my voice with his own at an incredibly fast speed, close to the recorder. Although the content could not be identified with any certainty, the energy and intonation behind it did not sound friendly. Perhaps this male was telling me off for asking too many questions. Perhaps this was the same male that exhaled the pair of open-mouthed hisses that Alicia had heard earlier.

Meanwhile, we were conducting our EVP session between the twin staircases that lead up to Willow Hall. When Victoria asked for a knocking response, a loud slap sound echoed through Citizens' Hall. When Alicia asked after Deanna, a second loud snap/slap erupted from Citizens' Hall. Within seconds of me asking a question of Harry, everyone acknowledged hearing distinct footfalls rushing across the floor of Citizens' Hall.

We decided to take a dinner break and once more let the surveillance and audio equipment document what happens on the property when people occupying physical bodies are absent.

Retrieving my recorder from the Mill Meeting Room upstairs, I was disappointed to find it had somehow been prematurely deactivated, even though the readout indicated full battery power. I left a recorder and a proximity alarm on the apron of the stage and positioned a large, plush teddy bear on the councillor's chair in full view of Camera 1 before exiting the building and locking it behind us.

Analysis revealed less than two seconds after I'd closed the doors dividing the Old Town Hall and Citizens' Hall, a distinct tap resounded a short distance from the recorder on the stage. While the team was away from the building, the camera also caught a wooden knock, a slap on the surface of the stage and a sound resembling a door slam (or a large object being dropped).

After dinner, the group returned to the twin staircases to listen for ghostly responses to a variety of music from different eras. Reactions varied from very subtle sniffing to a youthful-sounding cough and a grunt from a female or young male.

David checked on the rum experiment and found no changes in the liquid level. Less than two minutes after his departure, Victoria's recorder captured a footfall settling near the concession stand followed by deep, gulp-like noise.

Outside the jail cells, I set the surveillance camera up with a fresh DVD-R disc to record for the remainder of the evening. David volunteered to conduct a solo EVP session and positioned himself between the cell doors facing the glass wind chimes dangling freely before him, watching for motion not caused by his own movements. Leaving a recorder with David, I left to rejoin the others waiting on the second floor.

Within a minute of my departure, David reported feeling a weird tingling sensation travelling through the back of his head. As the footfalls of the team could be heard moving eastward, away from the auditorium above, David addressed the presence. "This place is still here because you put out a fire. Is that right?"

Unbeknownst to David at the time, there was a tap on the digital recorder followed by an extremely brief burst of EMI static in seeming response.

Upstairs, the remainder of the team had split up to ask questions using a script I'd prepared based on the names derived from the first investigation. Victoria, Joanna and Stephanie moved into the Mill Meeting Room while Alicia, Tim, Nicole and I remained in the Bower Room. I pulled out a pendulum and sat on a chair near the stage; Alicia held the RT-EVP recorder, and Tim began filming me using his cell phone.

"Can you show me 'yes,' please?" I asked. The pendulum started spinning in small clockwise circles. "Can you make that larger?" The pendulum obliged, but not by very much.

"Do you know why you're here?" Alicia asked. The pendulum direction quickly reversed, indicating "no."

"Do you know what happened to you?" she asked. The pendulum slowed to a neutral swing then rotated clockwise, indicating "yes."

"Are you male?" I asked. It continued swinging; yes.

"Are you Jimmy?" asked Alicia. It swung larger, stronger circles; yes.

"Jimmy, are you fourteen?" I asked. Yes.

"Is your last name Robertson?" Yes.

"Are you sure it's Robertson? Are you telling the truth?" Yes.

"Do you like it here? Is that why you stay?" Yes.

"Are you the caretaker here?" Alicia asked. Yes.

"Do you remember a fire?" I asked. Suddenly the strength of the pendulum swing began to ebb, and the rotations decreased in size.

I noticed that Tim was approaching as he filmed the session. "Are you scared of Tim?" I asked.

EVP: [Male; deep, growling] Tim.

"If Tim backed away, would you come back?" I continued. The pendulum swung in a neutral, nondescript pattern, but the recorder Alicia was holding captured the same deep male voice.

EVP: [Male] Yup.

"Okay, he's going away," I assured, grateful to see Tim was obliging.

"I'm sorry!" Tim apologized.

"See? He's polite!" said Alicia.

"Are you okay there, Jim? May I call you Jim?" I asked. The pendulum began to swing clockwise; yes.

"Does anyone call you James?" asked Alicia. The circles grew; yes.

"Do your mom and dad call you James?" The pendulum slowed to neutral/unsure.

I rested my right arm for a few seconds before settling back into position, but unfortunately, no further movement of the pendulum materialized.

The group began a standard EVP session using the prepared questions. Alicia asked several of "Carol" before passing the script to Nicole, who addressed "Annie," pausing for several seconds between queries in case responses none of us could hear were being recorded. Disappointingly, none were.

David returned from his solo vigil outside the jail cells and Tim left to take his place, bringing a copy of the questions with him to try there.

Joanna, Victoria and Stephanie then rejoined us. We all compared notes and agreed the building seemed very quiet, in stark contrast to earlier that evening. David observed that the initial heaviness he felt in the Bower Room was gone.

Victoria, Joanna and Stephanie excused themselves for the night, owing to the distances they needed to travel home. Tim returned and reported nothing from his solo vigil, and he and Alicia also left.

David, Nicole and I took our time packing up in the hope we might have one last unexplainable experience before leaving.

"Jimmy!" I called.

EVP: [Young male; sarcastic] We know!

None of my questions garnered recorded responses. David and Nicole joined me as I shut down the auditorium camera. Once again, while we were at a safe distance, a recorder left running in Citizens' Hall captured a click indicating movement nearby, immediately followed by a clear, urgent-sounding EVP.

EVP: [Male; hurried, warning whisper] Henry!

Then several light footfall noises were recorded before the three of us returned, packed everything up, thanked the spirits of the Acton Town Hall for hosting us and locked the building shortly after midnight.

Afterthoughts

After just two investigations, I came to the conclusion that asking the spirits of the Acton Town Hall to do something audible in order to prove they are present was an exercise in futility. Everyone—save Mrs. Duncan—that resided or chose to visit there for extended periods of time appeared to be very wise to their respective states-of-being and were content to exist without a need for attention.

Historical Hit?

Of all the clues The Searcher Group derived from its investigations of the Acton Town Hall, the most significant ones had nothing to do with its most famous ghost but with the spirit of a woman. That first evening, in addition to the audible sobs we heard, Joanna sensed that the woman's name involved the letters S-H. During the second investigation, Joanna managed to wrangle the married surname, "Duncan," and that her baby boy had died in infancy.

The newspaper archives of the *Acton Free Press* turned up the following death notice from April 16, 1885: "In Acton, on the 11th inst., Thos. Henry, infant son of Mr. Thomas Duncan, merchant, aged, 5 months and 9 days."

On the following page: "We extend our sympathies to Mr. and Mrs. Thomas Duncan, in the death of their only child, a most interesting little boy about six months old. It is only a few weeks since Mr. Duncan removed to Acton, and being almost entire strangers the sudden death of their little one is all the more keenly felt."

The next year brought some better news—a birth announcement in the June 3, 1886, edition of the paper: "In Acton, on the 29th inst., the wife of Mr. Thomas Duncan of a daughter."

However, in January 1887, tragedy struck the Duncans of Acton again with the death of Mr. Thomas Duncan:

> Our citizens were pained yesterday morning to hear of the death of Mr. Thomas Duncan, grocer. For some months it has been apparent that Mr. Duncan

was failing in health, but until a week ago he attended his business, and even until an hour or so before his death walked about the home. But that relentless enemy to the human frame, consumption, had fastened itself upon him, and almost imperceptibly the lamp of life was gradually extinguished. He was an honest, strait-forward [sic] businessman, and respected by all. He leaves a young wife and baby daughter to mourn their loss. We understand they are left in good circumstances. The whole community sympathizes with Mrs. Duncan in being obliged so early in life to bid goodbye to her loving partner.

According to the *Acton Free Press*, Thomas Duncan's funeral on Thursday, January 23 was "largely attended."

The following week came word that the entire stock of Mr. Duncan's grocery store was up for sale, and by late April came the notice: "Mrs. Thomas Duncan has sold her stock of groceries, glassware, &c., to Mr. L.G. Matthews. Mrs. Duncan will return to her father's home near Barrie."

The trail then ran dry as far as local news about the fate of the Duncan clan, with no indication of Mrs. Duncan's first name—nor her daughter's, for that matter.

Attempts to find the burial sites of Thomas and his infant son, Thomas Henry, in Acton also turned up inconclusive. Of the two graves marked "Duncan," cemetery records revealed only one of these plots was owned by an S. Duncan, with no indication as to who was interred there. I was surprised that someone so seemingly revered and embraced as an upstanding citizen inside a short span of time residing in Acton was—until now—essentially lost to history.

Thanks to Ancestry.ca, I was able to not only pick up the trail of Mrs. Duncan's life after leaving Acton, but also to skip back in time and corroborate the birth of Thomas Henry, who was born in the nearby town of Milton on November 2, 1884, to parents Thomas Duncan and Susanah Henderson—S.H.

While this match to Joanna's sense of our spirit woman's initials seems remarkable, there remained unresolved issues regarding two more pieces of information shared by Joanna: Mrs. Duncan's age—37—at the moment of communication, and the year—1871—she was allegedly communicating from. Mrs. Susanah Duncan passed away on October, 24, 1932, at the age of 63. This means she was 16 years old at the time of her son's death in the spring of 1885. In 1871, she was only a child.

Given that names and dates are the most difficult pieces of accurate, verifiable information to glean via psychic medium, what can we derive from this case? Did the numbers Joanna shared come from her subconscious? Were they filtered incorrectly from spirit through medium to the team like a bad game of Telephone? Were they random numbers shared on a whim by a spirit who was growing increasingly bored and unimpressed with our line of questioning?

We cannot dismiss the possibility that Joanna made contact with the 37-year-old version of Mrs. Duncan. There are hundreds of documented reports from around the globe by witnesses claiming to have encountered spirits of people they have known who have appeared much younger, hale and healthier than when their bodies actually expired. It is also not hard to imagine that a mother would continue to mourn the death of a child, even 20 years later. However, as investigators committed to researching historical facts, we cannot ignore information that is clearly inaccurate, either. Scenarios such as this one remind us that studying the paranormal is not an exact science.

~

Investigating the Acton Town Hall Centre was a genuine pleasure; I wished to confirm the presence of Jimmy, as so many people had claimed to have had paranormal experiences over the years that they attributed to James Robertson's spirit, rightly or wrongly. I feel we did meet someone named Jimmy, but whether he is *the* Jimmy is another matter.

The Searcher Group encountered several other spirit energies beside the beloved ghost of Jimmy. Certainly, more legwork is required to learn and confirm the surnames of Harry, Deanna, Patrick, Carol, Annie, Bart, Henry, Hannah, Jeff, Matthew and Stephie, but the reasons for Mrs. Duncan's manifestations are perhaps the strangest mystery at the Acton Town Hall. If Susanah Duncan had little or nothing to do with the Acton Town Hall in her physical lifetime, why did she choose to manifest herself there for the benefit of both investigations? Could having a medium present on both occasions have attracted her to the town hall so she could share her grief and be heard? Of course we can only speculate, but don't you just love a good mystery?

$\sim$

Chapter 3

Waterford Old Town Hall: First Investigation

Ty Cobb wanted to play, but none of us could stand the son of a bitch when we were alive, so we told him to stick it!
—"Shoeless" Joe Jackson,
Field of Dreams (1989)

⌒

Team: James, David, Peter
Guests: Michele, Denise M.
Hosts: Teresa, Jennifer, Denise J., Brenda

Wending my way along the worn, rural roads of Norfolk County one early Saturday afternoon in late May 2014, my mind skipped between admiring the spacious countryside under the warm sunshine and the thought of leading the next investigation within the hour.

Although every investigation is worthy of anticipation, I had three reasons in particular to look forward to the job ahead. The first was that Waterford itself was completely unknown territory to me and the team. All of us were coming into this investigation blindly, with no foreknowledge to influence our findings.

The second was that while arrangements were being made to investigate Waterford's Old Town Hall, I was warned that not even the local historian had heard of any ghost stories to come from the building. Rather than be discouraged, I was buoyed at the prospect that a visit by the team would reveal more to the story of the property than even its most devoted caretakers had ever imagined.

Waterford Old Town Hall, 2018

The third reason to anticipate this visit was the participation of a special guest psychic medium. Michele Hewer had assisted several Searcher Group cases in the past, but—until this investigation—had not been available to assist the team for about two years. Now she was my passenger on our sunny drive, and as is the routine for The Searcher Group employing anyone possessing psychic sensitivities, I remained silent on where we were headed.

The land on which Waterford's two town halls were built was sold to the District of Talbot for five shillings in 1847. The first town hall was erected within a year, but 50 years later, the single-storey building was deemed too crowded and dilapidated for the burgeoning village and township. Waterford taxpayers voted to demolish it in favour of constructing a new one on the same site, which was officially opened January 28, 1903.

Waterford Town Hall, 1906

The *Waterford Star* lauded the amenities of the new town hall, including a courtroom (furnished with gas lights), separate jury and witness rooms and a pair of holding cells on the first floor, while the second floor consisted of one large room that included a "nicely arranged" stage at the south end and ample seating for up to 500 people. The local fire hall was also based out of the town hall and remained there for almost a full century before obtaining its own building in 1990.

An addition was built on the north side about 1959 that housed the local police station. When police services became centralized in 1974, the space was rented out as office space for a time. Now it is home to the popular Old Town Hall Bookstore, specializing in the sale of used books; the proceeds support the operation of the building.

Today, though no longer used for municipal purposes, the building continues to host hundreds of patrons attending locally-produced theatre and visiting entertainers' shows, as well as yoga classes, seniors' card groups, dance classes and juried art exhibitions.

~

Michele and I arrived. Already present to greet us were James, David and guest Denise Miller, James' sister. Not having previously seen the interior of this building, I wasn't sure how many bodies we would need to explore it. Denise shared a strong interest in the paranormal, claimed to possess a sensitivity toward the unseen and was asked along on this trip to assist in the proceedings.

Leaving the team to get acquainted with Michele, I walked over to introduce myself to our waiting hosts, Old Town Hall Waterford Board members Teresa Sinkowski, Jennifer Burnett and Denise Jolicoeur. I was also introduced to a local historian just as she finished closing the bookstore for the day and was leaving the premises. She reiterated that during all the years she had been familiar with the history of Waterford, she had never come across any reports of ghostly activity associated with the town hall.

As the historian wished us well and departed, Old Town Hall custodian Brenda Dredge was introduced as the ninth member of our party. She had asked to join our investigation— not just out of fascination or curiosity, but also because she had a revelation to share involving one of her sons. A few years previous, Brenda's son arrived at the Old Town Hall after hours to help her move a heavy table following an event that had taken place there. While he waited alone in one of the rooms, from the corner of his eye he witnessed a figure move behind him. Assuming it was his mother, he was startled the next moment when she entered the room from the opposite direction.

"I've always felt that I'm never alone when I'm here cleaning," Brenda recounted. "There's always somebody here watching." She quickly added, "Not watching in a bad way, not staring. I know they're around, but it isn't uncomfortable."

While I was meeting with the town hall representatives several metres away, Michele began sensing a great deal of sadness emanating from the ground below her, immediately west of the cenotaph. James, David and Denise M. ensured that Michele could not read the historic information inscribed on the stone.

"Were people buried under here?" she asked, looking at the trio. "I feel like there are people reaching up; that's what it feels like. They may have died on this spot because when they come up, they show me their body was there."

Michele paused to concentrate and find the right words to describe her reading of the area. "I feel like somebody's died here—it was tragic, like a murder or an accident of some kind," she relayed before describing a chaotic scene involving many fires burning in the immediate vicinity and that she was hearing someone repeatedly yell, "Get to the water!"

Time was of the essence, so while David, Denise M. and I were given an introductory tour of the interior of the building to determine where to deploy the surveillance cameras, James and Michele conducted a perimeter sweep. As they began to walk northward, Michele saw a woman in a wartime-era nurse's uniform appear briefly at an upper-floor window before fading away. Walking around the building in a counter-clockwise direction past the bookstore at the north end, Michele sensed that where the present-day building is now there used to be one of a wider but shorter stature—possibly a house belonging to a family with lots of children. She picked up on the name Jacob. On the west side she began to feel ill—nausea, coupled with a pounding headache. James' recorder captured an obscure EVP of a woman using the words "weeping" and "head," but the ambient noise of the outdoors made it difficult to transcribe with much more accuracy.

Michele continued, sharing she felt many instances of death, sadness and combat fighting, and again she heard someone shouting, "Fire! Fire! Fire!" connected to the west side of the building. She pointed to a place where she felt there once was a door that led down to the basement and said she heard the name Jacob or Jacobson again, feeling he was very relevant to the area in the past.

At the south end of the building, Michele heard the sounds of horses but was quick to specify that they were not kept there. Instead, she pointed westward down Temperance Street and described a barn where they were actually stabled. Completing their perimeter sweep on the east side, Michele settled by the cenotaph and picked up on the surname Stanley.

Stepping over the threshold of the front vestibule, Michele sensed several energies inside the narrow space between the exterior and interior doors en route to the main lobby area. She heard the spirit people there warn her repeatedly about a disease (circa late 1700s or early 1800s) and that a cranky man warned her to get out.

As I shared the evening's strategy and safety precautions with everyone gathered in the main lobby, Michele was distracted, watching the antics of a cute little girl with dark, curly hair peeking at us all from just inside the vestibule doorway a short distance away.

Once the briefing was finished, I asked Michele to take the lead for the entire group. She opted to tour the basement first.

James and I directed her to the staircase and remained close by, digital recorders activated, as she grasped the railing and cautiously stepped lower into the building's depths, followed by the rest of the team and our curious hosts.

⁓

Stepping into the dimly lit footing, Michele sensed an overwhelming feeling of negativity. As the rest of the group settled at the base of the stairs, Michele started forward down a short passage, then turned to her right and stepped into a dark alcove lined with shelves and stocked with several large boxes of holiday decorations.

Standing among the cartons cluttering the floor, Michele said that though no one was present in spirit, she was visualizing the entrance once included a single door with a barred window, suggesting this space may have been used as a jail cell at one time.

Our Waterford hosts quietly took note of this observation; during our introductory tour of the building interior, they admitted to David and I that though there was no historical evidence to confirm the previous use of this small space, most of the locals believed it was once indeed a jail or holding cell.

Michele walked a few paces and stepped into a room cluttered with dozens more boxes, each one filled to overflowing with books that had been donated for sale in the bookstore. Here, Michele began to feel the return of the intense headache—possibly someone present in spirit sharing a head injury with her. She stopped to concentrate for a moment before sharing she had picked up on the name Trent or Trenton.

Inside a room housing the building's HVAC system, Michele envisioned many crates containing blankets and articles of clothing. She also picked up on the name Ken, and when pressed for a year, she gave 1904. None of our hosts recognized any of these particulars.

Entering the bookstore through its back door, Michele was quick to point out many spirits present, among them Margaret, Annie and a very prominent Shirley. Somehow the number 60 was associated with Shirley, though whether that indicated her age or referred to the year 1960, or something else entirely, could not be determined.

Michele wandered the aisles of the bookstore, commenting that she felt that a major rearrangement of the shelves and sections had recently taken place. When her back was turned away from the group, our town hall hosts quietly confirmed to me this was indeed true.

Stopping at the south side of the store, Michele informed us she was seeing a young, wavy-haired blonde girl, dressed as a boy, named Emily, sitting on a stool. She also described feeling the presence of someone who had a severe breathing/lung-related problem. As she finished relating this piece of information, Michele heard another male shouting at her from afar, ordering her once again to get out.

The reappearance of the aggressive male was weighing on the minds of the group as we exited the bookstore, retraced our steps through the basement and returned to the comparative warmth of the main floor.

~

Back on the main floor, James shared that he felt as if a burst of energy had just rushed right through him. Seconds later I felt an uncharacteristic tension in my abdomen. At that moment my digital recorder caught the disembodied voice of a male speaking between the voices of the group.

EVP: [Male; awed-sounding] You all walk...down the hall!

Michele was shown the open vault a few steps away from the stairs to the basement. Moving inside the vault, both Michele and James sensed a male retreating away from them into a corner. Michele added that she felt inclined to go deeper into an unseen space under the vault where she felt there were several letters from overseas preserved.

Next, James and Michele stepped inside the men's restroom. Here, Michele heard a female hum for a split second. Although no one else heard the same sound, it happened again mere seconds after Michele described it, and this time Jennifer and I heard the humming as well. Oddly, though both James and I were running digital recorders in this area, neither recorder captured the anomaly.

Leaving the restroom, Michele led us down the hallway into the former council chamber where a dozen card tables together with an aged upright piano occupied the large, sun-lit room. This space appeared now to be used for social gatherings. I watched as she slowly walked among the tables, followed closely by James and his digital recorder. The rest of the group stayed back and observed quietly.

Without being aware of the room's significance, Michele felt there were several stern, cigar-smoking male spirits standing about who did not approve of her presence. Glancing toward the north wall, she shared that the windows in it were originally taller. Again, when Michele's attention was focused elsewhere, I turned to our Waterford hosts and received a silent acknowledgment regarding both statements.

Drawn toward a storage space on the opposite side of the room, Michele sensed the spirit of an amiable Scotsman named Reginald Sinclair (or St. Clair) and began to walk with a limp, as if channelling the spirit's gait. She was miming holding onto something beside her, but she was not speaking.

"[A] walker?" I asked, indicating the invisible support.

My question seemed to jostle Michele from a brief trance as she mimicked Reginald's movement. "I get an...um, yeah, yeah," she replied, clearing some mental cobwebs.

EVP: [Male; very faint] Walker.

"[It's] either that or somebody has a limp," Michele continued. "Just when I started to walk, I felt like either somebody [moves] with a walker or has a limp, but it's like that."

"Reggie" claimed to be a decorated veteran, a captain who served during both World Wars with the Royal Navy and had died at the age of 92. It seemed that the spirit of his wife Margaret liked to frequent the bookstore located directly below the council chamber.

~

Leading the group to the second level, Michele stopped at the midway landing area, suddenly winded. She had just experienced a psychic blow—a stabbing sensation in her lower back. After taking a moment to steel herself, she continued upward and walked into the auditorium, where she immediately sensed the large, empty floor was completely covered with dozens of people resting in cots and makeshift bedding.

Michele stopped near the centre of the auditorium floor, away from the stage, and concentrated. "There's a gentleman," she said after a long pause. "He's sitting right here and he's patting a black cat. It's like he doesn't know that we're here. He's in a white t-shirt, grey pants—they're tight around the ankle— and he's wearing suspenders. He's just sitting there like this, not moving. The cat's aware of us, but he is not."

"How old would you say he is?" I asked.

"Early twenties, just a young guy," Michele replied. "I don't know what his deal is. He seems harmless enough. He's not acknowledging any of us." She squatted down and mimed stroking an invisible animal.

"You can feel the cat?" I asked.

Michele rose to her feet then sneezed twice. To the amusement of all, she explained that she was allergic to cats.

"Well, you touched it," I quipped unsympathetically.

Michele smiled, sniffed and agreed.

We moved to investigate a storage room under the seating area, where Michele didn't pick up on anyone even though this space included the window at which she sensed the figure of the nurse during her earlier tour of the exterior. As we closed the doors to the storage room behind us, James suggested we explore the stage next.

EVP: [Male; clear whisper] Stage.

James, Teresa, Michele and I ascended onto the stage. Michele reported that she was hearing much disembodied whispering coming from upstage, toward the back curtains. Although the air conditioning of the building had long been deactivated, James and I agreed we felt a localized cold spot near Michele's waist.

David and I left the group to retrieve and deploy the surveillance cameras. In our absence, Michele and James were shown a small room just off stage, where James felt someone touch his elbow and Michele claimed she was grabbed.

⌒

The late afternoon sun continued to shine through the main lobby as David and I deployed Camera 1 just outside the council chamber. From this angle, the system monitored the doors leading to the basement, the vault and men's room to the east and part of the counter top and our equipment boxes around the corner along the north-south passageway. Moments after activation, Camera 1 captured its first EVP of this investigation.

EVP: [Male; shouting] Peter!

Leaving a digital recorder running near the equipment, I carried the second surveillance camera system up to the auditorium. While David stayed behind with Camera 1 in the lobby area, the digital recorder captured a second disembodied voice, the intonation of which suggested the phantom male was curious about the surveillance system and might have been addressing David.

EVP: [Male] What *is* that?

Completely unaware of the voice speaking around him, David joined me in the auditorium to set up Camera 2. We chose a location among the raised seats at the south end of the building, pointing the camera northward. From this vantage point the camera monitored most of the auditorium, including a small balcony on the west wall, the main staircase leading to the seating area and the stage. Once the camera was operational, everyone exited the auditorium.

As we prepared for a well-deserved break, we said goodbye to Denise J., who had to leave the investigation for the evening. Teresa departed as well, but offered to return after dinner.

While the group congregated about the lobby, Camera 1 picked up on an otherworldly exchange.

EVP: [Male; calling] Danny!…Barbara!
EVP: [Female] Over here.

Upstairs, the microphone of Camera 2 was busy capturing evidence of tension among the auditorium seats.

EVP: [Male] Damn it. Get off the f**king chair.

EVP: [Male] You mean like that?

A loud bang erupted, possibly the sound of a retractable seat returning to its upward position.

EVP: [Male] Big chair.

Downstairs, everyone but Denise M. and I stepped outside for some fresh air. I stood on the landing of the stairs leading to the auditorium while Denise sat on a bench opposite, describing her own perception of spirit energies inside the front vestibule.

Partway through her explanation, I suddenly heard a pair of soft footfalls on the landing behind me. I felt as if someone had just stepped down from the staircase and had settled nearby. Unfortunately, questioning did not produce a response, so Denise and I joined the group outside.

After we exited the building, Camera 1 captured more spectral shouting.

EVP: [Male] Danny…Danny! Danny! Danny!

Meanwhile in the otherwise empty auditorium, Camera 2 captured the distinct sound of someone whistling, followed seven minutes later by a voice…

EVP: [Male] Hey, Danny?

…followed by the sound of a door slamming closed. Again, there was silence for several minutes, then another question.

EVP: [Male] You all want to eat?

After the break, the group split into two teams. James, Denise, Brenda and Jennifer moved upstairs to investigate the auditorium while Michele, David—armed with the parabolic microphone—and I returned to the basement, taking a digital recorder and the wind chime apparatus with us to place inside the bookstore. As we left the main floor, Camera 1 captured still more ethereal interplay.

EVP: [Male A; calling] Henry!
EVP: [Male B] Yeah, what?

There was a short pause.

EVP: [Male A; calling] Henry! Henry!

⁓

While David scanned the basement, listening intently through headphones connected to the parabolic mic, Michele experienced the return of the headache she felt earlier. Other than Michele picking up on the name Leonard, nothing more came of our EVP session.

Entering the bookstore, I positioned the wind chime apparatus in the centre aisle and placed a recorder nearby on a shelf full of books, pointed toward the glass chimes. We conducted an EMF sweep of the entire store and detected no electromagnetic anomalies. Likewise, no EVPs were captured the entire time I was inside the bookstore.

⁓

Two floors above us, James demonstrated to Denise, Brenda and Jennifer how an EVP session is conducted and moved about asking questions aloud while on the stage.

EVP: [Male] Yes there is.
EVP: [Male] What is the name?

Just then James' cell phone rang from his pocket.

EVP: [Male] What about that?

As the group conversed, several clicks, taps and ticks erupted from the opposite side of the auditorium, as if someone was tossing pebbles to misdirect the investigators' attention.

The team reconvened in the main lobby and agreed to leave for a dinner break. James activated one of his digital recorders and placed it inside the open vault. Ensuring everyone was outside the building, I placed a digital recorder on the upright piano in the former council chamber, along with the activated E. Probe 2.0 on a nearby table, and invited Reggie to communicate by speaking into the recorder and/or touching the sensitive proximity alarm. Outside in the lobby hallway, I turned on a CD of popular tunes from the 1940s. I exited the building last, locking the door behind me.

Over the course of the next hour, while the building was completely empty, the spiritual activity picked up. From inside the vault, James' recorder picked up a sound resembling a sharp footfall or a latch from one of the equipment cases being closed on the countertop outside in the hallway. Later, it caught what sounded like a door creak and a single footfall.

Inside the council chamber, several sounds (taps, clicks, snaps, wooden knocks, a dull impact resembling a leather jacket being dropped onto a table top) were recorded at varying distances from the recorder. Additionally, it captured a long, drawn-out breath and a short exhale, perhaps in relieved reaction four seconds after a loud bang was heard from outside the building. The proximity alarm did not sound the entire time.

Just outside the council chamber, Camera 1 captured a brief exchange that seemed to be inspired by the vintage music. One of the songs included a lyric mentioning "Danny," resulting in an appreciative-sounding response.

EVP: [Male; pleased] Yeah!
EVP: [Male; calling] Cara!
EVP: [Female] Yes.

Meanwhile, in the bookstore, the RT-EVP recorder caught many more small taps and clicks, what resembled a flick of a single page, a very subtle suggestion of fabric rustling and what resembled a single wheeze expressed from inside the room.

⁓

Arriving refreshed and energized after dinner, the group was greeted on the front steps by Teresa. She opted to remain for the final leg of the investigation and joined David, Jennifer, Brenda and I in the basement while James, Michele and Denise returned to the auditorium.

Reaching the midway landing up the main staircase, again Michele doubled over with a pronounced pain. Describing it as a punch to the gut, she rallied herself, proceeded up the remaining steps and entered the auditorium with James and Denise. There the pain returned in excruciating waves, prompting James to challenge the invisible assailant to affect him instead. No response as to who was responsible came through to Michele, nor was recorded as an EVP, but the bouts of pain occurred less frequently.

Spotting signs of movement near the control booth above them, the trio climbed the stairs to the seats, passed the surveillance camera and approached the small room. Michele described a very large male sporting a Fu Manchu-style moustache, a long beard and a bandana. She postulated that the abdominal pain she was experiencing was not a direct, malicious attack but rather a physical illustration of the agony this man had endured as his body expired. Pressing further, Michele sensed the male refer to himself as Timber—possibly a nickname.

James then experienced a poke in his abdomen and apologized to Timber for misunderstanding his possible intent to communicate using physical discomfort. Immediately after he acknowledged Timber's message, Michele's stomach pains vanished.

Asked why he chose to remain at the Old Town Hall, Timber's response (through Michele) was that he was "taking care of someone."

Gleaning no further information from Timber, the three returned to the auditorium floor. Four minutes later, James and Michele thought they heard someone screaming. Denise's digital recorder captured a drawn-out male exhale instead.

⁓

Meanwhile, in the basement, we activated the Spirit Box, sweeping every FM band frequency in a backward direction. I was keen to begin confirming the names Michele had shared with us throughout the investigation so far. Although much of what follows was not heard clearly in the moment, later analysis revealed that within a split second of the Spirit Box activation, it began picking up voices.

Spirit Box: [Male] David.
Peter: Hello?
Spirit Box: [Unknown gender] Hello.
Spirit Box: [Female or child] David!
Peter: Is somebody here with us, right now?
Spirit Box: [Male] Yes.
Peter: Is there a child named Emily here?
Spirit Box: [Female] Yeah.
Peter: Is there a Leonard here?
Spirit Box: [Female] Ja.
Peter: Can you say that again, please?

Pure static lasting for 21 seconds was the only response. The static continued over two more questions, but my next one seemed to pique someone's interest.

Peter: Was anybody hanged in front of the town hall?
Spirit Box: [Male] What?

But no more responses seemed forthcoming, so I deactivated the Spirit Box and the five of us moved into the bookstore. We closed the door to the basement and settled near the wind chimes and digital recorder. I activated the Spirit Box, and once again, someone unseen began talking before I even asked a question.

Spirit Box: [Female] All in!

Peter: Hello?

Spirit Box: [Female] Da-vid.

Peter: Did you say, 'David'?

Spirit Box: [Unknown gender] Yes.

Peter: Yes? Who are you?

Spirit Box: [Female] Emily.

Peter: Pardon?

Spirit Box: [Female; calling] David!

Spirit Box: [Male] They're going!

Spirit Box: [Unknown gender] We can…see you!

Spirit Box: [Male; clear] *Aujourd'hui?*

Peter: How many people—in spirit—reside at the town hall here?

Spirit Box: [Male; aggressive, faint] F**k you!

Spirit Box: [Older male] Eleven.

Brenda took this moment to point out that three centre glass wind chime pieces were swaying silently, while the ones flanking them were absolutely still. As everyone's attention focused on this subtle activity, the moving chimes slowed to a standstill.

Peter: Is that you, moving the wind chimes?

Spirit Box: [Male] No.

Peter: No? Who's moving the wind chimes right now? Go ahead!

Spirit Box: [Female or child] Okay, then!

Spirit Box: [Male] Luanne!

Although this exchange was not heard until later during audio analysis, I wondered if the male was trying to dissuade Luanne from complying with my request.

Peter: Can you tell us your name, please? Who is here with us?

Spirit Box: [Unknown gender] Leave me alone.

Peter: [Pointing to David] Can you tell me what his name is, please?

Spirit Box: [Unknown gender; slow, unsure] Ron…Fur…

Spirit Box: [Female or child] That ain't it!

Spirit Box: [Female] Uhhh…

Peter: His name's David. Can you say, "David"?

Spirit Box: [Female] Uhhh…

Spirit Box: [Female or child; excited] I did it!

It is unknown whether this person meant they had spoken David's name successfully earlier, or whether this was Luanne exclaiming that she had just started the middle wind chimes swaying again, despite the male's protest.

Peter: How can we help you?

Spirit Box: [Unknown gender; musical-sounding] Go home.

Peter: It sounded like, "Go home." Would you like us to leave?

Spirit Box: [Young male] Dave!

Peter: That sounded like, "Dave!"

Spirit Box: [Male] Yup. Dave.

Peter: What's the name of the man upstairs in the auditorium?

Spirit Box: [Male; super-fast] Wait a sec!

Spirit Box: [Unknown gender] Don't know.

Peter: Thank you, if you did answer. We're going to stop this session now. Goodnight.

As I shut the Spirit Box off, Brenda and Jennifer said they had watched the same middle-hanging wind chime pieces swaying throughout the length of the session. Again, when all of our attention turned to witness the phenomenon for ourselves, the active chimes slowed to a stop. Was our attention making someone uncomfortable?

David suggested I reactivate the Spirit Box to encourage more chime movement. Leaving the others to observe the wind chimes, I walked the aisles of the bookstore and activated the Spirit Box for a third time.

Peter: Please talk to us. Don't be afraid. We don't have much time here.

Spirit Box: [Female] Cathy?

Spirit Box: [Female] Walk away.

Peter: Is there anything we can do for you?

Spirit Box: [Male] I dunno.

Peter: "I don't know"? I don't know, either. Are you happy here? [At this point Brenda indicated silently that the wind chimes had resumed their isolated movement] Is there a little girl named Emily here? Is there a man named Leonard here?

Spirit Box: [Male; gravelly-voiced, slow] Get…out!

Spirit Box: [Young woman or child; friendly] Hello!

Peter: Is there a bully here at the town hall?

Spirit Box: [Male] Yup.

Hoping to catch an unexplainable sound the whole group would hear in the moment, I stopped the loud static hiss blaring from the Spirit Box, throwing the entire bookstore into sudden silence. The contrast was jarring to our ears, putting us all on high alert for anomalous noises. After a few moments we asked some more questions, but we didn't hear any responses and neither were any EVP replies recorded.

We gathered our equipment and made our way through the back of the bookstore, returning to the cold, dark concrete aisles of the town hall basement. As the group waited for Brenda to finish arming the store's alarm system, she backed out of the door we had all just passed through and turned to face us, astonished. "Call me crazy, but I swear somebody just told me goodbye."

Descending the main stairs, Michele stopped on the mid-point landing and turned to look behind herself. She had sensed a fourth set of footfalls and announced the presence of the angry spirit; apparently he was now trailing Denise. James aimed his camera in his sister's direction and captured a large orb-like anomaly hovering behind her. For safety's sake, everyone used the handrails as they descended the staircase leading to the lobby.

Shortly afterward, our team emerged from the basement and James quickly updated us with their encounter with Timber in the auditorium.

Before calling it a night, we decided to hold a final impromptu pendulum session. "Is there anyone here in spirit with us right now?" I asked the room. The pendulum swung clockwise; yes.

EVP: [Male; quiet] Me.

"Would he like us to know his name?" I asked. The pendulum began to slow to neutral/unsure.

EVP: [Male; clear whisper] No!

"He doesn't want us to know his name?" I asked, wanting confirmation.

I looked up toward Michele; she was staring blankly toward the former council chamber. I had seen this look many times before tonight—she was listening to something in her head. She blinked and teetered on her feet as I spoke to her directly.

"As you're asking questions, I'm [hearing the answers] before you get the answer. I know the man is here, and he definitely doesn't want you to know his name," she said.

"Is this the bully I'm talking to?" I asked.

EVP: [Male] [A deep, hoarse grunt]

Michele nodded to me in the affirmative, then turned away.

No more replies came through the pendulum, so I ended the session and we all looked back at Michele. When she came to, Michele shared that she had picked up on the name Gerald or Gerry and another name similar to Simon associated with the angry male. Michele felt Gerry admit to her that while he was in the physical, he was an egotistical philanderer who had several girlfriends in town while still married. He claimed he was confronted by the fathers of these girlfriends, overtaken and murdered, ultimately dying from a pair of knife wounds. The location of this alleged assault was not specified.

Through Michele, Gerry conceded that while his first instincts were to continue with his angry, aggressive ways, he recognized the need to reform when he found himself shunned by the spirit community populating the Old Town Hall and relegated to the basement. Hearing this, I couldn't help but recall a similarly shunned ghost mentioned in the popular 1989 film *Field of Dreams*.

Our time was up. As James jokingly cited "union rules," the team separated to collect and pack up the equipment. Michele excused herself to use the restroom while our Waterford hosts discussed the evening's adventure.

After several minutes, Michele returned and approached Teresa, Brenda and Jennifer, saying a name sounding like "Benjamin Razooski" came to her inside the restroom. While the surname Zaluski was one belonging to a local family, none of our Waterford hosts was familiar with any members with the first name Benjamin.

Having retrieved and packed all our gear, we said our farewells, expressed our gratitude to our hosts and went our separate ways. We all had much to reflect upon.

Afterthoughts

The preliminary investigation of the Old Town Hall in Waterford was a first of its kind for the property and an interesting and memorable experience for all involved. It was exciting to discover that a building without a previous reputation for being haunted certainly was.

I shared our findings with the local historian I had met upon our arrival in the hope she would be able to help us verify Michele's readings and some of the names captured by our equipment. Despite her personal skepticism regarding the paranormal, she acquiesced (under the proviso of anonymity) and provided some interesting historic facts:

- On Michele feeling like people were or are buried on the property: "It is unlikely that anyone is buried on the town hall site. That said, the Anglican church across the street is built on the former town graveyard. The cemetery was moved to its present location at the southeast part of town (and bodies exhumed) in about 1907, and the church was built in 1909."

- On the nurse-like figure Michele spotted briefly in the (present day) auditorium storage room window: "No nursing was done here as far as I know. During World War I, bandages were prepared and sent overseas for a time from here."

- On Michele "seeing" instances of fire and hearing multiple voices shouting, "Get to the water!": "Waterford had a lot of fires, including a couple of minor fires in the hall—one during a meeting about improving fire protection in the town!"

- On the possibility a home with a large family once existed at the north end of the present-day town hall: "No—the north end was added in 1958 for municipal purposes; the police station was the lower part where the bookstore is now."

- On Michele picking up on the name Jacob: "I actually came up with very few Jacobs right in town. Jacob Goble, the first returning officer for Townsend—there's a record of him being sworn in in 1842 at a Township meeting. In the 1901 census, there wasn't a single Jacob-like surname in Norfolk County. In 1911, there are a couple, but not near here. Jacob Goble—I'm guessing a descendant of the returning officer—who collected taxes, would have remitted these taxes to council in the hall."

- On Michele hearing sounds of horses from the south end of the building and pointing down Temperance Street, describing the location of the horses' shed: "From early times up until the 1950s there was a drive shed behind the current location of the post office. People coming to church, town hall events, etc., needed a place to park."

- On Michele picking up on the surname Stanley near the cenotaph: "Best I can find is a boarder called Herbert Stanford in 1901. I think there were Staffords who lived across the street."

- On the repeated warning of disease (circa late 1700s/early 1800s) by spirit energies inside the main door vestibule: "There was barely anyone here late 1700s/early 1800s; there were some nomadic [First Nations]. The first white birth in Townsend Township is thought to be something like 1794, but there was only a mere scattering of people, then."

- On the small storage room in the basement rumoured to have been a cell: "Not that I know of. There was precious little serious imprisonment here—just a holding tank."

- On the cigar-smoking male spirits that didn't want Michele in the former council chamber: "I have found that the town was actually quite tolerant and supportive of women's involvement. Political rallies held at the hall usually explicitly said 'Women Welcome' even before women could vote, and I don't imagine they would have shooed out a woman in quite that way. As a matter of fact, I expect they would have considered such behaviour ungentlemanly."

- On decorated Captain Reginald Sinclair/St. Clair: "I found an enlisted man from B.C. in the First World War by that name, but he had no connection to here. There was a Sinclair who owned a piece of land in the mid-1800s; that's all I have. We would have noticed a decorated veteran of both wars; [such a person] would have been a matter of general knowledge. As my son said, there's probably only a handful in the world."

- On Michele "seeing" the auditorium floor covered with cots: "During 'Old Boys Reunion' in 1906, people slept on cots in the hall."

- On Michele sensing the name "Leonard" in the basement: "Leonard Sovereign [was] an important figure in town— one of the first mill owners, depending on which version of the story you hear."

Of all Michele's visions and impressions shared here at Waterford's Old Town Hall, my favourite hit of hers was that of the auditorium full of cots. To me, this was such an obscure, rather unexciting piece of information to simply make up on the spot for the sake of saying something under the scrutiny of a roomful of (likely) skeptical people. And yet, buried in the fifth column of the June 28, 1906, edition of the *Waterford Star* is a single sentence that reads: "100 cots will be placed in the Town Hall by Mr. Babcock of Brantford."

None of our hosts that evening was aware of this mundane fact. The only person this vision struck a chord with was a thoroughly knowledgeable—and extremely skeptical—historian who wasn't even present for Michele's walk-through.

Not surprisingly, the team looked forward to returning to the Old Town Hall to address our unseen observers personally and perhaps meet some new ones.

～

Chapter 4

Lebovic Centre for Arts & Entertainment—Nineteen on the Park (Former Stouffville Town Hall): First Investigation

In addition to unfinished business, some ghosts haunt so that they will be remembered.

–Donna Lynn Hope

~

Team: Richard, Paul, Joanna, James, Peter
Hosts: Ashley, Maureen

A long journey awaited the team this warm day in early September 2014. A rather tempestuous rain storm had swept through southern Ontario the night before. Evidence of its fury was apparent as James drove past muddy, overflowing creeks and fallen tree limbs toward the township of Whitchurch-Stouffville. Bringing him up to speed as his passenger, I described the historical background of the investigation site ahead.

Erected in 1896, Stouffville's original town hall housed a marketplace on the ground floor and a concert hall on the second. In 1923, local businessman Sidney Schmidt converted the concert hall into a silent film cinema, naming it the Auditorium Theatre. The ground floor space alternately became an auto garage, a bowling alley and a billiard parlour—all within a span of seven years.

When the theatre was forced to close due to the onslaught of motion picture "talkies," the upper floor was used as a dance hall for a short time. However, Schmidt and his love of the cinema soon inspired local businesses to help fund a complete remodelling of the building's interior in 1930. Most of the second floor was removed and the entire building was converted to a larger theatre space, lovingly named the Stanley Theatre after Sidney's eldest son.

Stanley Theatre circa 1942

Lebovic Centre for Arts & Entertainment, present day

The building underwent more renovations in 1957 when new owners Ted Topping and Harold Spofford added restroom facilities and renamed it the Park Theatre. As television began to dominate the field of entertainment, the cinema closed again two years later and the property was sold to the Village of Stouffville. The historic edifice hosted council meetings until 1970 and accommodated municipal offices until 1998 before being left to stand derelict for the next eight years. A proposal to restore and develop the old town hall as a multi-purpose arts, culture and entertainment facility for the now-incorporated Town of Whitchurch-Stouffville came about in 2006, and three years later, the doors reopened, admitting the public to what is now the Lebovic Centre for Arts & Entertainment—Nineteen on the Park.

James and I arrived for an 11:00 AM meeting with acting
cultural facility and programming coordinator Ashley McIntosh and former employee Maureen O'Halloran. Ashley and
Maureen were eager to introduce us to the building and immediately led us into the darkened, spacious auditorium, where
attempts to activate the lighting from the main floor proved
unsuccessful. It appeared that the rain storm a few hours before
had somehow affected the ground-floor switches.

We doubled back through the main lobby and proceeded to
the second floor to access an alternate set of lights, climbing
a brightly lit, exposed brick staircase adorned with framed vintage posters depicting dozens of theatrical and cinematic images
from the past. The concrete steps led to the wood-floored upper
lobby area—a warm, sunlit space that revealed a small outdoor
balcony just beyond a pair of heavy glass security doors, overlooking the gardens and water features of Civic Square and the
town's iconic clock tower.

James and I were led past a community room and a pair of
restrooms and up a few more steps to the U-shaped catwalk area
overlooking the auditorium. Here several darkened flood and
spotlights stood poised at downward angles, ready to operate for
the next event. The edges of the catwalk were bordered with
counters on which sat numerous mixing board devices and
a master control panel. A metal cabinet stood in a shadowy corner, chock full of tech equipment, gear and tools. Various
lengths and widths of cable and wires snaked along the floor,
safely laid out of the way of foot traffic.

When the general lighting for the auditorium was activated,
the shadows retreated into the corners, revealing an ornately
carved wood ceiling. Ashley explained that it was discovered
hidden under a drop ceiling during the most recent renovation
and was incorporated into the new architectural plans. Not only

aesthetically pleasing, it is also lauded by audiences and visiting performers alike for its acoustic properties.

As the four of us discussed the renovations, several loud snapping and popping noises began to sound sporadically from the auditorium below us. I asked Ashley if this was normal; I was concerned that analysis of the recordings we would be accumulating in the hours to come might be hindered by these sounds if they remained consistent. She said that though such noises have been noted in the past, late at night following an event, this was the first time she'd heard them in such rapid succession and quantity as we were hearing them at that moment. James and I wondered if someone was already trying to get our attention.

On that note, I began to inquire into the kinds of activity that have been experienced in the building.

"I'm former staff," Maureen began. "A lot of times I'd be here by myself, closing up alone. After all the patrons left, it was an unsettling feeling up here, like heavy on my chest, just at night. I always felt quite anxious, just up here—nowhere else in the building."

Ashley nodded. "I'll be the only person in the building, and the booth has been locked while I'm not up here, and the things that I've had out are not where I left them. There are only five keys to the entire building, and only two of us have keys for up here."

Ashley continued to describe how the door to the stairwell we had just ascended has been known to close behind her of its own volition, mostly when she is alone upstairs at night. On separate occasions, Maureen and another staff member witnessed the same phenomenon. No one was anywhere near the door when it closed.

EVP: [Male] [Panting exhale]

Ashley explained that during October 2013, the Lebovic Centre hosted a family-friendly Hallowe'en event featuring an amateur ghost-hunter group. The event was very informal and operated in the vein of good-natured entertainment; the members of the visiting group brought popular devices currently on the investigators' market for the enjoyment of the participants.

"Ashley and I came in before the group came in and the projector was on, where it had been turned off," Maureen shared, indicating a large digital projector under the counter, aimed downward into the auditorium. "We turned it back off and then it kept flashing back on through the night. We have our theories. I know we may sound crazy…"

"You're talking to crazy," I said, indicating James and myself.

The women laughed, then shared their idea that the mysterious operator of the digital projector was none other than the theatre's dedicated, long-standing owner and licensed projectionist, Sidney Schmidt himself. Later research revealed that Mr. Schmidt was so loyal toward his work that he missed but three shows during his entire career, from the silent films (1923) to the "talkies" (1933 onward). He was forced to retire at 75 years of age in 1959, which coincided with the theatre closure and conversion to municipal offices.

Returning to the topic of the Hallowe'en event the previous year, Ashley shared that almost from the outset, the organizers experienced odd and interesting things. Certain equipment—including a Spirit Box—failed to operate while inside the building, but once taken back outside, it functioned normally again.

During an Ovilus demonstration, when the spirit of Sidney was asked if he had any relatives in the area, the device emitted the words "ACROSS," "RIVER" and "BRIDGE." What the ghost-hunting guests did not know at the time was that

Mr. Schmidt's son Stanley happened to reside just south of the building opposite a small bridge spanning Stouffville Creek, which runs just outside the premises.

Presumably to keep the mood light and entertaining, a member of the ghost-hunting group then asked if Sidney was a "party guy." The Ovilus allegedly responded with the words "SILLY" and "GIRL."

I noted a security camera suspended over the auditorium and turned back to Ashley. "Ever catch anything on that?" I asked.

"Nothing that I've seen [live]," she replied. "But I looked at it one day because a painting in the front foyer ended up on the floor, and we were wondering when it came down and [why] the glass on the front of it didn't break." She went on the say that the security footage showed a large, framed painting suddenly come loose from its wall hanger and drop just over one metre to the floor during the early hours of the morning. It was recovered the next morning, miraculously intact. Unfortunately, the original video footage had long since been recycled and the painting itself was also no longer on site. That incident also happened in October 2013.

Retracing our steps back to the main floor, Ashley and Maureen stopped to point out the open stairwell door near the upper lobby. This was the same door that had a habit of closing itself when no one was around it.

I stepped across the threshold and tested the stopper, finding it wedged firmly. I then removed it, allowing the door to swing freely to its closed position. Interestingly, each time we tried this, the door would not close completely but always stopped just short of touching the door frame.

"Where is the door stopper found when this closes on its own?" I asked.

"It ends up coming with the door," Ashley answered.

Using the wedge to prop the door open again, James experimented by kicking the stopper loose toward the threshold, as per Ashley's description. As the door swung shut, the traction of the stopper grinding along the floor slowed the momentum of the door. This time the gap between the door at rest and the door frame was even wider. In order to fully close this door—with a bang loud enough to be heard from the catwalk area—someone would need to pull or push it shut using a significant amount of force.

We propped the door open again, and Ashley recalled that during the restoration of the building in 2007–2008, a construction worker actually resigned part-way through the renovation process, citing that he felt uneasy about working on the premises but not elaborating further. As this new piece of information was discussed, I heard a gasp from the lower stairwell behind me. The hairs on the left side of my head began to rise as I called attention to this unexpected sound. Although no one else heard it in the moment, my digital recorder did. Upon review, the noise resembled a female or a child exclaiming in surprise.

⁓

We returned to the main lobby, where Ashley showed us a series of archival photographs of the building through the years, leading up to its present-day appearance. She revealed that the original southern end of the building was shortened considerably to free up more space for parking outside and replaced with a concrete-based, modern-day annex, complete with a basement—something that had not existed on the property prior to 2007.

Maureen and Ashley then led James and I back into the auditorium to continue our introductory tour. As we walked southward, my digital recorder captured a curious directive.

EVP: [Female or child] Right side! No!

At the entrance to the basement, loud cracking sounds resounded from the opposite end of the auditorium and the catwalks above. These sounds seemed to originate from wherever we were not.

"That's what I often hear when I'm walking through this space," Ashley shared. "I hear sounds from up top; it just sounds like somebody's working up there, or packing."

I decided to experiment and stomped along the spring-loaded auditorium floor, trying to reproduce any of the snaps or cracks we were hearing, but to no avail.

"Today is the most I've heard with this many people in the building," remarked Ashley. "Normally, that's what I hear when I'm all alone."

James set his digital recorder on the auditorium risers before we all turned toward the basement door. Noting that all four of us were about to descend, I joked about being locked down there during the investigation. In seeming response, my recorder captured the sound of a child (or perhaps a crazed, elderly woman) giggling animatedly.

The basement was brightly lit and spacious, divided into quadrants of varying sizes to accommodate storage for the local theatre company and other groups that made use of the building. After a quick look around, we made our way back to the main floor.

Meanwhile, the atmosphere in the auditorium had become highly charged as James' recorder captured a series of loud snaps, cracks and sounds resembling small objects forcefully whipped to the floor and smashing apart. As we all stepped back into the auditorium, James spotted a shadow darting along the catwalk between the stage light fixtures.

While he moved to investigate, Maureen showed me the kitchen located at the back of the building. On multiple occasions, while washing dishes or tidying the kitchen after an event, she heard footfalls approaching from the direction of the auditorium. But whenever she went to the kitchen door to greet the person drawing near, the footfalls would invariably cease, and there was no one in sight.

~

The introductory tour of the premises complete, James and I deployed surveillance Camera 1 to record the expanse of the auditorium pointing at a low angle, while Camera 2 was positioned inside a corner of the catwalk aimed to watch the north and east sections.

While readying the second camera alone on the catwalk, I asked, "Mr. Schmidt, are you here with me right now?" The recorder I had placed on the nearby soundboard counter caught a light, female-sounding exhale or sigh.

Leaving the cameras and digital recorders running, everyone exited the building shortly before 1:00 PM. We parted ways with Maureen; Ashley joined James and I for lunch several blocks away. There we met up with Joanna, who would now join the investigation without any preconceptions, biases or foreknowledge of the building's history.

During the hour the building was supposedly vacant, a digital recorder left on a chair in the upper lobby caught several instances of inhales, exhales, shifting and shuffling sounds, as well as wooden knocks and metallic taps of varying intensities. There were also occasional bangs, likely originating from the auditorium. However, no visual signs of movement—not even floating dust particles—were caught by either of the cameras surveying each level of the auditorium.

~

Ashley, James and I returned to the former town hall with Joanna and reunited with Maureen shortly after 2:00 PM. A few steps into the auditorium, Joanna commented that the energy felt dense, likening it to a space full of people, lowering the oxygen level.

Backing up a few paces, she turned to open the door to the practice room and suddenly doubled over as if winded. "Oh, heavy in here!" she gasped.

"Are you okay?" I asked, concerned.

"Yeah, it just hit me, that's all," she panted. "I think there's more than one in here."

"What do you mean by 'hit'?"

"Their energy is hitting me hard. Think of waves of energy coming at you and you're trying to push back."

The practice room was jam-packed with stacks of chairs, folding tables and a baby grand piano. Joanna pointed to the corner behind the piano. "I [sense] an older male and female," she panted, trying to recover herself. "I feel like they worked here at some point and they decided to stay [after death]. But they're terrified right now."

"Of us? Why?"

"Sometimes they think we can get rid of them and move them forward, and they don't want to [go]."

I tried my best to reassure the unseen pair of our unobtrusive, peace-keeping intentions.

Joanna began to describe them. "I get an older female, silver grey curly hair," she said. "She's also short-to-average [height]. And the male I can't zero in on him so much, but he's a small build as well. I get a darker skin tone. Maybe [in their] sixties? Seventies? I don't get them from that long ago, that's the weird thing."

James began taking photos inside the practice room as Joanna and I backed out. I followed her as she toured the kitchen and dressing room and glanced into the restrooms, but she shook her head as she went, unable to sense spirit energy inside any of them.

"No, it's all in there," said Joanna, indicating the practice room. "They're the strongest energies right now."

Ashley said the practice room was not used very much, which might explain why the alleged spirit couple seemed so shocked to have been found there—perhaps their customary retreat had just been discovered.

Moving deeper into the auditorium, Joanna scanned the room before lowering her eyes and mounting the risers. She had spotted something but was averting her eyes as she walked slowly up the centre aisle between the seats. She turned and pointed to a chair marked E3. "He's sitting here," she said with a shiver. "Male...tall...slim...short brown hair, kinda combed to the side. Robert, I'm getting. Forty or fifty-ish [in age]. Again, not going that far back in history; 1960s? '70s?"

"Does he know you're here?" I asked, holding my recorder near seat E3.

"He just doesn't want to talk to me," Joanna chuckled. "He was hoping I didn't notice him. But he's not moving, either. I see his shirt: white with some striping on it, collared, short-sleeve, casual—like you would wear over jeans. I don't feel like he was employed here."

"Robert? Is that your name?" I asked carefully.

"He doesn't want to look at us, but he is acknowledging."

"Okay, you don't have to look at us, sir. We're just here to visit."

"It's like we're annoying him."

"Are you trying to watch a film or a concert?" I asked. I looked back at Joanna, whose expression indicated that pushing for a response this early upon meeting would likely be in vain. "We'll leave you if you are. Sorry to disturb you."

Meanwhile, Camera 1—stationed a few metres away—captured a disembodied male voice calling out an indistinguishable name that none of us perceived.

Glimpsing more movement from the catwalk above us, James excused himself to return upstairs to take photos of the area.

Joanna turned to Ashley and Maureen to review the spirit energies she'd sensed thus far. "They don't seem like destructive spirits. They could bother you or make sounds—annoy you—but I can't see them do anything destructive. They seem content to be here and share the space. I'm not picking up on anything negative here. They may be active, but not necessarily negative. They wouldn't do anything to harm you; I'm not picking up on that energy."

Camera 1 caught a fraction of a disembodied conversation.

EVP: [Male] Yeah, I get them.

Given the quantity of earlier snapping and cracking noises, I found it interesting that none occurred in Joanna's presence. Ashley, Maureen and I followed Joanna as she continued her tour, sensing nothing atypical about the main lobby or the stairwell. Once inside the upper lobby, however, Joanna did pick up on a pressure she had described in previous investigations as a residual trail left behind by spirit energies as they travel. She marvelled at how she did not detect this sensation in the main lobby directly below us.

James joined us on his way downstairs and reported that after the four of us had exited the auditorium, a single footfall and a new round of snaps, pops and clicks erupted—once again coming from the opposite side of the theatre.

Camera 2 watched as Joanna, Ashley and I walked past it to explore the catwalk. Maureen stopped and leaned against the north wall to observe us for a few moments in full view of the camera.

"There's a lot more pressure on my head [here]," Joanna said off-camera, indicating the top of her head.

"As you said that, I'm getting the first inklings of my hair standing up on end," I conceded. "Right now it's getting stronger."

At this moment, Maureen stepped away from her resting place against the wall and walked past the unblinking eye of Camera 2 to join us on the catwalk. As she passed the lens, a distinct inch-wide orb of light appeared from the wall and fol-lowed Maureen, rising upward at a 30-degree angle. The orb sped up and then disappeared into the crown of Maureen's head before she exited the shot.

An EVP session yielded no results, and no more orb-like particles were captured on video, even though all four of us walked past the camera again, stirring the air as we moved.

～

We were overdue for a break and stepped outside to Civic Square, leaving the equipment to continue to roll without us. Over the 20-minute period the building was empty, both sur-veillance cameras gathered some interesting phenomena. Heavy footfalls resembling someone wearing work boots were recorded marching along the catwalk. On the main floor of the auditorium, more audio phenomena were captured.

EVP: [Male; calling] Ben!

This voice was followed by a loud bang very close to Camera 1, and the same male shouted something indistinguishable before calling again.

EVP: [Same male] Harry!

There were no verbal responses recorded; however, a short time later, a small yellow light appeared and drifted along the floor parallel to the eastern wall before disappearing.

Meanwhile, a recorder left behind on a chair in the upper lobby caught a series of shifting and shuffling sounds preceding some light metallic rattling resembling the noise of a refreshment cart being pushed about, its contents shaking and clinking against each other.

Richard and Paul arrived and entered the Lebovic Centre for the first time. They paused to survey the 6600-square-foot space while James and I brought more equipment inside. Maureen excused herself for the evening and left.

Meanwhile, Camera 2 recorded a warning shout on the catwalk…

EVP: [Male; shouting] Everyone get back!

…followed by another pair of loud bangs next to the camera. As the team began to file back inside through the south door, someone issued another warning.

EVP: [Young female] Get out!

A third tour of the building began; Richard and Paul were shown the main lobby, the staircase and the upper lobby.

Ashley suddenly remembered that she had forgotten to tell us the glass security doors leading to the short balcony over Civic Square had a history of opening themselves after hours. "I didn't think to mention them," she said, shaking her head in disbelief. "I get called whenever the [building] alarm system goes off, and I'll get a call when the doors [in the upper lobby] are open. Maybe I shouldn't be blaming my staff."

Richard, a veteran security specialist, inspected the doors, noting they were composed of heavy glass and polished nickel with a self-closer attached. The deadbolt lock appeared to work perfectly. Ashley added that originally there was a single window in this location, replaced by the doors in 2008.

Paul encouraged me to leave a recorder inside one of the restrooms (a source of water energy), so I began a new recording and left it on the counter of the women's washroom for the next 85 minutes. Upon review of this recording, close to the 32-minute mark, a clear EVP was captured while the second floor was otherwise deserted.

EVP: [Female; clear, quick whisper] Hello!

Richard decided that a third camera system should be deployed in the main lobby, so James left to retrieve another system. I moved into the semi-darkness of the catwalk alone to refresh the discs for Camera 2. Leaving my recorder on the counter nearby, I knelt before the DVD recorder. My eyes adjusted to the dim light as I peered at the remote control, trying to locate the buttons needed to end the recording and finalize the DVD.

Without warning, just over my right shoulder, a fluorescent safety light under the counter turned on, providing me with ample illumination. Grateful for the aid, I expressed my appreciation aloud to my invisible assistant just as James entered the catwalk area to join me. I pointed out what had just occurred, and we immediately seized the moment to attempt EVP communication.

As the pair of us asked questions, Richard arrived and quietly approached us on the catwalk. As he moved closer, I glanced at the monitor of the camera system and spied a sizable mist-like orb appear to pass right through James' body and zoom toward Richard before disappearing. Regrettably, the DVD-R was in the process of being finalized, so this anomaly was not recorded on the disc.

Examining the opposite side of the catwalk, James observed that the underside of another section of the counter was also alight. Ashley joined us and said that the safety lights could only be activated via a touchscreen panel on the control board. She pointed out the computerized device on the counter, enveloped in darkness. It was turned off.

Moments later, the fan of the digital projector began turning itself on and off. Ashley recalled a similar occurrence during the previous year's Hallowe'en event, adding that a repairman had been called in to remedy the phenomenon. "That's not normal," she assured us. "The [repair] guy said it should not come on unless the projection system is on. They couldn't find anything wrong with it."

Exiting the catwalk area, James took photographs of a hatchway that led to the rooftop. Believing he had captured the image of a face, he was about to take more photographs in order to confirm or debunk it. Raising his camera, his recorder caught an all-too-familiar warning.

EVP: [Male] Watch out!

Immediately after James depressed the camera shutter a third time, another comment came.

EVP: [Young male] Tss! Tss! Point it, snake!

Everyone then retreated downstairs to the main lobby, where Richard deployed the third camera system. Less than six minutes after the team's departure, the recorder left behind on the catwalk counter captured several pieces of audio evidence over the span of 17 minutes.

EVP: [Male] He's here!

This exclamation was followed by a tapping sound near the recorder.

EVP: [Female; pained-sounding grunt, far from the recorder] Don't!

EVP: [Several males; shouting in unison] We will!

EVP: [Male; comical falsetto] Turkey!

EVP: [Male] Secret!

EVP: [Female; loud, breathy] They saw him.

~

We walked Richard and Paul through the basement, where a brief burst of EMI static was caught on my recorder immediately after a comment was made about Paul's ability to spot flaws in building construction.

I moved deeper into an adjacent storage room, where a freestanding framed vertical mirror stood at the end of a table. I pointed out the mirror to Richard, as mirrors and reflective surfaces are an ongoing mystery in terms of paranormal research.

He grinned in appreciation as I placed a digital recorder on the table aimed at the reflective surface before walking away to rejoin the others near the base of the stairs.

In the course of the group's conversation, Paul cracked a joke and Richard laughed. A loud, sharp hissing sound erupted near my recorder as if someone disapproved. None of us heard this hiss at the time, and James' recorder did not pick up this same anomaly, which ruled out the possibility that it was an explainable environmental noise.

⁓

I retrieved my recorder from the table, and everyone moved back upstairs into the auditorium to try an EVP session there. Settling at the foot of the seating risers, James attempted to communicate with Robert, but Joanna said that he was no longer present. The projector fan began to operate on its own from the catwalk above us, this time with increased frequency.

"Is there anyone here who wishes to speak with us tonight?" James asked.

Camera 1 captured a direct response.

EVP: [Male] Not me.

The same camera system also picked up many more incidences of loud banging, yet none of us heard these noises in the moment. Joanna settled into seat E3, concentrating on Robert's energy. Camera 1 continued to record phenomena as we asked our questions.

EVP: [Same male] Benny...Harry...Benny!

"Can you tell us the name of the man near where Joanna is seated?" I asked.

EVP: [Same male] Jake.

Richard left the auditorium to explore the catwalk area alone and reported that both of the underside safety lights were still activated.

I began to hear a series of light, metallic rattling sounds coming from the north end of the auditorium and called attention to them. Ashley explained that this noise was common, made when someone is walking up and down the risers. This explanation would have been satisfactory, except none of us was moving on them.

Ensuring that everyone nearby remained still, I moved closer to the risers and peered into the dark shadows beneath them, trying to pinpoint which set of narrow crosspieces supporting the structure were the primary source of the rattling. Directly opposite me, Richard reappeared from the main lobby walking south; he confirmed hearing the same rattling noises.

I asked for a noise louder than the rattling sounds. In seeming response, a loud door slam resonated from somewhere far from the team (subsequent checks revealed all interior doors remained unmoved). The metallic rattling began again, lasting six seconds before subsiding.

I decided to try an EVP session. "Is that you knocking on the risers?" I asked. Silence.

"Am I speaking with a man?" Again, my question was met with silence.

"Am I speaking with a child?" An instantaneous—albeit brief—rattle sounded from under the risers.

"Yeah?" Short rattle.

"Are you a boy?" Short rattle.

"Older than 10?" Short rattle.

"Are you a teenager?" A short set of rattles.

"Do you work here at the hall?" Silence.

Joanna rose from her seat and walked down the riser steps, during which time—ironically—no rattling sounds occurred. In fact, there was complete silence from the riser crosspieces over the next minute as James requested communication using the projector fan.

"We're probably confusing the person because James is speaking," I suggested. As if in response, a short burst of rattling began. Simultaneously, the projector fan activated.

"Turn it off," James ordered from the foot of the risers.

The fan remained on, but a short rattle emanated from the darkness under the risers. Another loud thump came from elsewhere in the building. Again, no one had moved. Some faint rattling sounds began, then stopped as Joanna pulled out her cell phone to use its camera function.

"Is it okay if Joanna takes a picture of you, please?" I asked the darkness as Richard joined us. There was no response, but I thanked the unseen entity anyway.

A light rattle seemed to reply before yet another loud thump resounded just outside the auditorium. "What was that?" I asked. "Did anyone move?"

Camera 1 caught a response.

EVP: [Female] No.

"Do you have enough energy to say your name into this little box I'm holding?" I asked, indicating my digital recorder. My request was met by complete silence from the riser crosspieces.

"Would you, please?" Light, hesitant rattling.

"Are you afraid of us?" Immediate rattling, increasing in intensity.

Again, Camera 1 captured voice phenomena from the solitary male spirit.

EVP: [Male] What is your name?…Ben.

More banging sounds unheard by the team came before another EVP.

EVP: [Same male; impatient] Benny!

Joanna shot a pair of short videos, the first of which caught a few orb-like objects rushing past her.

James—who had ascended to the catwalk area—continued to attempt communication using the projector. "Can you put the fan back on for us?" he asked.

The digital recorder I was carrying captured a sharp reply.

EVP: [Male] No!

I asked a series of questions but was met with silence. I wondered if time had run out for this session. "Hello? Are you still here?"

EVP: [Male] Yes!

The rattling immediately began anew. I asked whether Sidney Schmidt was with us in the building and received some hesitant-sounding responses. Pressing onward, the rattling replies grew in intensity.

"Are you afraid of [him?]" I asked. Before my question was even finished, loud rattling emanated from the metal cross-pieces. When James and Richard seated themselves on the risers, the rattling stopped.

Richard reported hearing sounds of movement from one of the corners of the catwalk. The recorder perched on the counter-top captured a response that both James and I heard as a disembodied voice.

DV/EVP: [Female; cheerful, friendly] Hello!

Although we asked further questions, nothing more was heard or recorded, so we decided to break for dinner. Hoping to capture some spirit interaction while we were away, we locked the building behind us and headed across the street for dinner. Over the 80-minute break, our equipment captured a variety of environmental noises from subtle to obvious: wooden knocks, chain link shaking, riser rattling and a male breathing rounded out the collection of discarnate data. All of these sounds ceased when the group returned.

~

As the team settled in the auditorium, our discussion of the films *The Conjuring* (2013) and *Annabelle* (2014) seemed to inspire a pair of responses.

EVP: [Female] Anna…a-belle.

EVP: [Male] Marie, fall off.

We began a Spirit Box session near the risers.

Peter: Hello?

Spirit Box: [Male; shouting] Yell at it!

Peter: Who's this? Can you tell us your name, please?

Spirit Box: [Older female; slowly] Anne…Harvey.

Peter: I'm sorry, what's your name, please?

Spirit Box: [Young male] Mike!

Peter: What's the name of the woman who's here with us besides Joanna and Ashley?

Spirit Box: [Female] Emily.

Spirit Box: [Unknown gender] Heard me again.

Spirit Box: [Older female] Reginald!

Spirit Box: [Female] Why can't…you…find…him?

Peter: Robert?

Spirit Box: [Male; immediate] Yes.

Spirit Box: [Male] F**k...this.
Peter: Can you use this to speak to us, please?
Spirit Box: [Unknown gender; unknown accent] Joanne.
Spirit Box: [Male] Hey, Joanne.
Spirit Box: [Male; calmly] E...nough. [Door-closing sound]
Peter: Robert, are you watching us right now?
Spirit Box: [Male] Sure.
Spirit Box: [Unknown gender] You aren't...watching.
Peter: Would you like us to leave?
Spirit Box: [Male] Go on...home.
Spirit Box: [Male] Joanne...[Thump sound]
Spirit Box: [Female; clear, sarcastic] Insightful.
Spirit Box: [Female or child] [Is] that it?

I turned the Spirit Box off. The team then took turns asking questions, but we neither heard nor recorded any responses. I attempted a pendulum session next but was not successful.

I asked, "Robert? Would you like us to leave?"

James' recorder captured a vague response.

EVP: [Female or young male] Get out. Discuss.

~

Joanna left the investigation at 7:50 PM. While James, Richard and Paul took a break outside, Ashley and I conducted a second Spirit Box session in the main lobby.

Peter: Hello?
Spirit Box: [Female; stern/impatient] What do you need?
Peter: Who am I speaking with?
Spirit Box: [Child] Mom?
Peter: Who? Can you say that again, please?
Spirit Box: [Child; loud, urgent] Mom!
Spirit Box: [Female] Where'd they go?

Spirit Box: [Unknown gender] I don't know.

Spirit Box: [Unknown gender; boastful] *I* do!

Peter: How many people reside here at the Lebovic Centre in spirit?

Spirit Box: [Male; quiet, stern] Jacob.

Peter: Is there a little boy who likes to hang out here?

Spirit Box: [Male; instructing] Lay low.

Peter: What's the name of the lady who likes to sing in the auditorium?

Spirit Box: [Unknown gender] Natalie.

Spirit Box: [Female; indifferent] Whatever.

Peter: Is Sidney here?

Spirit Box: [Female] What?

Spirit Box: [Male; friendly] I've got ya!

Spirit Box: [Male] Hello!

Peter: Who works here full time?

Spirit Box: [Female; speaking carefully] Ahhh…

Spirit Box: [Male; bluntly] Her.

Peter: [Pointing toward Ashley's workstation] Who sits in this chair and uses that corner?

Spirit Box: [Female] It's…Ashley.

Peter: Ashley?

Spirit Box: [Unknown gender] Told you.

Peter: What's Ashley's last name?

Spirit Box: [Female; distant] McIntosh.

Spirit Box: [Male] Get outta here.

Peter: Who likes to play with the soundboard upstairs on the catwalk area?

Spirit Box: [Male] Dave.

Spirit Box: [Male] Go away.

Spirit Box: [Male; distant] Fred!

Peter: Fred?

Spirit Box: [Female; coy] Maybe.

Peter: Did you say, 'Fred'?

Spirit Box: [Male; very quickly] No.

Peter: Do you mind if we stay all night?

Spirit Box: [Unknown gender] Go home now.

Peter: You really want us to leave and stop asking questions?

Spirit Box: [Female A; extremely faint] Go.

Spirit Box: [Female B; clear, pleading] Don't go!

Peter: Don't go?

Spirit Box: [Unknown gender] Go away!

Spirit Box: [Female A] Pfft! Buzz off!

Spirit Box: [Male] Prick!

Spirit Box: [Female B; distant] Don't go!

Richard joined Ashley and me inside the main lobby.

Peter: Do you have a message before we go?

Spirit Box: [Male] See ya later!

Spirit Box: [Male; quiet] Go.

Spirit Box: [Male] Wait.

Spirit Box: [Female] Where are you?

Peter: Okay, we're going to try talking to you…

Spirit Box: [Female] What?

Peter: [Continuing]…without this [device], all right? Thank you.

Spirit Box: [Unknown gender; protesting] No!

Peter: Pardon?

Spirit Box: [Male; raspy, creepy whisper] Beat you!

I turned the Spirit Box off. James and Paul returned, and a second attempt at a pendulum session proved futile. "Well, I'm going to say goodnight to you now," I said, pocketing the pendulum.

Richard observed a small puddle of water on the lobby floor near the electrical outlet powering Camera 3. No one recalled spilling water or leaving a condensation-covered bottle on the floor at any time during the course of the evening.

James' recorder captured a parting request that no one heeded.

EVP: [Male; slow drawl] Ss-taay! [Pause, then louder and clearer] Sss-taaay!

The hour growing late, the weary team began to pack the equipment up. James' recorder captured the loud thuds of this activity, but also a disembodied observation.

EVP: [Female or young male; whispering] Heavy!

Finally, Ashley armed and locked the building. The team expressed its gratitude for the opportunity to investigate, and everyone left the premises. We all had long drives home.

Afterthoughts

We were already familiar with the reports of footfalls and feelings of unseen presences, but what we experienced and were able to document in a matter of hours far exceeded our hopes for verifying a haunting at the former Stouffville Town Hall. The spirits seemed to be well aware of why we had come to investigate and were only too pleased to make themselves known to us, albeit from safe distances.

The unexplained appearance of the water puddle in the main lobby toward the end of the investigation is worth considering. Whereas we cannot dismiss its presence as a simple oversight, in many cases water appears as a byproduct of spirit manifestation.

Researching the names provided to us through EVPs would prove daunting because most—with the exception of one—were simply first names and very common ones at that: Ben/Benny, Harry, Jake, Marie, Mike, Emily, Reginald, Joanne, Jacob, Dave and Fred. The exception was the older female who clearly identified herself as "Anne Harvey" at the outset of the first Spirit

Box session. Subsequent research resulted in a historical hit when I came across an obituary for an Anne Harvie, a Stouffville resident from 1954 until her passing in 1977. Although a connection with the building could not be immediately established, her funeral took place just across the street.

Additionally, the male who said, "Hey, Joanne," during the first Spirit Box session might very well have been addressing Joanna. Could the speaker have been Robert, finally ready to communicate?

We soon formulated plans to return to the former Stouffville Town Hall.

~

Chapter 5

Old Caledon Township Hall: First Investigation

It's a big spooky place when you're in it alone. It's like you can hear all the whispers of all the voices of all the actors who ever played here. Kind of creepy.

–Benjamin R. Smith

~

Team: Richard, Paul, Joanna, James, Victoria, Peter
Guests: Bill, Beth
Hosts: Linda, Jeannette, Janet

The team pulled into the parking lot of the Old Caledon Township Hall on a particularly cold evening in December 2014. We were greeted warmly by two members of the Caledon Townhall Players (Linda and Jeannette), a former member (Janet) and a newspaper reporter (Bill), accompanied by his wife (Beth). Everyone seemed eager to meet us and curious about what we would find.

In customary fashion, Joanna had been kept in the dark concerning this location. The team congregated at a coffee shop in north Brampton an hour before being led to this evening's site. Joanna remained in her car waiting patiently as the rest of the team was admitted into the building, stepping through a small lobby before proceeding into the 142-seat theatre.

Old Caledon Township Hall, 2014

It was obvious that many changes had been made to the former courthouse and township hall over the years. Erected in 1875, the red-brick building also served as a library and hosted meetings of the Church of England as well as countless social and public events, even though no indoor restrooms or running water existed on-site until 1992.

With the opening in 1963 of new municipal offices, the former township hall was leased to the Caledon Townhall Players (CTHP) and has been maintained by the amateur theatre group ever since. The building received an Ontario Heritage designation in 1982, which proved to be its salvation when proposed widening of nearby Highway 10 secured its safe relocation 20 metres south and 40 metres east of its original foundation in 2003. The move of the historic building afforded CTHP the opportunity to construct much-needed basement space, and an addition built onto the south side functioned as a small, comfortable green room for the cast and crew of CTHP—complete with washroom facilities.

Twin staircases descend to the spacious basement. Here the team was shown the dressing rooms and a large communal lounge dubbed the Loonie Café, complete with a kitchenette. The lounge space was warm and inviting; its walls were decorated with dozens of framed images from the archives of the CTHP, including cast and crew photos and original production poster art. Spread about the room were several photo albums brimming with additional memorabilia. From the lounge, another staircase winds up and around an elevator that leads back to the main entrance. Additional restroom facilities, costume storage and a furnace room contribute to the seeming maze of corridors and rooms below the stage.

⌒

Paul set to work immediately, deploying Camera 1 in the Loonie Café, positioning it to aim across the room opposite the kitchenette. The room seemed quiet and far enough away from the excited chatter between hosts and guests to enable clearer interpretation of the audio during analysis later. Almost immediately, the camera microphone picked up an impressive number of EVPs spoken by a single male over an 18-minute period.

EVP: [Male] James.

A long pause followed with no response, until he called again…

EVP: [Same male] Jimmy.

…followed by another lengthy silence before he tried again.

EVP: [Same male] Jim.

After a short pause, the male's search for his associate began to sound more urgent…

EVP: [Same male] Hey, Jim!

…but even this call did not elicit a reply.

Camera 2 was deployed upstairs at stage right, aimed toward the auditorium, the front door and the partially open mezzanine. The mezzanine was divided into thirds and housed an eight-seat balcony, a props room and a control booth in which the sound and lighting control boards sat dormant.

Satisfied that all was well and that the lock-up procedure was understood, Linda excused herself for the evening, leaving us in the capable hands of our hosts Janet and Jeannette. James went to fetch Joanna.

～

Unbeknownst to the rest of us, Joanna had already met her first spirit occupant of the premises. While waiting inside her car, a weathered-looking male carrying a shovel approached her, curious about her presence. Joanna lowered her car window and perceived "David" as a personable groundskeeper with squinting eyes whose timeworn appearance was owing to excessive smoking and alcohol consumption. He wore a red lumber jacket and a cap from which a curl of grey hair sprouted, dangling over his forehead.

When she asked David why he chose to remain behind on the property, his reply was simply, "This is all I know."

The groundskeeper's image dissipated as Joanna shifted her focus to James, then approaching her car. James logged Joanna's encounter with David as the pair made their way inside the building. Stepping inside the front entrance, Joanna's heart began to race.

"Do you feel anything right here?" asked James.

"I do, but I don't know if it's coming as I acclimatize myself," she answered.

EVP: [Male; loud] [Drawn-out exhale lasting three seconds]

"It's a different feeling," Joanna continued, completely unaware of the intense hiss fading away over her words. "My heart's racing. I have a feeling that something doesn't want me here."

"Why is that?" asked James.

"Fear."

"What would they have to fear from you?"

"Some fear [me] because they think I'm going to get rid of them."

"This building is much bigger than it looks," James said, scanning the theatre.

"Oh yeah?" replied Joanna.

"Yeah," nodded James.

EVP: [Unknown gender] Yeah!

James and Joanna walked together along the main aisle of the house. The high level of anxiety Joanna had initially picked up on seemed to fade as distance grew between her and the front entrance; however, she reported feeling a new, heavy sensation take its place as they neared the stage.

Mounting stage left, James stopped short over a short stretch of the floor where the black painted surface was more scuffed and worn. "Whoa, I just felt tightness in my jaw as we stepped up here," he frowned. "I'm feeling a chill right here and a tingly sensation in my feet."

Joanna nodded, looking around. "Yeah, it's heavy here. It's like we stepped into another dimension. I'm definitely picking up on a male." She eyed the exposed wood of the stage and concentrated. "Something is going on [here]. They stand there and observe."

As soon as Joanna finished speaking, the various sensations James was experiencing ceased.

Joanna turned to Richard as he walked over. "We need to test this spot," she said, indicating the worn surface of the stage. "This is a heavy, high-activity spot."

Richard and James understood what Joanna was suggesting: this spot could indicate the presence of a vortex or portal between our respective worlds.

"Ask Peter; he's got his meter," Richard suggested.

"I'm starting to feel that numb, tingling feeling again," James frowned, indicating his jaw.

I was summoned and returned to the stage to take EMF readings, paying particular attention to stage left and the scuffed area. Although James suspected an unseen source of electricity was the cause of the curious sensations, there were no spikes of the Gauss meter needle, and an inspection of the underside of the stage floor revealed empty space for several metres in all directions.

"The name Henry just popped into my head," Joanna blurted. "He's the male that keeps coming out on stage."

"Are you getting anything from Henry as to how long he's been here or what he does here?" asked James.

"No, but he's definitely interested in theatre. He's curious and attends the shows and may have been part of a production because he seems familiar with them."

I left James to record Joanna's tour and descended alone into the brightly lit basement, taking EMF readings and noting high spikes of the Gauss meter when passing under fluorescent light fixtures along the way. I arrived at the Loonie Café and began an EVP session in front of the surveillance camera, introducing myself and politely inviting conversation. I settled behind the counter of the kitchenette and was soon joined by Joanna and James.

Joanna had not picked up on anything peculiar until she reached the kitchenette. There she began to feel vestiges of the intense anxiety she had felt inside the front entrance, directly above us. "It's weird because it's like my head feels like there's a high frequency pitch going on," she shared, scrunching her face, trying to find the words. "It *feels* like that; I don't hear it, but it *feels* like that."

Upstairs, from her vantage point on the stage peering westward, Victoria caught a fleeting glimpse of a small point of light darting between the seats of the small balcony area of the mezzanine. Immediately she began an EVP session. "Anyone want to talk with me?" she asked the empty air.

It was Camera 2 that captured an otherwise unheard reply behind her.

EVP: [Female] Me.

James and Joanna returned to the ground floor via the staircase leading back to the main entrance. Next opening a door marked "Employees Only," they stepped into a short corridor leading to the lone staircase that accessed the mezzanine. As the pair moved toward the narrow stairs, Joanna stopped abruptly.

"I found another one," she informed James, indicating the open space that extended under the stairs. "A female with long, curly brown hair. She's hiding from us."

James moved into the storage space cautiously, speaking words of assurance.

Joanna straightened with a revelation. "Rhonda," she uttered. "You know that high frequency pitch I got below? I think that was her voice. She's talking right now, but I can't make it out. She's freaking out, almost delirious. That's the anxiousness I felt at the front door."

"Are you getting anything about Rhonda, like a time period?" James asked as he and Joanna climbed the steps to the mezzanine.

"She's not from too long ago. Maybe the 1970s?"

~

Meanwhile, in the basement, I retraced my steps and conducted an EVP session in the dressing rooms before ascending the staircase and arriving at stage right. Victoria was already onstage, taking photos and watching James and Joanna moving along the upper mezzanine, opposite. Paul sat among the seats of the house, concentrating on the ambiance of the theatre.

I placed my digital recorder on a narrow table at mid-stage and turned to take photos of the house and mezzanine. James and Joanna sounded quite animated as they walked through the props room and into the lighting booth. I aimed my camera at the auditorium, panning slowly from right to left, settling on Victoria standing still at stage left.

At that moment the camera began to hesitate before the shutter would engage, so I stopped to examine the viewing screen. The target-finding function, represented by a rectangle-shaped graphic, was rapidly attempting to focus—not on

Victoria, who was clearly standing within sight, but on a spot in front of her—in the open air over the seats. The graphic undulated and blinked, changing dimensions from square to rectangle, trying to focus on an unseen subject for several seconds before it disappeared and then reappeared surrounding Victoria.

While this was happening, the recorder on the table behind me captured a friendly greeting.

EVP: [Female or young male] Hello!

⌒

Simultaneously, inside the mezzanine control booth, Joanna spoke up. "There's another male here," she noted. "Not to offend, but he's got a bit of a beer gut."

She and James laughed before she continued describing the gentleman. "White sweater with a V-neck, black trousers, dark or black hair, goatee or small beard," Joanna relayed. "I'm thinking [he's from] the '70s again and could be connected to Rhonda."

"Do you have a personal relationship with Rhonda?" asked James of the unseen male.

"He indicates 'no,' but I'm feeling some vibes indicating denial on his part."

"Can you tell me what your name is? I'm James."

"I'm Joanna," Joanna said, pausing to concentrate before relaying the reply: "Bob."

"My last name is McCulloch. Can you tell me yours?" asked James.

"I got Handoff or Handolf," Joanna replied after a moment of silence. "He's a nice guy; a lovely gentleman. At first he was hiding from us, but not anymore."

⌒

Across the theatre I placed a pair of proximity alarms between the table at mid-stage and the edge of the apron, hoping a curious spirit might trigger them at some point in the evening within view of Camera 2.

James and Joanna called out to me from the mezzanine with an update on the names they'd amassed thus far. While they did this, James' recorder picked up a third person with them who couldn't resist correcting Joanna.

"So the one onstage coming in and out," Joanna began. She turned back to James. "What was his name, again?"

EVP: [Female; British accent, clear] Heather!

"Henry," James recalled.

~

Downstairs, Bill and Beth were conducting an interview with Paul and Richard as they walked through the Loonie Café, where Camera 1 captured a running commentary on the presence of the visitors.

EVP: [Male] How many people?

The foursome stopped moving briefly, unaware they were being observed.

EVP: [Same male] Yeah, still here.

As the party exited the basement, the camera audio recorded the male's voice once more.

EVP: [Same male] They are leaving now.

~

Upstairs, Paul caught up with James, Joanna and Victoria to discuss the layout of the theatre. While they conversed, a fifth voice chimed in, unbeknownst to anyone.

EVP: [Young boy] Hi! Come on!

Next door in the green room, Janet relayed some of her eerie experiences in the Old Caledon Township Hall to me. She described instances of small objects falling to the theatre floor from the props room, a levitating hammer, cups of screws and nails inexplicably spilled during set construction and even a cast member's car keys vanishing from one place only to reappear in another during a rehearsal.

We were joined shortly afterward by Bill, Beth, Jeannette and Joanna; they settled in with us to continue Bill's interview.

Out in the auditorium, Richard stood alone on the stage while Victoria wandered the main aisle, asking questions. Behind Richard, Camera 2 recorded a lone EVP that did not correlate with any of Victoria's questions.

EVP: [Female] Hug.

Richard joined Victoria and slowly wandered along the main aisle, studying the design of the rows of seats while listening carefully to the silence between Victoria's questions. Within moments the stage camera captured a bright orb-like object that appeared from the south wall and zoomed directly toward Richard, then turned and flew across the auditorium in the opposite direction before vanishing.

Richard entered the green room and waited for a break in the interview conversation to broach the subject of the auditorium seats with Jeannette.

"They're not original," she replied. "They came from another theatre."

"That's what I was going to guess," said Richard. "They look like they're an Art Deco type of design, from the 1930s."

"If I'm not mistaken, they came from a theatre in Owen Sound," Jeannette said, jotting a note down for herself. "I can find out and let you know if it's important."

"It could be," said Richard, "because you don't know if you brought somebody with those chairs."

⁓

Downstairs, in the Loonie Café, Camera 1 recorded 22 minutes of silence before Paul entered the lounge. His presence seemed to provoke a panicked reaction.

EVP: [Male; urgent-sounding] Get back! Get back from there!

It is unknown if this order was directed at Paul or at another spirit who may have been in Paul's path.

⁓

Upstairs, Richard, Victoria and I looked on as Joanna pointed out the area at stage left where she had detected Henry to Jeannette, Janet, Bill and Beth.

Jeannette's eyes widened in realization. "This is where I flew!" She explained she was mysteriously tripped up at the same location on stage during a performance of the comedy *Sex Please, We're Sixty* in 2012.

"You've said that it was a comedy," said Richard. "Would you say it was a little risqué?"

"Oh, it was *very* risqué, oh yeah," smiled Jeannette. Janet nodded in agreement.

"Maybe whoever it was didn't appreciate it," Richard suggested with a small shrug.

⁓

Nearing 6:00 PM, Bill and Beth decided to leave for the evening. Bill's notebook was filled with enough information for a lengthy article about the team and our investigation of the Old

Caledon Township Hall. We bade them goodbye and decided to go get food to bring back with us to eat before resuming our investigation.

I wished to leave a recorder somewhere on the mezzanine before heading out, so Janet joined me upstairs. I introduced myself to the spirits and reiterated our amicable intentions as visitors, hoping to calm Rhonda as well as glean a response from Bob.

We moved into the control booth, where Janet reminisced about performing sound-mixing duties. Here I heard a faint female hum or whine, seemingly in response. Unfortunately it was not caught on my recorder, and we moved back into the props room where I invited Bob and Rhonda to communicate using the recorder I was leaving behind on a wooden box in the middle of the room. Forty-two seconds later, I received a response that might have been from Bob.

EVP: [Male; whispering] That's me.

Unaware of the voice, Janet and I left the recorder behind and returned to the main floor. Jeannette walked Janet through the building and reviewed the lock-up procedure before leaving for the night. Richard and Paul volunteered to stay behind while Joanna, Victoria, Janet, James and I left to seek sustenance. They sat among the house seats and quietly conversed.

Over the 25-minute period the Palmisano brothers were the sole physical occupants of the building, the mezzanine recorder captured numerous wooden knocks of varying intensities, speeds and quantities. Whoever was doing the knocking seemed to be carefully increasing the strength behind each set of raps, as if gauging the volume that would attract Richard and Paul's attention from the auditorium below. Incredibly, neither seasoned investigator heard a thing the entire time.

As the rest of us returned with our dinners, Paul and Richard left to get their own. We then assembled in the green room to eat and talk, away from the cameras and recorders. Dinner over, the silence of the mezzanine broke as the voices of the team returning to the auditorium seemed to provoke yet another series of progressively louder knocks; it was as if someone was once more daring one of the investigators to hear them and respond. Again, none of us did.

⌒

The team settled about the house to conduct an EVP session. I called upon Henry from the stage, but the only recorded responses were light knocks and the rustling of fabric past the mezzanine recorder. While the team remained silent, a loud smack and three loud knocks were recorded originating from the props room—again, unnoticed.

From his position on the stage, Richard suggested that if hangings took place on the property during the period the town hall served as a courthouse, they may have happened at or very near the location of the theoretical "vortex" at stage left.

This idea inspired James. "Does anyone know the name of someone who was hanged here?" he asked.

EVP: [Male; whispering] Howard.

⌒

Paul suggested we move to the basement to try communicating there. Everyone settled about the Loonie Café, asking questions and leaving sufficient silence between our queries to accommodate EVP responses.

I looked to Richard, who was bent over a side table, concentrating. He had placed his magnetic compass at the end of the table closest to the women's dressing room and was studying it intently. He caught my glance and motioned for me to join him.

Although the dial was turned northward, the compass needle would not line up correctly. Instead, it wavered between south and southeast and would not settle. Richard pushed the compass a few centimetres westward. The needle returned to true north and settled to a stop.

Richard picked up the compass and moved methodically about the lounge, pinpointing the extent of the magnetic anomaly affecting the device's readings and finding that it enveloped a fairly large area. I followed and carefully scanned the area with the Gauss meter, but I detected no distinguishable electromagnetic energies.

While this was happening, my recorder caught a series of EVPs in close succession. First, an exasperated male made himself known.

EVP: [Male] [Short sigh] Whatever.

Five seconds later came the sound of receding, running footfalls, echoing as if someone was rushing down an empty tiled hallway. In the midst of the fading footfalls, another disembodied voice spoke up.

EVP: [Male; whispering] Running.

The team moved south toward a short alcove outside the door leading to the men's dressing room. Paul pushed the door open to take a picture inside the dressing room, then let the door close gently behind him. One look at his face indicated something had just happened, but it was Janet who frowned and spoke up first.

"I'm feeling weird," she said, scrunching her face and shifting restlessly in place.

Paul was immediately intrigued. "Just now? In this area?"

"Yeah, just in this area," Janet replied.

"I agree with you," nodded Paul, indicating the men's dressing room behind him. "It's because there's a male here. I just heard a disembodied male's voice when you guys were over there. It wasn't a very old voice. It said, 'Hey!' as I was opening the door to take a picture."

"Something's happening here," Joanna and Victoria said, almost in unison. They settled deeper into the alcove.

"Yeah, there's a male here!" said Paul, growing excited.

Joanna frowned, trying to get a reading. "What's going on?"

"I don't know," said Victoria, looking concerned.

It seemed both women sensed something was amiss, yet neither could vocalize what they were experiencing. A palpable tension began to fill the air.

"Sir?" I began.

Just then, Richard called out from just outside the alcove, peering down at the compass in his palm. "It's going back to north now," he reported.

"What's your name?" asked Paul.

As Joanna shared feeling a sensation in her ears, the surveillance camera across the lounge recorded a response.

EVP: [Male A] Jimmy.

"What's your name?" I called out as well.

EVP: [Male A] Jimmy.

"Should we be careful?" Richard asked.

EVP: [Male A] Upstairs.

Our subsequent questions were met with silence, and nothing more was recorded by any of our equipment while we were present. The team and Janet left the basement shortly afterward, leaving the surveillance camera to record one final exchange.

EVP: [Male B] Jim.
EVP: [Male A] Dan.

~

Back upstairs, Richard and I broke away from the group, ascended to the mezzanine and settled into a pair of fold-down chairs overlooking the theatre. Paul clambered onstage and in true class clown fashion began asking for song requests from the women sitting among the house seats while James continued to wander, holding his digital recorder.

Richard shared a gut feeling with me that someone was electrocuted in the original crawl space under the building, and now their energy was responsible for the magnetic anomaly in the present-day basement.

I activated the Gauss meter I had brought, resting my wrist on the balcony rail to hold it steady. Deciding the mood seemed calm enough, I attempted communication. "Rhonda?" I asked. Next door in the props room, unbeknownst to Richard and me, the digital recorder caught an immediate knock in response.

"Ma'am?" Another single knock.

"Are you too young for me to call you 'ma'am'?" I asked. A third, rather tentative knock was recorded but not heard live. Four seconds later, an impatient-sounding, harder knock erupted. Incredibly, this too went unheard in the moment by everyone present.

"Rhonda, did you act in a show here?" I continued. "Did you help backstage, somehow?" The props room remained silent.

"Did you pass away on this property?" As soon as I said "pass," the recorder captured a very hard knock, as if the listener had anticipated my question or perhaps was upset by the concept of passing away. Yet again, this knock went unheeded by any of us.

Richard headed down to the auditorium. I meandered through the props room and into the control room, talking as I went. "You can help us help the theatre people get to know you, but we need to hear from you," I reasoned. "Are you able to gather as much energy as you can and move something for me? Rhonda, can you help us, please? Can you put aside your anxiety for us for a moment and—"

A single knock from a corner of the control room behind me interrupted my request. "That's it," I said encouragingly.

I heard a faint exhale from the props room. I quickly confirmed that no one below me in the house had sighed loud enough for me to hear. Two more knocks came from the same corner behind me.

"Is that you again, Bob? I haven't cornered you, have I? I don't mean to. I'll back off." I retreated back to the control room threshold, my back to the props room. "I was hoping you could use some more energy to move something. Something small enough that you can—"

I shivered violently as a cold sensation ran up my back. As I reacted, two faint taps sounded from the wall.

"Is that you in there, or is that the weather causing the building to settle?" Silence.

"Bob?" I asked cautiously. There was a faint tap.

"Are you knocking there? Do you have more energy than that?" A loud knock sounded from the wall.

"Thank you!" I replied, buoyed by the seeming direct response.

From the stage came the familiar electronic voice of James' device, the Ovilus III. Once activated, the Ovilus spouted the word "SHOULD," prompting James to ask after its meaning. Silence filled the mezzanine between my own questions.

"Bob? Are you down there with James right now?"

OVILUS III: SOLO

"Do you mean *I'm* solo?" I asked. A single gentle knock came from the northwest wall of the control room.

"Yeah? Is that what you mean?" I was met with more silence. Either my efforts were in vain or I was competing with someone's fascination with the Ovilus III, across the theatre.

"You're knocking so randomly, Bob; I can't believe that's you. Can you knock really hard, please?" A second wave of coldness shot through my spine, this time spreading farther outward, wrapping around my back and along both arms.

OVILUS III: MOMMY

"Is Rhonda afraid of me? Do we have her name right?" I asked. Another tentative knock came from the control room. Further questions were met with silence on the mezzanine.

I decided the Ovilus III was too attractive by comparison. "Bob, if you can hear me, can we play a joke on James right now?" I whispered in a conspiratorial voice. "Can you make that machine say 'turkey'?"

OVILUS III: DISASTER

"I'm starting to think so," I sighed.

I reset the recorder in the props room and left the mezzanine. Within two minutes of my absence, it captured a snapping sound followed by three very hard wooden knocks. After eight minutes, I returned to the mezzanine to collect the recorder. It was time to pack up and call it a night.

When I got back downstairs, Richard and Paul had packed away Camera 1. They were in the process of doing the same to Camera 2 on the stage when I placed a recorder down on the apron at stage left, pointing it toward them (experience has taught me that when the cameras are no longer in operation, it often pays to continue audio recordings up until departure from the investigation site).

"Did anyone see any movement in their peripheral vision this evening?" I asked everyone present.

James squinted toward the mezzanine balcony. "I just saw a grey shadow move from left to right up in the [balcony] there."

"Yeah, when we came in, I saw a light behind the second chair," shared Victoria, indicating the mezzanine above.

OVILUS III: COMMON

Joanna and I chuckled at the device's interjection. "That's common, is it?" I called out. "Bob? Remember that code word? Could you please have that device say it before we leave?"

OVILUS III: MERCURY

"That wasn't it," I smiled, "but it sounded close!" (Later I discovered that "turkey" is not among the 2000+ words programmed into the Ovilus III's data bank. The reader may decide whether it was simple coincidence that the device spouted the similar-sounding "mercury" or not.)

As Richard and Paul finished packing the second surveillance camera into its tote box, Victoria walked past me into the green room next door to use the restroom. James and Joanna began to wander westward along the main aisle, away from the stage.

Paul scanned the stage, looking for any stray equipment. He pointed past me toward the green room. "We gotta grab that bag of garbage before we leave," he instructed.

"Yeah, in the green room," I agreed.

"That always goes with us," he said.

"Yeah, yeah. Oh yeah," I replied, fully aware of our clean-up protocol.

DV/EVP: [Female or young male; loud] Bye!

All present stopped what they were doing. Paul was the first to speak. "What?"

Richard turned around, frowning. "What was that?"

Janet—who was in the process of turning stage lights off from the top of a step ladder—looked over her shoulder. "Somebody just call me?"

"I just heard 'why'" I reported.

Richard nodded. "Yeah, 'why.' That's what I heard."

I peered around the arch of the stage to see Janet. "Did you just say 'why,' Janet?"

"I didn't say anything!" Janet sounded bewildered.

"It was a woman's voice," recalled Paul, his eyes wide. "That was loud and clear."

"I thought it was Janet speaking, it was so clear," I said.

"Yeah, so did I," agreed Richard.

It was a surreal moment; time seemed to stand still as each of us tried to analyze what had just happened. Seizing the opportunity to continue communication, we asked more questions of the otherwise quiet theatre, but nothing more was heard or recorded.

I turned and entered the green room just as Victoria emerged from the restroom, completely unaware of the excitement. I quickly updated her as to what she'd missed, gathered my equipment, my coat and the small bag of garbage. When I returned to the auditorium, everyone was abuzz, comparing perspectives with each other as they carted their belongings toward the main door.

We all thanked and bade goodnight the spirits of the township hall and stepped out into the parking lot amid a windy, bitterly cold night. Satisfied the lights were off and all our equipment was out of the building, Janet locked up behind us.

Afterthoughts

In the brief period The Searcher Group investigated the Old Caledon Township Hall, it appeared that not only was it definitely haunted, but also that a few spirits seemed willing to try communicating with us.

Like many other sites we've investigated, we managed to collect strong audible evidence of physical movement occurring in areas where none of the investigators, hosts or guests were present.

The widespread (and ultimately temporary) field of magnetic interference in the basement was another fascinating event. Did its sudden disappearance coincide somehow with the activity encountered by the team toward the end of the investigation? Could this have been part of the theoretical portal?

Richard's observation regarding the house seating was correct: the chairs were indeed imported from outside Caledon. After contacting several CTHP members, one with access to the theatre group's membership meeting minutes archives was able to ascertain that the seats arrived in fall 1986 from the Capitol Theatre in Toronto. I contacted a historian known for his extensive documentation of theatrical locales from Toronto's past, but he was unaware of any deaths that might have occurred at the Capitol at all, let alone before 1986.

Joanna's ability to sense first names of several spirit people was a terrific starting point for conducting EVP sessions early in the investigation. Catching definitive evidence of Jim and Dan's names through EVP recordings also worked in our favour.

Without discounting Paul's hearing a disembodied male's voice address him in the men's dressing room in the basement, arguably the most intriguing *recording* was that of the voice spoken clearly from the stage, heard live by seven people. It is very rare in this field to capture an EVP that is also heard in the moment.

Disembodied Deliberation

After the initial thrill and with the aid of audio recordings to review the event, what really happened is cause for discussion. Firstly, everyone who heard the voice—or rather, misheard it— agreed it was someone who possessed a vocal timbre similar to Janet's. At the time, we were convinced that Janet had asked, "Why?" as a response to Paul's wish to remove our dinner refuse from the property. Not many people expect their guests to exit with their trash, so someone unfamiliar with our team's protocol certainly might be inspired to ask why we would be bothered to do such a thing.

However, earlier in the evening at the conclusion of the dinner break, Paul had actually informed Janet of our trash-removal protocol. Instead of questioning our practice, Janet seemed grateful that we would do this, especially because the building would be empty for the better part of a month after the investigation concluded. So there should have been no reason for Janet to question Paul when he asked me to retrieve the garbage bag as we packed up. Nevertheless, enough time had passed between the dinner break and the tear-down time that we cannot rule out human forgetfulness.

Careful post-investigation audio analysis revealed another possibility. James' recorder captured the voice in question from his position on the opposite side of the theatre. Analysis of my and James' recordings convinced us this voice belonged to a pre-pubescent boy casually saying, "Bye!" It would be a logical sentiment for someone to utter, given the team was preparing to leave for the night. After all, my recorder captured a youth's voice on the stage earlier that evening whispering hello, and the same voice later greeted the team with a cheerful, "Hi! Come on!" which James captured.

Perhaps, at the end of the night, the spirit of a boy stood on the threshold of the alleged vortex onstage, bade us farewell and then exited through the invisible doorway. This theory would explain the lack of responses to the bevy of questions we asked afterwards—he was no longer present to reply.

~

Suffice it to say, this was an extremely successful introductory visit for the team. We had a series of first names to use for the next visit, which is always an encouraging start for any location under investigation. And the possible existence of a portal or vortex between realities meant we would need to return with specific equipment in order to confirm and measure the unseen source of energy. We had much to look forward to and prepare for when planning our return.

~

Chapter 6

Lebovic Centre for Arts & Entertainment—Nineteen on the Park (Former Stouffville Town Hall): Second Investigation

Ghosts are some of the loneliest people you will ever meet.
   –Thomm Quackenbush, *A Collector of Spirits*

~

Team: Richard, Paul, Joanna, David, James, Peter
Host: Ashley

A bright, crisp winter afternoon greeted the team on its return visit to the former Stouffville Town Hall in January 2015. Thanks to the enormous amount of data collected during the team's initial visit four months earlier, the team arrived ready to address the building's spirits directly.

James, Richard, Paul and I arrived first and were admitted to the building by acting cultural facility and programming coordinator Ashley McIntosh shortly after 1:00 PM. We entered the auditorium to find long, black curtains spread across the width of the southern wall in readiness for an event later that week. Paul suggested using the curtains to camouflage the ground-floor surveillance system, and he and Richard set to work assembling Camera 1.

As I established a base camp in the main lobby, James began a solo sweep and found himself drawn to the second floor. He climbed the staircase cautiously, digital recorder in hand, sensing he wasn't alone. He toured the upper lobby, the community room and the restrooms. Upon entering the men's restroom, James' recorder picked up someone acknowledging his presence—or perhaps mistaking him for someone else.

EVP: [Female; breathy] Hey, Handsley!

Joanna and David arrived on site shortly afterward, and James returned to follow Joanna's walkabout with his recorder. Drawn to the auditorium risers, Joanna once again picked up on the spirit of "Robert," who seemed more receptive to communicating this time.

"I don't feel him sitting; I think he's the same guy," Joanna said. "It's either Robert or Richard. Again, I get the plaid shirt, more of a casual look—white with stripes and jeans."

"What kind of a time era?" asked James.

"I think '67. He has a goatee and light brown hair. Not much of a goatee, but scruff. He is still clean-cut and he's educated. Late 30s/early 40s."

"Are you here to perform, listen to music or see a play?" asked James, addressing the area Joanna was focusing on.

"A play," replied Joanna. "I feel he has a technical background, which I'm trying to understand. It may have something to do with the sound system. He's definitely technical."

"What do you think of the new technology that's here?" James asked.

"He's greatly impressed and wishes he could have played with it [in his time], too." Joanna paused, concentrating. "I also think he is up and about inspecting…That's it!"

Joanna turned to Ashley, who was observing from the auditorium floor at the foot of the risers. "Do you know if there have been any issues with the sound system here?"

"As far as working or not working?" Ashley clarified.

"Yeah."

"We had a fire in one of our big speakers recently," Ashley replied, pointing to a large amplifier connected to the southwest corner of the catwalk, overhead. "The only thing that [the tech crew] could figure out is that one of the wires had somehow become loose, causing an arc. This was about two or three weeks ago."

"It was totally accidental," Joanna shared.

"Tell him to leave that alone because it cost me 5000 dollars," said Ashley in a good-natured but semi-serious tone.

"Richard or Robert was a tech guy here in '67 and was doing something with sound systems or electronics. He is loving what you've got here and he got a little too close to it. I don't think he was playing with [the speaker], just tinkering."

"It was such a strange occurrence, too," recalled Ashley. "The [tech/repair] guys said that the entire bolt had worked itself loose inside the speaker. They said it was so odd because they have had speakers up for 20 years and never had that happen. The way it came loose started a fire."

"[The spirits] may not know the effect their energy will have on an electrical current," Joanna suggested.

"Ashley, would you forgive him for what he did?" asked James.

"Oh, absolutely. Just don't do it again. I'm not angry at all."

"Do you accept her forgiveness, Robert or Richard?" James asked, turning back to the risers.

As James finished asking this question, a clear, mechanical-sounding voice overlapping his own was caught on his recorder, followed by a fainter, hollow-sounding voice.

EVP: [Male] Please don't come here.

EVP: [Male] Jame[s].

If the first male was asking James to keep away from him and his favourite seat, he was probably relieved when Joanna and James did just that and proceeded with their walkabout. Meanwhile, Camera 1 filmed Richard and Ashley conversing a few metres away. In the course of their discussion, the camera audio recorded three EVPs.

EVP: [Male] Yeah, right.

EVP: [Male] You b**ch.

EVP: [Male] Rick.

Regrettably, Richard and Ashley's voices were too low to determine exactly what was said that may have evoked some or all of these replies.

⁓

The team and Ashley prepared to leave for a late lunch on Main Street, just a three-minute walk north of the building. I deployed a recorder in the washrooms off the upper lobby and left a proximity alarm in the adjacent community room. James left his recorder activated on a corner counter of the auditorium catwalk. He felt that he was not alone, so before he left, he addressed the unseen presence: "You're following me too, aren't ya?"

EVP: [Male] Yes, I am.

While the building was empty, several instances of activity were recorded. On the catwalk, James' recorder was tapped four times within a 10-minute period. These taps were followed by sounds of movement, including one resembling someone sitting down in a nearby chair.

Inside the upper lobby restrooms, my recorder also captured sounds resembling movement: metallic banging sounds that were not HVAC-related and a distinct, dull thud of an object being dropped on the floor.

Concurrently, a third recorder in the main lobby restrooms clearly captured this same loud, dull thud, followed by a second thud 40 seconds later. Four more impacts followed, all within four and a half minutes of the original sound. About a minute and a half later, a seventh impact sounded like a softball being bounced off a wall.

The recorder in the upper lobby washrooms also captured the distant sound of a woman calling from inside the building.

EVP: [Female; distant] Hello!

Four minutes later, a toilet or urinal in one of the restrooms flushed by itself. The restroom facilities of the Lebovic Centre are not of the automated sort.

Meanwhile, Camera 1 once again picked up the male voice in the auditorium calling for three other men.

EVP: [Male] Help me!…Henry?…Ben?…Jake?

The male voice got no response to his pleas for help, but the lighting of the auditorium grew brighter for several minutes before returning to its original level of illumination. The blinds on the windows lining the room to the room were all drawn closed.

~

The team and Ashley returned to the building after a 70-minute recess. While Joanna and James moved to the second floor, everyone else hung back in the main lobby. Joanna and James passed the washrooms as they made their way to the auditorium catwalk. As they entered the catwalk area, the restroom recorder captured a disembodied exclamation.

EVP: [Male; jeering] Missed me!

The male sounded as if he had just narrowly evaded the investigators in time to avoid detection.

Downstairs, Camera 1 caught the now-familiar voice of the auditorium spirit yet again before the room fell completely silent for a 20-minute period.

EVP: [Male] Henry?

Everyone gathered inside the auditorium. Ashley, James and Joanna toured the south-end addition while Richard replaced the recordable DVD for Camera 1. Paul and I asked questions aloud while David monitored a Gauss meter and noted EMF fluctuations.

I stepped up onto the risers. "Robert?" I asked, "Do you remember me from the last time we were here?"

EVP: [Male] I forget.

Paul suggested turning our attention to Jake. A familiar ticking sound—unheard since the first visit—erupted from somewhere on the empty catwalk.

"Is that you up there?" I called.

"This just jumped up to two," reported David, referring to the Gauss meter. He stood motionless on the floor of the auditorium, watching the needle of the meter intently as he joined in on the questioning. "My name's David. I'd really like it if you came close to me. You don't need to be afraid. I'll know you're here if you come close to me."

The needle spiked to 2 milliGauss (mG) once again, up from zero. "That's very good," said David, encouragingly. "Could you come close to me?" The needle spiked to 4 mG before dropping back to zero.

From there, the needle began bouncing in small jumps. I likened these minute fluctuations to a person rising and falling on the balls of their feet in excited anticipation, ready to reply— or run. "Jake, do you have enough energy to speak to us?" I asked.

"Try asking for Ben," Paul suggested when no responses seemed to be forthcoming.

"What's Ben's last name?" asked Paul, hopeful that some-one amongst the spirits would volunteer some useful information. "Ben, are you here with us tonight? Are you with Jake? Ben, what's Jake's last name?

"I'm getting a three," David shared, his eyes trained on the EMF meter.

I produced a pair of small LED flashlights, one with a green casing, the other red. I activated them and then loosened the inner connections between battery terminals and lamps of both devices. In this manner, the slightest change in pressure on the face caps of each flashlight would bridge or break the connection and light or darken the tiny lamps. Leaving the green one lit, I placed both flashlights on a table standing near David and stepped away.

"Do you see the flashlights on the table?" David asked. He paused, registering a sudden sensation. "I'm getting the weirdest chills, all the way through my back," he shared calmly.

David's eyes darted from the meter in his hand to a sudden movement near the green flashlight. "The light just got brighter."

I nodded; I had witnessed that too. "Can you turn it off, please?" I asked.

The red flashlight sprang to life in a flash and went dark again. Simultaneously, a sharp tick sound erupted from the EMF meter, indicating another spike of the needle.

"Can you use those flashlights to let us know that you understand what we're saying?" I asked.

Suddenly the red flashlight illuminated. The needle of the meter jumped to 2.5 mG in seeming response. Joanna settled on a riser seat with Ashley and James and suggested that David move closer to the flashlights. Paul and Richard stood and observed from a few metres away.

"Ben?" I asked, watching the green flashlight. "Do you have enough energy to turn that flashlight off, please?" The Gauss meter needle registered 3 mG then dropped, hovering just shy of 2 mG but never falling completely back to zero.

"Ben, what's your last name, please?" I asked.

"Back up to three and jumping," reported David.

"You see that grey box David's holding? The closer you get to it, the more noise it'll make. Can you make it go to five?" The needle didn't move.

"Ben, are you a little boy?" The Gauss meter needle ticked to just short of 3 mG.

EVP: [Unknown gender; faint] Uh-huh.

"Did you work in the bowling alley?" I asked, looking to David as he nodded, silently indicating another hit on the meter. "Do you remember when they took out the bowling alley and it closed?"

"You got a reaction up to three on that."

"Do you remember Mr. Schmidt?"

David nodded. "A couple of ticks."

"Is Mr. Schmidt here with us right now?"

"Whoa! Ticked to three," David said.

"Ben, do you know someone named Robert here?"

The meter immediately responded with a loud tick. "That was three," said David.

"Is David touching you right now? Can you touch him back, please?"

The meter ticked again. "Three," David repeated and slowly extended his free arm outward, feeling the air about him carefully. The Gauss meter responded with several faint, static-like ticking sounds. "These feelings are so weird. Shivers."

"He's standing in your [energy] field," said Joanna.

"Is that you touching me?" asked David, continuing to stay focused on the meter. "Can you do that again?" The needle spiked past 3 mG in response. "Very good, thank you!" said David, pleased.

The meter needle rose, dropped and hovered between 3 and 2.5 mG as David took a seat at the bottom of the risers. "I'm getting waves of…changing energy," he said, trying his best to describe what he was feeling.

I moved to a seat behind David so I could monitor the EMF readings over his shoulder. The meter had dropped back to zero.

"Ben, this is Joanna. Do you know me?" The Gauss meter needle rose to 2 mG, then dropped.

"There's an older couple here, and they like to hide from us," she continued. "I think they're in the practice room. Do you know them?" There was no response of any kind.

"The lady has curly grey hair," Joanna continued. The meter needle ticked once as if in agreement. "Do you know her?"

"Two and a half," reported David. "Some steady ticks."

"Is her name Shirl?" asked Joanna.

Two seconds of silence passed; then SQUEEEEEEEE! Everyone started in surprise as the meter squealed loudly, the needle spiking all the way right before dropping abruptly back.

"Are you serious?!" I gasped. "That went to six!" It was an amazing moment. I had never before witnessed such a sudden reading from this device—so far from an obvious source of electromagnetic energy—in the four years that I'd used it.

As if to acknowledge what I'd just reported, the needle jumped to 3 mG and then dropped just below 2 mG as if awaiting the next question or comment from the team.

"Is there an older gentleman that's with her?" Joanna continued. The needle jumped, accompanied by a pair of tick sounds.

"Do you know why she is afraid of us?" she asked. Another pair of tick sounds came from the meter but farther apart, as if answering hesitantly.

"Is she nice to you?"

"Nothing," I shared, eyes on the meter. "It's staying steady at two."

"Is she not very friendly with people?" Joanna asked.

A creaking noise, like that of someone's weight slowly coming to rest, emanated from the west side of the catwalk above us. "Is there somebody standing above us right now?" I asked.

As if the novelty of communicating using the Gauss meter had worn off, none of our remaining questions received any particularly exceptional or relevant responses. Noting the entire session took 40 minutes, Richard called for a well-earned break, and everyone exited the auditorium for the main lobby.

～

Not one to rest for long, I wandered the catwalk alone asking after Mr. Schmidt and noted that Paul was downstairs in the auditorium, also wandering quietly. As he turned to leave,

Camera 1 captured a male voice saying something indistinguishable before it recorded some clearer EVPs.

EVP: [Male] Andrew?

EVP: [Female] Andrew?

EVP: [Male; surprised-sounding] Anna?

I watched silently from the catwalk as Paul exited the auditorium, headed back to the main lobby. I was unaware my recorder was capturing a disturbing plea.

EVP: [Female; faint, whispering] Help me!

After requesting communication with Jake, Sidney Schmidt and then Harold Spofford, the video projector fan inexplicably began to operate—the first of several times that evening for the remainder of our visit.

I also noted that the under-lighting of the corners of the catwalk counters was once again activated, though no one had touched the main control panel to switch them on. Between the lights and the projector fan, it seemed like someone was showing us the extent of their abilities for a second time.

Camera 1 caught some indistinguishable whispering as I exited the catwalk soon after. Once I was gone, a male's voice muttered his frustration.

EVP: [Male] I hate it.

Joanna left shortly after 5:00 PM. We attempted another EVP session without her, but our questions, called out from the catwalk and the auditorium below, were getting no recorded results.

Ten minutes into the session, James was on the catwalk setting up a shot of Richard and Paul in the auditorium below when he reported witnessing what looked like a pair of disembodied feet rushing past the brothers through the viewfinder of his camera. Lamentably, the anomaly vanished before James could depress the shutter.

Simultaneously, Richard shared that his own camera was inexplicably trying to focus on a space above the chairs and that it registered "Blink Detected" from his position facing James. No visual or audio evidence of this phenomenon was captured by Camera 1, watching from the opposite corner of the auditorium.

Two minutes later, as James wandered the west-side catwalk, he smelled the scent of a burning cigarette that dissipated as soon as he called attention to it. Approximately a minute later, Richard reported a fleeting perfume-like fragrance near the emergency exit door.

Everyone exited the auditorium, and yet again the microphone of Camera 1 caught a now-familiar voice.

EVP: [Male] Come here.

This command was followed by the sound of door handles being rattled behind the camera.

Someone suggested a dinner break. I decided to move the proximity alarm to an alternate location, as no one seemed interested in it inside the community room. Recalling that the glass doors at the north end of the upper lobby have been known to open themselves, I positioned a chair directly between the two doors, 10 centimetres from the glass to ensure that no externally produced vibrations against the door would affect the alarm. I stood the device upright on the seat, leaning it against the back support of the chair.

I took a number of control photos of the alarm set-up, then placed a digital recorder nearby. I exited the upper lobby and rejoined the team downstairs. We vacated the building soon after to dine across the street again.

Less than a minute after the town clock chimed 6:00 PM, the alarm activated. The recorder captured the shrill noise for 25 minutes and 8 seconds before it finally stopped. While the alarm sounded, several noises suggesting movement were also recorded in or around the upper lobby by the digital recorder.

Downstairs, the moment the alarm began, the auditorium camera caught the sound of a door opening, then several EVPs.

EVP: [Male] Hey.

After a long pause, there was some indiscernible whispering near the camera.

EVP: [Older male] Hey, Benny.
EVP: [Male] Go over there.
EVP: [Male] We can't.
EVP: [Male] Ben.

After another long pause came the sounds of shuffling and, again, a door opening.

EVP: [Male] Anna? [No reply]

In the upper lobby, the digital recorder caught a subtle sound suggesting fabric rustling seconds before the E. Probe alarm sounded a second time. This happened at approximately 6:45 PM, just as we were returning at a leisurely pace from across the street.

Entering the building through the main doors, David was the first to hear the alarm. I quickly moved upstairs and deactivated it, taking photos and asking questions. No responses were recorded.

Resetting the alarm and returning it to the chair in the upper lobby, I returned to the main lobby where the evening's final experiment—a scripted EVP session—was organized.

Richard and Paul entered the auditorium first, using the script I had prepared to ask after Ben and Jake. Although no direct replies were recorded in relation to the questions, once more Camera 1 captured the unanswered inquiries of a lone adult male.

EVP: [Male] Henry?

The auditorium light brightened then dimmed, undetected by the Palmisano brothers.

EVP: [Same male] Ben?

When Paul and Richard returned to the main lobby, David and I went next. We ascended to the catwalk to ask after Harry and Anne. All seemed quiet until the questions began; then we noted loud clacking, snapping, thuds and knocking sounds through the duration of our inquiries. Immediately after I asked if Harry remembered the team, the overhead lights brightened slightly.

Then, as David asked questions of Anne, we observed the parted black curtains directly opposite us drop smoothly in unison to a closed position. We chalked this up to a possible HVAC-related phenomenon—perhaps the air system had blown the curtain panels open to begin with? But moments after the curtain edges converged and settled, a black, foot-long shadow appeared on the floor behind the west-side panel. I watched as it slid along the floor a few centimetres before completely disappearing. David's eyes were on the script, so he missed seeing this phenomenon for himself, but I was certain someone had just been standing behind the curtain.

"Is Jake here now?" asked David.

EVP: [Male] Yes.

Completing his questions for Anne, David observed that one curtain had parted and peeled backward. The HVAC system was likely the cause behind this, but the other half of the curtain remained absolutely still and unaffected. It looked as if someone was holding one of the panels open to let someone else pass, or perhaps to enter the auditorium themselves. David and I exited the catwalk, leaving a digital recorder on the countertop.

Next, Ashley and James entered the ground floor of the auditorium to ask questions of Sidney Schmidt, Mike, Emily and Natalie, with some interesting results. Addressing Sidney, James asked, "Were you the one that was turning the [fan] off and on on the projector?"

Immediately the projector fan sprang to life from the catwalk above. "Was that you that turned the light on on the catwalk for Peter?" James followed up.

EVP: [Male; dismissive tone] Ya got me.

The most exciting results were recorded during questions James asked concerning the phone numbers once attributed to the Auditorium Garage (1922–28) and the Stanley Theatre (1933–57). "Can anyone here remember the telephone number of the Stanley Theatre? Does anyone remember if the number was 95?"

The theatre space remained silent. "Was it maybe 100?" James prompted. At this, the recorder on the catwalk counter captured a single click sound, though neither James nor Ashley heard it in the moment. James continued, "Or 140? Or perhaps 175?" No responses came of the last two numbers.

"Can anyone here remember the telephone number of the Auditorium Garage? Do you remember if it was the number 80?

Or was it 110? Or perhaps 135? Or maybe it was 170?" James asked. The catwalk recorder caught a second single tick sound following 170, but it was too subtle to be perceived by Ashley or James in the auditorium.

Although there were no vocal responses to the line of questions, Camera 1 caught a male's voice calling three times for Jake.

Apart from two dull thuds as Robert was addressed, no other sounds were captured by the catwalk recorder until Ashley and James exited the auditorium for the main lobby. Once they were gone, the subtle sounds of rustling fabric and a third thud were recorded, sounding very close to the microphone.

Richard and Paul returned to the auditorium to question Ben and Jake. During this period, a series of male panting sounds approaching the catwalk recorder were captured that may have been perceived as whispers by Paul and Richard as they reported hearing as much. The ground floor camera captured these noises as well.

Once Richard and Paul exited the auditorium, David and I returned upstairs to the catwalk area to put questions to Mike, Emily, Natalie and Robert. James and Ashley also entered the auditorium and stood quietly to observe. Again, notable thud sounds erupted far away from us during this line of questioning, but no cooperative EVPs were captured by the catwalk recorder or the Camera 1 microphone.

Our time at the former Stouffville Town Hall had come to an end. While the team was packing up its equipment and disassembling Camera 1, James and David explored the basement briefly but recorded no audio anomalies. By 8:10 PM, the team and Ashley were back outside in the south parking lot, and the building was locked and secured.

Afterthoughts

Our two investigations of the Lebovic Centre were extremely successful in verifying the staff reports of hearing disembodied footfalls. Not only did we record them audibly, but we also witnessed brief manifestations of walking feet. To whom these lower limbs belong remains a million-dollar question.

Apart from the positive responses validating historic facts and the names of the spirits gleaned from the first investigation, the highlights of this second investigation were numerous and exciting.

Tech Talk

One of the first encouraging hits of the afternoon came early as Joanna re-established contact with Robert (or Richard) and collected information from him concerning a recent freak fire originating from an auditorium speaker that none of us had been made aware of prior to this investigation. It also appeared that an entity was meddling with (or perhaps drawing energy from) the lighting system a few times on this visit; this activity was caught on camera twice and once by David and me toward the end of the evening.

The communication established between Ben and the team through energy spikes registered on the Gauss meter was the most memorable highlight for all present. The acknowledgement of the name "Shirl" as indicated by the strongest wave of energy was promising confirmation of Joanna's encounter with this woman earlier in the visit. None of us had ever witnessed such behaviour from this device, and the results were encouraging.

Then there's the interest in the proximity alarm. Once the E. Probe 1.0 alarm is triggered—depending on its sensitivity setting—it tends to keep going, piercing the air with a high-pitched beeping that would drive anyone mad inside a minute of hearing it. I was quite pleased to discover upon analysis that the first time the alarm was triggered, it stopped itself after 25 minutes while the building was devoid of corporeal presence.

Was an entity consciously touching the device to test its ability to sound the alarm? Did the sound frequency or battery power feed it energy as it continued to handle the device? Is it possible that a spirit wasn't even aware of the alarm and had simply decided to stand at the window (as it was pre-renovation) for 25 minutes before stepping away?

As inconceivable as it is to me that anyone—physical or in spirit—would consciously allow that aggravating noise to continue as long as it did, I lean toward the first theory. The reason for this involves the triggering of the alarm the second time, which occurred within minutes of the team's return to the building. I can imagine the spirit standing on the second floor, spying us approaching, then triggering the alarm to illustrate to us what it was capable of doing because we were absent for the first demonstration.

Spirit Summons

Our best guess is that it was Robert who was captured calling out for Henry, Ben, Jake and Andrew inside the otherwise empty auditorium throughout the course of the evening. For the most part, the caller did not receive direct responses, save a brief exchange with Ben and an unidentified older gentleman. He did seem surprised by the appearance of Anna, who arrived to inquire after Andrew as well. The sheer number of names to come from just two investigations at this location was very exciting to us. In our experience, it usually takes several visits to discern who is who and what their names are, but not in this case; it seems there are several souls present who continue to call the former town hall home.

Physical Manifestations

There were at least two instances wherein James sensed he was not alone on the second floor, and both were corroborated via responses (a female, then a male) captured by his digital recorder.

Someone was bold enough to attempt to manifest themselves visually in the presence of the team. James spotting the lower legs of a person hurrying past Paul and Richard through his camera viewfinder was unexpected. My glimpse of a foot-sized dark shadow appearing, shifting then disappearing at the foot of the static curtains was a personal thrill for me, marking my first direct sighting of a partial apparition in the field.

This investigation also included stray and fleeting odours on the catwalk (cigarette smoke) and in the auditorium (perfume), sensed within minutes of each other. These fascinating olfactory manifestations marked another Town Hall Tour first.

⁓

If longtime owner Mr. Sidney Schmidt does return to his former workplace, it is likely he only visits. However, following this visit, we were confident we had narrowed down a small group of regular spirit people residing on the property: at least two grown men, a woman and a young boy. Placing Robert in the late 1960s–early 1970s meant he might have been a municipal employee while the building was housing local government offices. Was technology part of Robert's job or perhaps a hobby outside the workplace? As for Shirl and Andrew, we now had two new names to research.

⁓

Chapter 7

Waterford Old Town Hall: Second Investigation

Yesterday, upon the stair,
I met a man who wasn't there.
He wasn't there again today,
I wish, I wish he'd go away...

—Hughes Mearns, "The Psycho-ed"

Team: Richard, Paul, Joanna, James, David, Peter
Hosts: Brenda, Jennifer

The return to Waterford in spring 2015 seemed surreal to me as I drove southward through a zigzag route of country roads, followed by Richard and Paul. It had been almost a year since the team first investigated the Old Town Hall in Waterford, and I was eager to apply what we'd learned previously—hopefully to achieve some worthwhile results.

We pulled into the parking lot of the former town hall where David waited patiently. Our hosts, Jennifer and Brenda, were stepping from their cars as we arrived. The day was sunny and warm for early April, but the occasional gust of cold wind necessitated jacket closure. As I introduced the Palmisano brothers to our Waterford hosts, a group of groomsmen in black tuxedos rounded the corner of the building and arranged themselves on the main steps, employing the impressive architecture as an attractive backdrop for photos.

Bypassing the wedding party blocking the main entrance, we entered the building through a side door and found ourselves in a dimly lit stairwell. The stairs led up to the auditorium while a door to our right led into the boardroom, where we established our base camp. David and I then showed Paul and Richard the main lobby, pointing out the vault, the staircases, adjacent rooms and the placement of the ground-floor surveillance camera the year previous.

With James' arrival, I left the others and exited for the parking lot, digital recorder in hand. Just as I reached James, Joanna arrived. The groomsmen were gone, so after exchanging salutations, James moved his equipment into the building while I stayed back with Joanna. I encouraged her to share any psychic sensations she might pick up on because this was her first visit here. As it happened, she sensed a strong male presence nearby that had apparently come from inside the town hall to greet her.

"I do feel they're an aggressive person in terms of in-my-face," said Joanna, posing defiantly to illustrate the spirit's stance. "Like, 'Oh you're here, eh? What're ya gonna do?'"

Joanna continued, describing the spirit's physical appearance. "He's a big, surly fellow—shaved, if not slightly bald, off the top. He's wearing a white t-shirt, grey, nondescript pants—loose, lighter material…kind of dressier pants they would wear in the '50s. He's not aggressive in terms of being negative—I want to be clear on that. In fact, he's probably done a lot for the town and is proud of that, but he demands a certain amount of acknowledgement and respect."

Keen to begin gleaning historical information, I suggested we introduce ourselves.

She shared that a reply was already forthcoming: "I was just going to ask his name, but initially I just got a Harold or something like that."

"My name is Peter. Do you remember me from last time?"

"He's like, 'Oh yeah.'"

"Would you share with us your surname, please? Mine is Roe."

"He's saying it; I'm just not zoning in," Joanna frowned, concentrating. After a short pause, she spoke hesitantly. "Fitzgerald?"

"Harold Fitzgerald?" I asked, not doing a very good job at disguising my amusement at the rhyme.

"I think he says his parents had a sense of humour," laughed Joanna.

Inviting Harold to tour the exterior of the building with us, Joanna was immediately drawn toward the nearby stairwell and the shrubs that were planted alongside it. "I think he said these all used to be flowers. The ladies of the town would volunteer to tend a flowerbed…. I guess no one volunteered to do it anymore, so they put shrubs there."

Inside the building, Camera 1 was already operational, stationed in a corner shooting the main staircase leading to the second-floor auditorium. As David and Richard were around the corner setting up Camera 2 outside the men's room pointing westward down the opposite hallway, Paul wandered about the main lobby and the front vestibule, taking in his surroundings.

As he turned to rejoin the others, he noticed a man dressed in black, wearing a dark fedora (with a shock of grey hair protruding from under it), climbing the first few steps toward the auditorium. Assuming this person was a groomsman from the wedding party, Paul continued through the lobby without paying any further attention to the male's progress toward the second floor, but hindsight stopped him in his tracks. Realizing he hadn't heard the sound of footfalls, he quickly doubled back only to find the staircase empty and silent.

Paul demonstrates the position of the ascending male spirit.

As Paul reported his sighting to Richard and David, Camera 1 recorded an orb of light exiting the council chamber, turning abruptly, then vanishing up the stairs. Then came the first EVP of the investigation.

EVP: [Male] Dave, is that you?

Outside, Joanna and I continued our tour of the building exterior. As we were still accompanied by Harold, I pressed for information. "Harold, would you tell us please when your body passed?"

"I got two numbers right away: 45 and 65, overlapping," said Joanna.

"Were you aged 45 in 1965? Or the other way around?"

"Yeah!" Joanna brightened. "Sixty-five in 1945."

"That's when your body passed?"

"'Yes sir,' he said."

We walked westward and ascended the main staircase. I thought of the team inside. "Harold, is anybody with the other guys right now, following them around?" I asked.

"He says it's just him today," Joanna shared.

Inwardly I hoped that wasn't the case as we entered the former town hall through the small vestibule, stepped past Camera 1 and set our things down inside the boardroom. While we settled, Joanna shared that Harold had stopped following us and was back in the main lobby waiting for us to re-emerge. I wondered if Harold was somehow unable to follow us into the newly renovated section or if he simply preferred not to join us there. Had we vanished from his perception when we entered the boardroom?

⁓

Joanna and I started our interior tour from the south end, entering the kitchen where—to my great relief—she immediately picked up on another spirit's energy.

"This is a different person. This is not Harold," Joanna said.

"I wonder if Harold can perceive this person, because he said he was the only one here tonight," I wondered aloud.

"They might be from different eras," suggested Joanna.

She concentrated, exhaling. "This one's lighter...definitely female...a bit hunched...Lindsay. Long, grey hair...older, but was always very active in terms of volunteering and things like that. I believe it was a cancer that ended her physical life. Very loving, giving, but I don't think she had too much family, so this place felt more like her home, which is probably why she did so much here."

"Lindsay, do you remember me from the last time we were here?" I asked.

"She's very humble; she's like this," said Joanna, clasping her hands together and bowing slightly in a formal, polite greeting. "Like, 'Yes.' Different mannerism; very sweet."

"Lindsay, would you share with us your surname, please? I'm Peter Roe."

Joanna paused, concentrating and listening. "I got Smith, but..."

Just then, my digital recorder captured a hiss or exhale sound nearby that neither of us heard in the moment.

Joanna began to doubt what she was hearing psychically. "I don't know; Smith is so commonplace, right? Is it just in my head, or...?"

EVP: [Unknown gender; whispering] No.

"Is Joanna correct?" I asked the empty space to my right.

"Yeah, apparently," confirmed Joanna.

"So your name is Lindsay Smith?"

"Anne," Joanna blurted. "Lindsay Anne Smith."

"Thank you. What year is it, Lindsay? I'm wondering what year your body passed away."

"I got like 1987 or something like that."

"Did you grow up here in Waterford?"

"Yes, including her husband, as well. I think he died quite early on in their marriage."

EVP: [Female; distant-sounding] Yeah.

"What was his name, please?" I asked, pushing for further information to validate later.

"I got Frank," Joanna replied.

"Is he buried here in town?"

"Yes," Joanna said after a brief pause.

"It's really nice to meet you. Do you know Harold?"

"She does, actually."

"Can Harold see you or communicate with you?"

"She doesn't see him."

"But you know of him?"

"Yes," Joanna responded.

"How is that? Can you hear him?"

"No."

"Lindsay, did you have any children?"

"I'm getting that they had one small child that passed," Joanna said, pausing to concentrate. "I guess when the husband passed, she was on her own."

"What year did your husband pass, please?"

"Before 1940, so he would have died soon after they got married, I would think." Joanna paused. "What's that? Oh, war maybe. I don't know if he actually fought in the war, but he was in the military. I know there are auxiliary units of some type, but something happened—an accident or something, and he still ended up dead."

"Well, we're sorry to hear that. Do you have a message for us?"

"No, she's content," Joanna reported, then relayed Lindsay saying, "Feel free to walk around."

We explored three other rooms in the south section of the building. Apart from some residual energy left behind by Lindsay in the props and costume rooms, Joanna didn't pick up on any new spirit energies. We returned to the main lobby, where Joanna said that Harold was no longer there.

⁓

The rest of the team and our hosts were upstairs in the auditorium while I showed Joanna the rest of the main floor. She did not detect any other presences until we walked into the former council chamber. Once across the threshold, she broke into a broad smile and sat down at one of the square card tables set up around the room.

She turned to address a chair directly to her left. "Sorry to keep you waiting!" Joanna illustrated that Harold was impatiently drumming his fingertips on the table surface.

She was amused by his antics, but I wanted to glean as much information as I could in case our connection was cut short. "Do you know Lindsay?" I asked.

"He goes, 'Yeah.'"

"We were speaking with Lindsay," I said.

"Hm. Okay. I don't think he sees her."

"Harold, is there anybody else here in the room besides the three of us?"

Joanna giggled. "He said something funny: 'Why, do you see another person?'"

"No, I'm not that gifted, unfortunately. Harold, the last time we were here, we got a sense that there was somebody who was a bit of a bully; he kept shouting at us to get out. Is that person still here?"

"He did this," said Joanna, raising her right hand in the air as if volunteering himself.

"That was you?" I said, surprised. "Why did you act that way?" I asked.

"Somebody showed disrespect, or he felt disrespect. Was somebody laughing or joking or something?"

"Not that I'm aware of, but if that was the case, I apologize on behalf of the team if somebody said or did something disrespectful to you or if you felt defensive that we were here."

"That's what it was," confirmed Joanna.

"Well, we certainly didn't and don't mean any harm."

"He's like, 'Okay.'"

I wanted more information concerning the spirits we'd met during the first investigation. "Harold, are there any children here in the building? I'm thinking of one little girl in particular. Do you know who I'm talking about?"

"I got two [names], Elizabeth and Samantha, and I don't understand why...and she's got like a nice Sunday dress. He's well aware of her."

"Is there anybody in the basem—"

Joanna cut me off. "He knew what you were going to say! He's like, 'You're not gonna find much down there.'" She paused, concentrating. "I think the problem is he's not aware of anyone else. So in his mind, you're not going to find anyone."

"Are you aware of the bookstore below us?" I asked Harold.

"I don't think he knows anything about it."

I recalled what used to be where the bookstore is now. "Do you know of the police station?"

"Yes, he knows of the police station."

"Are there children in the police station right now, playing around?"

"No."

Meanwhile, after deploying Camera 3 on the stage of the auditorium, the other three members of the team were on their way back to the main floor when David's cell phone rang. Near the base of the stairs in the main lobby, Camera 1 captured a seeming response.

EVP: [Male] It's too loud.

Several metres away inside the former council chamber, Joanna and I thanked Harold and left for the main lobby. There she was introduced to our Waterford hosts, and Richard updated the group, stating that all three cameras were up and running.

I followed Joanna up to the auditorium, where she sensed multiple energy sources but was unable to elaborate further. I did not share Michele's previous perception of the floor blanketed with beds or cots.

Joanna used her cell phone camera to film the auditorium and caught several dust particles. One in particular stood out, floating horizontally about one metre parallel to the floor and then angling up the stairs toward the seats at an identical height before disappearing from view.

~

Downstairs, Paul wandered into the brightly-lit former council chamber. His attention was suddenly called toward a corner where a pair of disembodied voices was whispering something indistinguishable to each other. As Paul stepped closer to investigate, the hushed conversation ended as quickly as it began.

~

Brenda joined Joanna and me upstairs in the auditorium and unlocked the entrance to a small balcony for us. We climbed the narrow staircase and settled into a couple of the chairs that filled the space. Here Joanna sensed both male and female energy but experienced difficulty focusing on either.

A loud alarm from the main staircase outside the auditorium signalled the arrival of Richard, Paul, James and David. An EMF meter app on David's cell phone was indicating a large spike of electromagnetic energy at the top of the stairs that disappeared within a few seconds of its detection. Jennifer joined us as we all congregated inside the auditorium.

In the lobby below, Camera 1 recorded a disembodied exchange.

EVP: [Female] Benny?
EVP: [Male] Dan?…Dan?

A very loud bang erupted from somewhere on the main floor.

EVP: [Male; nasty-sounding] Give me that chair!
EVP: [Male] Henry?…Hey.

Roving shadows began appearing from inside the former council chamber.

Upstairs, while everyone explored the auditorium, Camera 3 captured voices that no one heard in the moment.

EVP: [Male] Yeah.
EVP: [Male] Henry, get right out of the back, like this.
EVP: [Female; youthful-sounding] Dan?
EVP: [Male] Danny?

James and I tried to establish communication onstage but were not successful. Joanna joined us but could not pick up any spirit energies, either.

Richard, Paul, James and I moved back into the main stair-well and attempted an EVP session. I asked if I was correct in identifying one of the spirits as Jacob. Camera 1 recorded a response.

EVP: [Male] No.

Richard and Paul returned to the main lobby first, discussing the figure Paul had seen ascending the stairs earlier. Again, Camera 1 caught a curious disembodied comment.

EVP: [Male] I want to see him.

The Palmisano brothers descended into the basement. Several minutes after Joanna, Jennifer, Brenda, David, James and I left the auditorium, Camera 3 on stage captured an all-too-familiar parting order.

EVP: [Male] Get out.

Joanna led our Waterford hosts and the rest of the team into the basement and seemed drawn northward, making a bee-line toward the bookstore where Richard and Paul were. "They brought me right here," Joanna explained when I asked why she felt compelled to bypass the rest of the basement along the way.

She took a seat behind the bookstore desk and began coughing, asking if anyone else was having trouble breathing. No one was, though I made a mental comparison to Michele's perception of a bookstore spirit with lung-related difficulties during our previous visit.

Joanna then shared she was feeling a dull pain in the right side of her head but stopped short of calling it a full-blown headache. Unknown to Joanna, Michele had been conscious of someone suffering a head injury outside the store.

Joanna "reads" the bookstore.

"I think whatever caused their death is something here," said Joanna, trying to find the words to explain. "Something to do with breathing, 'cause I'm having a hard time talking right now. It's extremely dry air or something."

"Along the lines of an asthmatic?" I asked.

"No, not quite asthmatic, no," Joanna frowned. "It's different. Like there's something in the air, like if there was a fire, it could've been smoke or something...fumes?"

"Do you get a gender yet?"

"I'm thinking it's the little girl...she's what, eleven? Ten?"

While the bookstore was crammed with most of the team and hosts, James returned to the main floor and entered the former council chamber, asking after Reggie, the spirit that Michele claimed to have met during the first investigation: "Are you here, Reggie?"

EVP: [Male] I'm here.

James proceeded to ask about the spirit alleged to loiter inside the vault but received no responses. As he exited the room, James thanked anyone unseen for participating, at which point a spirit he couldn't hear called after him.

EVP: [Male; loud, breathy] Hold back!… Hold!

~

It was time for a much-needed break. Richard, James, Paul, Jennifer and Brenda returned upstairs. Before David, Joanna and I left the bookstore, David's EMF meter app began detecting spikes of energy at the east side of the room.

Joanna advanced into the aisle cautiously, picking up on a young male spirit named Brian. "Slim build…straight brown hair…short…quite young, too," Joanna said. "Maybe 14 or 15 [years old]?"

"Can you tell us your last name, Brian?" I asked. Silence. "Do you know what year it is, Brian?"

"I get the '80s," replied Joanna, finally.

"Why do you stay here, Brian?"

"He feels safe here."

Seconds later, David reported a sudden drop in the energy reading. "He's gone," he said, and Joanna concurred. I left a digital recorder behind on the desk, pointing the microphone toward the centre of the bookstore, before we all headed upstairs.

When the three of us joined the others, we found that they had stopped to chat near Camera 1. I asked that the conversation be continued next door in the boardroom, away from the camera microphone. An immediate disembodied response was captured, seemingly satisfied.

EVP: [Male; pleased] Great.

Moments later when the main lobby was empty, another exchange was recorded.

EVP: [Male] Barbara.
EVP: [Female] Rec room.
EVP: [Male] Barbara?
EVP: [Female] Yes.

And downstairs, the recorder on the bookstore desk captured a loud, wooden-sounding knock erupting from somewhere deep within the aisles. This was the first of more knocks, flicks, taps and raps of various intensities captured over the next half-hour; some sounded as if they originated far from the recorder and some seemed to come within centimetres of it. One significantly loud thump followed by subtle sounds suggested someone had moved around the desk

Following the break, Richard and Paul were climbing the stairs to the auditorium when they heard the sound of a young female singing musical scales from within.

At the same time downstairs, Camera 1 captured a male voice.

EVP: [Male] Go up.

A few minutes later came another exchange.

EVP: [Male] Henry?
EVP: [Male] Yes, yes, I'm here.
EVP: [Male; yelling] Yeah! Yeah!

Meanwhile, Camera 3 captured several responses to Richard and Paul's inquiries as they attempted to communicate with the female they had just heard.

Paul: We heard you singing. Give us your full name!

EVP: [Young female] Mary Ferrin.

Paul: Is there a little girl here?

EVP: [Male] Mary.

Unfortunately, no further responses were captured at this time. Was the male spirit responsible for suppressing further communication by Mary?

Then as David and I ascended the stairs to the auditorium, Camera 1 captured more evidence of a social interaction between a dominant male spirit controlling more subservient spirits, presumably from the safety of his station in the main lobby.

EVP: [Male] Go with them.

Upstairs, during a lengthy series of questions, Camera 3 captured an all-too-brief exchange instigated by David.

David: Is there someone here who would like to talk to us?

EVP: [Male] Sure.

Meanwhile, in the bookstore, the recorder on the desk caught a number of footfalls seeming to emanate from the former council chamber overhead, nine minutes before James returned to perform another solo EVP session.

Nearly 20 minutes after he left, a loud, metallic, scraping squeal—similar to a heavy object being shifted in an adjacent room—cut through the silence of the basement, its cause and point of origin unknown.

～

The dinner hour was near. Most of us had gathered at base camp in the boardroom and were waiting for Joanna and James to return from the second floor when suddenly a hard, loud impact erupted from the closed stairwell area. It sounded like something sizable and solid had fallen. Richard, Paul, David and I moved to investigate.

Cautiously opening the door to the stairwell, we discovered that a snow shovel had inexplicably toppled across the walkway, and its handle had knocked over one of the winter boots on the first step. Moments later James and Joanna came down the staircase, confirming they were nowhere near the area when the shovel fell.

We wondered if someone unseen had knocked the shovel down in a panic to leave the building. With the group of us in the boardroom and James and Joanna at the top of the stairs, perhaps this person felt cornered. We took some photos to document the incident, then prepared to head out.

By 6:20 PM, the building was securely locked. Jennifer returned home for dinner while Brenda accompanied the team for a meal at a restaurant about a block away. As was our custom, all forms of surveillance were left to record throughout the building while we were gone.

The air outside remained cool as the sun began to set, casting a blanket of orange-red over the main street of Waterford. Over the course of its existence, The Searcher Group has noted that the frequency of paranormal activity tends to increase with the coming of nightfall, and thankfully the events of this evening did not disappoint.

While devoid of corporeal people, the digital recorder on the bookstore desk continued to log the occasional tick, tap and knock. Another wooden-sounding footfall-like thump came from the council chamber above, followed by a sharp rap on the desk itself, near the recorder. Then came a voice.

EVP: [Male; mechanical-sounding] Weird place.

About 30 seconds later, a pair of solid impact sounds—not unlike someone stumbling into something hard, hollow and wooden on the floor—were also captured somewhere in the vicinity of the recorder.

Inside the vault on the main floor, a recorder James had left running recorded no activity. However, a few metres away, over a 22-minute period, an unexplainable buzzing sound overtook and interfered with the audio of Camera 1, making EVP detection impossible. Cameras 2 and 3 recorded no audible or visual anomalies.

~

Following dinner, David bade everyone farewell and left for the evening, while the rest of us re-entered the now-darkened building. As the lights were illuminated, Camera 1 captured an unsolicited taunt or challenge.

EVP: [Male] Find me.

Each of the surveillance systems was stopped temporarily as recordable DVDs were replaced with new ones. Then everyone met at base camp to discuss the next phase of the investigation.

The group divided into smaller parties to attempt short communication sessions in various parts of the building simultaneously: namely the bookstore, the former council chamber, the main lobby/vault and the auditorium. Each group was furnished with a list of prepared questions to ask aloud near a recording device in an attempt to evoke and capture a response.

Richard, Paul, Joanna and Jennifer moved upstairs; James remained alone on the main floor, and Brenda and I withdrew to the basement. As everyone took their places, Camera 1 recorded the following exchange.

EVP: [Male] Henry.
EVP: [Female] Peter.

There was silence for two minutes.

EVP: [Male] Cara, is that you?

Just then James passed the camera as he patrolled the main lobby, asking, "Can you tell me what your name is?"

EVP: [Male] No.

James' questions in the former council chamber went unanswered.

⁓

Downstairs, Brenda and I entered the bookstore through the back door of the basement. I flicked on the main light switch; a sharp pop and a quick flicker of light announced the death of the light bulb. The store remained in shadow, illuminated only by the dying rays of sunlight. We stepped deeper inside and settled at the desk, satisfied there was sufficient natural light to read from the script of questions. I activated my Spirit Box.

Peter: Shirley, are you here this evening?

Spirit Box: [Female; distant] Yeah.

Peter: Can you tell me the full name of the person with the breathing problem, please?

Spirit Box: [Female; faint] Bob…move on!

Spirit Box: [Male] No.

Peter: Is there someone named Annie here tonight? What's your last name, Annie?

Spirit Box: [Female] Howe!

Peter: Is there someone named Luanne here?

Spirit Box: [Female; loud, coy] No!

Peter: Or do you prefer to be called Annie?

Spirit Box: [Female] Whatever!

Spirit Box: [Male] No.

Peter: Did you live here in Waterford?

Spirit Box: [Older female; clear] I did.

Peter: Pardon?

Spirit Box: [Male; calm] Our home.

Peter: Yes? What street? What was your house number?

Spirit Box: [Male; clear] One.

Peter: One? Is your body at Greenwood Cemetery?

Spirit Box: [Unknown gender] Uh-huh.

Peter: Is there a little girl here?

Spirit Box: [Unknown gender] Two.

Peter: Emily, are you here?

Spirit Box: [Young female; British accent, clear] Peter!

Peter: Can you say that again, please? How old are you?

Spirit Box: [Female] Ten!

Peter: Sorry, one more time.

Spirit Box: [Older male] Go home.

Peter: Do you like to read the books here, Emily?

Spirit Box: [Older female] She does.

Spirit Box: [Female] Hey, Mom.

Spirit Box: [Older female] Babe…

Peter: How did your body die, Emily?

Spirit Box: [Young female] I'm…ill.

Peter: How do you feel? What's your last name, please?

Spirit Box: [Young female; loud] Em-ly!

Peter: Can you say that again, please?

Spirit Box: [Female; faint, pleading] Emily, don't!

Spirit Box: [Unknown gender] You're wrong.

Peter: That was very good. Can you try again? What's your last name?

Spirit Box: [Unknown gender] I can't.

Spirit Box: [Unknown gender; garbled] I know!

Spirit Box: [Female] Shut it off!

Peter: What's the name of the man who is angry when we visit here?

Spirit Box: [Female; quickly, low voice] Harold.

Peter: Did you say, "Harold"?

Spirit Box: [Female; upbeat] I dunno!

Spirit Box: [Female] Help 'im!

Spirit Box: [Female] Oh yeah.

Peter: Does he scare you?

Spirit Box: [Unknown gender] Uh-huh.

Peter: Uh-huh? Is he a bully? Can he hurt you?

Spirit Box: [Female; quiet, matter-of-fact] No.

Peter: Okay, I'm going to stop this and take this [Spirit Box] upstairs.

Spirit Box: [Female; casual] Okay.

Peter: Bye for now.

I deactivated the Spirit Box, left the list of questions on the desk for the next group and exited the bookstore with Brenda.

⁓

Arriving on the main floor, we took the place of James, who went up to the auditorium. I wandered the main lobby under the watchful eye of Camera 1, asking questions. "What is your name, please?" I called out.

EVP: [Male; angry] Jesus Christ!

As Richard and Paul proceeded toward the basement stairs, I mentioned the burnt-out light in the bookstore. Richard retrieved one of his flashlights from the boardroom. As he did, Camera 1 captured another comment.

EVP: [Male] The creepy one.

Inside the former council chamber, Brenda and I attempted another EVP session. The silence of the main lobby was broken by a single-sided exchange captured on Camera 1.

EVP: [Male] Benny…they are coming.

EVP: [Male] Come here, Barbara!

After another switch-up of locations, Paul found himself sitting alone on a bench in the main lobby. Alerted by movement in his peripheral vision, he turned to see a shadow shifting along the floor of the otherwise empty (and well-lit) council chamber. Paul raised his eyes in time to see a darker shadow figure lean around the open door to peer back and forth into the lobby, as if scouting for a clear escape.

Behind Paul, Camera 1 recorded an admonishment of the shadow figure from the main lobby.

EVP: [Male; exclaiming] Henry!

As Paul watched, the shadow figure withdrew just as Richard appeared nearby, completely oblivious to the activity taking place behind him. The brothers rushed to the council chamber only to find the room completely empty.

⁓

Upstairs in the auditorium, Brenda quietly settled as I activated the Spirit Box for a second time. It seemed as if someone was eager to begin conversing even before I had a chance to speak.

Spirit Box: [Male] Hi!
Peter: Hello?
Spirit Box: [Female] Ready there.
Peter: You're ready?
Spirit Box: [Unknown gender; faint] Uh-huh.
Peter: Who's here with us right now?
Spirit Box: [Female; pleasant] Good evening.
Peter: What is your full name, please?
Spirit Box: [Male; clear] Ronald.
Spirit Box: [Female; panicked] None of this!
Spirit Box: [Same male] No!
Spirit Box: [Same female; scolding] Gonna find you!
Spirit Box: [Older female; annoyed] Hell with it!
Peter: Did you say, "Ronald"?
Spirit Box: [Female] Yes.
Spirit Box: [Unknown gender] We did.

Peter: You did?

Spirit Box: [Female; frustrated] No!

Peter: What are you doing here in the town hall, Ronald?

Spirit Box: [Female; clear] Nothing.

Spirit Box: [Young male] Who are you?

Peter: Could somebody play a note on the piano for us, please?

Spirit Box: [Musical notes resembling a trumpet or horn]

Spirit Box: [Older female] Eugene.

Spirit Box: [Unknown gender] Nerd!

Without warning, I deactivated the Spirit Box, plunging the auditorium into silence as Brenda and I listened for movement in the room. When we didn't hear anything, Brenda excused herself and left to find a replacement for the burnt-out light bulb in the bookstore.

As the Spirit Box session was happening upstairs, Paul and Richard entered base camp in the boardroom. The atmosphere was quiet and—according to both—felt empty as Paul moved to retrieve a cup of coffee.

Suddenly, a pair of loud thuds resembling hard footfalls erupted from the staircase behind the closed door. Paul and Richard threw open the door and took several photos, but no one was present and the camera captured nothing odd. This time the snow shovel and winter boots remained undisturbed. Richard wondered if someone had just rushed upstairs or perhaps out of the building altogether.

From its position on the stage, Camera 3 recorded me as I closed the door leading to the balcony and turned to address the open space around me, holding my recorder. "Okay, I'm all alone, here."

EVP: [Unknown gender; youthful] No, we're here.

Without hearing this voice at the time, I continued asking questions of Timber and the unnamed fellow Michele had encountered squatting on the floor with a cat. No responses were recorded as I took several more photos, investigated the control booth and then returned to the auditorium floor.

Glancing at the empty piano by the stage, I posed another request. "Would someone hit an 'A' key on the piano, please?" I asked. "Right now."

Although I heard no response at the time, audio analysis of my digital recorder revealed that almost on cue, a rapid drum beat faded in from the silence, accompanied by an indiscernible, hollow-sounding male chant reaching a peak volume before fading away again—all within the space of 1.5 seconds. This anomaly was not captured by Camera 3 nearby, thus dismissing the possibility that it was the blaring stereo of a vehicle speeding past the building that somehow I had not noticed in the moment.

～

As the team packed up its equipment, Jennifer left the lock-up procedure in Brenda's capable hands and headed home. Cameras 1 and 2 were shut down and disassembled; Richard and Paul returned upstairs to the auditorium to deactivate Camera 3 and I followed, pausing at the stage, where I spotted a loonie resting on the edge of the apron. I quickly ascertained that no one else had noticed its presence the entire afternoon or evening—including Brenda, who had swept the stage before our arrival.

With the last of the equipment packed up, the lights were doused and Brenda secured the premises, officially ending our second visit.

Afterthoughts

This investigation was extremely successful in terms of the amount of activity and direct responses picked up by the recording equipment. It deserves repeating that Joanna had no prior knowledge of the investigation location other than that the team meeting place would be the parking lot of the Waterford Old Town Hall. Joanna does not personally know Michele, nor did she have any foreknowledge of Michele's involvement with the first visit, nor of any of her experiences at this site.

Shuffling Shovel

Given the number of times the team and hosts used the side entrance doors and stairwell without incident, the toppling of the snow shovel long after anyone passed through the area was an interesting note of possible paranormal activity.

The loud impact sound heard by Richard and Paul coming from the same staircase later in the evening suggests that a) paranormally speaking, this may be a high-traffic area, or b) because this area was not monitored by a camera or audio recorder, perhaps it became the sole means of safe escape or entrance for the duration of our investigation.

Wandering Souls

Paul's sighting of the male figure ascending the stairs from the main lobby at the outset of the investigation, as well as shadow activity and hearing disembodied whispering confined to the former council chamber was exciting to note, especially recalling the shadow figure Brenda's son witnessed a few years previous.

The Better to Perceive You, My Dear

Part of our work involves validating names of spirits, their current social roles among each other and their connection to historical facts. While we are performing these tasks over several years, we also observe patterns unique to the paranormal world that emerge from investigating different locations.

One such phenomenon we have consistently encountered is that some spirits are unable to perceive their fellow tenants by sight (or, in other cases, not at all). Many times we have captured exchanges where ghosts sound as if they're present in the same room, yet they call out for each other as if feeling about blindly in a fog.

An example from this investigation occurred shortly after the dinner break. The main lobby camera recorded a male saying, "Henry," followed by a female saying, "Peter." After this, the male asked, "Cara, is that you?" Similarly, Lindsay and Harold claimed to know of each other, yet neither could hear the other.

Role Call

Based on the impressive number of recurring names and voices captured by our equipment, it seems there was one male in particular ruling the main floor. He was heard ordering other males (Ben and Henry) to follow the investigators and then became rather incensed ("Jesus Christ!") when pressed to reveal his own name (which may be Harold, as was spoken by a female during a Spirit Box session and by his own admission earlier to Joanna).

A number of females were present as well, including Barbara and the younger female, Mary, who gave us her surname—Ferrin—to research. Acknowledgements from Annie and Emily a second time inside the bookstore were interesting to note as well.

Whereas we couldn't take Joanna's input as gospel without historical or factual backup, it was interesting that she picked up an 'E' name for the young girl ("Emily" by Michele, "Elizabeth

Samantha" by Joanna) as well as had breathing difficulties in the bookstore, just as Michele had during her visit. The brief head pain Joanna felt sounded similar to the recurring headache Michele experienced outside the bookstore near the back door.

Historical Hurdles

Unfortunately, confirming Harold's existence proved difficult. There is no record of a long-standing Fitzgerald family in Waterford, nor did the street he claimed he lived on ever exist. We found a Gerald S. Fitzgerald (1928–1995), but this was where the similarity ended.

As for the Smiths, there were droves of "Frank Smith"s found among military records accessible through Ancestry.ca, but none of them listed Lindsay as a spouse. No one associated with the former town hall recognized the name Lindsay either, which was curious given her claim to have worked as a volunteer there for several years.

Because we captured Mary's surname on camera, hers was the most promising lead we came away with after this visit. However, it turned out to be one of the most exasperating leads to pinpoint. We found variations of Mary (Margaret, Maud, Maggie) and Ferrin (Fehrman, Perren, Fearman) dating back as far as 1847 (long before the construction of the town hall) too numerous to list here, all residing in townships and counties outside of Waterford. We will require more data from her to narrow our research parameters.

~

For a place that boasted no public reports of a haunting, the Waterford Old Town Hall proved to be quite the opposite and earned top billing on Paul's personal list of most haunted town halls over the course of our team tour.

Based on the apparent willingness of the young female, Mary, to communicate, coupled with the amount of activity recorded and sensed inside the former council chamber, we requested one more investigation. Apart from applying the new names our equipment captured, we needed at least one more chance to focus on Mary, to try to establish a meaningful dialogue and glean more specific information to help us narrow our historical search for proof of her time among the physical.

Chapter 8

Old Caledon Township Hall: Second Investigation

In the past few centuries, science has made us aware that the universe is stranger and more interesting than our ancestors realised. It is an amusing thought that it may turn out stranger and more interesting than even the scientists are willing to admit.

—Colin Wilson, *The Occult*

~

Team: Richard, Paul, James, Peter
Host: Jeannette

The return to the Old Caledon Township Hall was much anticipated by the team, especially after the evidence and experiences we had during our introductory visit. We decided to keep the team smaller than before to reduce the possibility of audio contamination as well as to observe any environmental differences with a change in participant dynamics.

Our host this evening was Jeannette Massicotte of the Caledon Townhall Players. Jeannette had been with us on our previous investigation, during which she shared that she felt that she had been tripped-up mid-performance during a production in 2012 of a particularly risqué farce. And in the same vicinity of Jeannette's embarrassing incident, various members of our team had experienced odd sensations; Joanna had sensed the presence of what might be a phantom door or dimensional portal, still in use by a male entity named Henry. This time around, we hoped to conduct tests and experiments on this small section of the stage to try to scientifically measure any energy fields that might ebb and flow emanating from an otherwise unseen source.

~

It was a sunny mid-afternoon in late May 2015 when Richard, Paul, James and I arrived at the Old Caledon Township Hall. Jeannette admitted us into the building, then set herself up in the green room to toil quietly over piles of paperwork, deliberately keeping out of our way.

The surveillance cameras were rearranged to shoot the opposite directions than on the first visit. Camera 1 was deployed from the very back row of the house, directly under the small mezzanine balcony. From this corner, most of the seats were in full view, as was a majority of the stage, which was once again open to the back wall and clear of all set pieces.

Paul, Richard and I descended into the basement and found the tiled floor damp with condensation, making it slippery. We trod carefully as we walked through the Loonie Café lounge to the kitchenette to set up Camera 2. Paul decided to aim it eastward; not only was most of the lounge in view, but so were the restroom entrances and the doors to the dressing rooms beyond.

I set the wind chime apparatus in view of Camera 2 and left a recorder in the women's dressing room. As soon as the surveillance system was operational, the camera captured evidence of an unhappy observer.

View of the theatre house as Richard moves toward the stage.

EVP: [Male; demanding] Get out!

Similarly, while we were in the basement, Camera 1 upstairs captured otherwise unheard activity.

EVP: [Male] Dan…Dan!

The three of us rejoined James upstairs on the stage. Prominent scuff marks gouged in the black painted surface of the stage marked the suspected portal, where we had all felt unexplainable sensations and where Jeannette felt herself being tripped up. I placed a Devil's Toy Box in the centre of the site, then left a recorder on top of the glass cube. I half-hoped that if someone emerged from the portal, they would interact in some fashion with the mirror trap. At this moment the recorder captured a disembodied comment.

EVP: [Male] Hunters.

With our equipment in place, the team went straight to work and conducted an EVP session, asking questions of the people we had encountered previously: David, Dan, Jim, Bob, Rhonda, Howard and Henry. Richard ascended the staircase to the darkened mezzanine balcony while James inspected the small box office just inside the front entrance. Paul and I wandered about the house, listening intently for responses between our questions.

A consistent pitter-patter of water drops began to emanate from the direction of an emergency exit. Paul lowered his camera and we both turned to investigate. The sound continued as Paul and I approached the door frame, searching for a source. There were no puddles and no traces of liquid anywhere to be seen, even though we felt we were mere centimetres away from the origin of the noise. Within seconds of our arrival, the sound ceased. We opened the exterior door to confirm there were no signs of water anywhere near the building.

Richard returned to the main floor and James wandered downstairs. Paul and I encouraged the source of the dripping sound to recommence, but we were not obliged. We wondered if our reactions to stray sounds were being tested by someone observing us—or if we were intentionally being distracted.

Downstairs, Camera 2 recorded James wandering about the lounge. He was not alone.

EVP: [Male; beckoning] Jimmy, come here!

James walked slowly throughout the adjoining rooms of the basement, asking to hear from the men whose voices we'd heard during our previous investigation. Camera 2 recorded a short exchange.

EVP: [Male] Jimmy!

James: Is Howard here?
EVP: [Male] No.

~

Upstairs, I settled against the apron of the stage. As I turned my head to look over my right shoulder, the light in the stairwell behind the stage was blocked by a five-foot-tall male wearing a blue plaid shirt, rushing past the door frame toward the green room. Attributing the split-second sighting to a natural trick of parallax, I attempted to recreate my glancing action several times but could not replicate the illusion of a person hurrying by, let alone the amount of detail I attributed to my sighting.

We decided to continue the EVP session downstairs. Before leaving, I deployed the E. Probe 2.0, leaning it upright against a case of bottled water on a small table about midway down the aisle of the house, in full view of Camera 1.

Once back downstairs, I moved the recorder from the women's dressing room to the lounge and placed it on a side table near the wind chimes. The Loonie Café was very still, and the air was cool and humid as we all took up positions around the room. Our questions seemed to go unanswered, save one posed to Jimmy.

Peter: Was that you who said, 'Hey!' to Paul last time?
EVP: [Male] Yes.

Meanwhile, the recorder atop the Devil's Toy Box on stage captured various noises that were not detected while the team was present. As James' voice drifted from downstairs, a loud smack—similar to someone's shoe kicking a solid object—erupted near the recorder. Smaller sounds of subtle movement and shifting were interrupted six minutes later by a loud snap resembling a wooden rod striking a solid surface, also very close to the recorder.

~

The team returned to the theatre auditorium. Paul ascended to the mezzanine to take photographs while James observed Richard and me climb onto the stage. As I activated my Gauss meter, a familiar tingling sensation spread across the back of my head. I stopped moving and realized I was crossing the purported portal area, yet no anomalous readings registered on the EMF detector. Without measurable corroboration, I chalked my feeling up to subconscious suggestion.

Infrared photo of Richard noting Geiger counter readings. The Devil's Toy Box and a digital recorder lie nearby at left.

Richard produced a Geiger counter and a notepad. He placed the Geiger counter on a section of the study area and recorded the meter readings before shifting the device a few centimetres upstage. The needle inside the gauge was reacting to an energy that seemed to be emitting in short wave lengths. Richard worked silently, frowning in confusion at the varying readings, noting the time between tests and recording the results.

He picked up the Geiger counter and moved it 60 centimetres closer to centre stage, at which time the needle dropped and remained at zero.

I decided to do the same with the Gauss meter and placed it on the floor next to the Devil's Toy Box. Immediately the needle jumped past 2 milliGauss and ticked, indicating a low surge of electromagnetic energy that should not have been present. Another look under the stage confirmed the absence of anything electronic or electric below the wooden floorboards for several metres in all directions.

"Interesting," murmured Richard as he reviewed the readout results. "I wonder if this *is* a portal. I was trying to see the fluctuation. I wouldn't say it opened and closed; it's more like a spasm." He wondered if perhaps there were particular times of day when the portal—if that's indeed what this was—opened fully.

Downstairs in the Loonie Café, the recorder I had left by the wind chimes recorded something small and solid strike the tabletop next to it and bounce away—as if someone had hurled a pebble at the device in frustration.

The lounge was then quiet until the team began its descent. Then Camera 2 captured a male uttering a warning to someone else.

EVP: [Male] They are coming again.

After an unsuccessful attempt to elicit responses with more questions, I elected to remain alone in the Loonie Café to conduct a pendulum session. Richard and Paul wandered up the back stairs to the stage, while James used the front staircase leading to the main entrance.

As soon as James left, my Gauss meter—placed atop a nearby table—produced a single tick sound, indicating a split-second surge of electromagnetic energy. Although no replies came through the pendulum, the Gauss meter needle spiked again as if in reply to my asking after the spirit of Jimmy. When I asked, "Jimmy, are you an actor?" Camera 2 captured a frustratingly brief response.

EVP: [Male] No.

I was getting nowhere using the pendulum, so I left the basement a short time later. As I exited, someone sharply tapped the plastic casing of the recorder.

~

Upstairs, Camera 1 watched as James took multiple photos of the auditorium and moved slowly through the house.

EVP: [Male] That's okay.
EVP: [Male; calling] Danny!

The team regrouped near the stage, discussing investigation strategy and a plan for dinner. Paul inspected a framed seating plan listing the names of donors supporting the Caledon Town-hall Players. He scanned each one, looking for possible connections to Jimmy or Dan. When he called out loud, "Are there people from the name plaque here?" Camera 1 recorded an unexpected, disconcerting reply.

EVP: [Male] We are here from hell.

Sitting at the back of the house, Richard began to hear whispering nearby but was unable to determine its source or content. Camera 1 recorded this indecipherable exchange. Twelve minutes later, a second male voice was captured.

EVP: [Male; calling] Jimmy!

Several minutes later, a woman's voice—sounding as if she had only just arrived—was also captured by the house camera, followed by a reply.

EVP: [Female] Is Danny here?
EVP: [Male; astonished] Jenny Frost?!

That was the end of this exchange, but for the second time during our Town Hall Tour, we had someone's full name on digital record—an incredible rarity in this field of paranormal intelligence-gathering. We had also gained further evidence of social interaction between spirit energies. However, we had no idea this fantastic catch had been made at the time.

As we prepared to leave the former township hall for dinner, two motion detector lights were deployed in view of Camera 1 between a pair of ladders leaning against the back wall of the stage, aimed away from each other. The E. Probe 1.0 proximity alarm was activated and placed on the edge of a short, black dividing wall next to the staircase leading down to the dressing rooms—the same wall where a youthful-sounding disembodied voice directed a greeting into a digital recorder during the first visit. After new DVD-R discs were loaded into both surveillance cameras and set to record, the team and Jeannette exited and secured the building.

Within three minutes of our departure, sounds of movement were recorded. Within four minutes, the shrill blare of the alarm erupted and—unfortunately—remained activated for the duration of the dinner hour, effectively overpowering any possible audible exchanges between Jimmy, Danny or Jenny.

The alarm was loud enough to be heard through the main door as Jeannette re-admitted us into the building. Before

I reached the stage to reset the device, Paul observed the stage-right motion detector had also been activated. Someone had just been—or perhaps still was—in the vicinity.

I silenced the proximity alarm, reset it and thanked the person responsible for triggering the alarm. I apologized to Paul for the annoying noise ruining his analysis of the dinnertime surveillance footage, at which point Richard turned from examining Camera 1 and declared that it had been inexplicably deactivated in our absence. It appeared that someone was adept at interacting with our equipment.

While technical hiccups like these in the midst of an investigation are old hat to the team, Jeannette was amazed at the activity that was transpiring. She inquired about the theoretical origins and nature of spirit energies and why anyone would ever choose to return to a place such as the former township hall after death.

Within a second of Richard explaining the appeal of locations that people have emotional connections to, Jeannette was suddenly overcome with a feeling of sadness that was not her own. It was if someone unseen was present among us and had decided to illustrate Richard's words for her benefit. It was an incredibly moving outburst none of us had expected—leastwise, Jeannette.

After she had fully recovered from this abrupt emotional spell, Richard, Paul and Jeannette began a search for names corresponding to those of our spirits among the dozens of framed cast photos and theatre memorabilia adorning the main floor.

James entered the green room and replaced the batteries in his digital recorder. Again, he was not alone. A recorder I had left in there before dinner caught the creak of a floorboard, then a voice that James did not hear.

EVP: [Young female or child; greeting] Hey!

Jeannette returned just then to continue her paperwork and stopped short, eyeing the files she thought she'd stacked in neat piles before leaving for dinner. They were now separated and strewn about the coffee table. However, because no definitive activity was electronically documented (the recorder did not catch sounds of paper shuffling, shifting or falling), we could not count this observation as evidence.

⁓

With a third fresh DVD-R disc set to record through Camera 1, we resumed the investigation downstairs, settling into the Loonie Café to conduct another EVP session. This time we used a pair of LED flashlights as an alternate means of communication, trying to coax yes or no responses by encouraging an entity to turn the lights on and off. This experiment did not work, nor were any EVPs captured.

The west side view of the Loonie Café. Richard peers out from the kitchen where surveillance has been deployed.

Using a compass, we retraced our movements of the initial investigation and this time observed no anomalous fluctuations of the needle.

Partway through the proceedings, I carried the wind chime apparatus up to the stage and placed it directly over the alleged portal in view of Camera 1 before rejoining the team in the basement. If any energy were to cross this area, perhaps it would affect the sensitive glass chimes.

After a half-hour, the session in the basement lounge had not garnered any noticeable results; the team returned upstairs to try its luck there. Seven minutes later, a couple of distinct snapping sounds were caught very close to the digital recorder left behind in the Loonie Café.

⁓

I decided to visit the mezzanine alone, hoping to connect with Rhonda or Bob. Meanwhile Paul donned the parabolic microphone and slowly panned the dish around the house as he wandered, listening intently through a pair of headphones. James took a seat facing the stage, snapping photos of the theatre, and Richard moved around, quietly observing.

As he walked toward the exit leading to the green room, Paul stopped short as he heard a male voice utter, "Get back!" through the parabolic mic. He could not determine if the order was directed at him or toward a second spirit person he was unwittingly approaching. Camera 1 likewise captured this voice as an EVP.

James rose from his seat and fired his camera in the direction of Paul's encounter but failed to capture visual evidence of a phantom presence.

Paul took a seat in the front row, scanning the room with the parabolic microphone. "Anyone want to talk with me?" he asked.

EVP: [Male] Me.

EVP: [Male] Danny, come here.

EVP: [Male] Danny, it's the September bottle.

Paul listens for disembodied responses through the parabolic microphone.

Meanwhile, James ascended the stage and reported he felt something touch the top of his head.

Leaving a digital recorder in the props room midway along the mezzanine, I took a front-row seat in the balcony and proceeded to ask questions. "Is your name on one of these seats?" I called out. "What's the seat number and which row, please?"

Paul's eyes widened as he arose and turned to look up at me from the main aisle, still listening through the parabolic mic. "It sounded like a nine," he said, walking westward, counting the rows of seats. "It could've been the ninth row back."

"What's the seat letter?" I asked.

"You wanted the ninth row back?" Paul asked the unseen participant, taking a moment to listen for a reply. "J? J9? What's your name?"

Instead of a verbal reply, a loud snap erupted inside the props room beside me, and a loud stomp came from somewhere onstage.

"Is there anybody up here with me, watching the theatre?" I pressed. "It's a nice view, but it's pretty hot. Can you feel temperature? How are you feeling right now?"

Again, Paul's eyes widened as he listened through the parabolic mic. He returned my gaze, nodding. "Hot," he said.

"Hot? Was it a male's voice?" I asked.

"Yeah."

Although more questions were asked, no further replies were detected. I retrieved the recorder from the props room and rejoined the others on the main floor. We decided to head back to the basement with the P-SB7 device.

Paul and Richard used the front set of stairs to the basement. Camera 1 recorded James and I exiting through the door to the green room on our way to the back staircase leading to the basement. The moment James disappeared through the door, a short, glowing figure standing about one metre high emerged from between the backstage curtains, opposite. Whatever this entity did next remains unknown because for the second time that evening, Camera 1 suddenly went dead.

~

As Richard, James and I settled in to conduct a P-SB7 session in the Loonie Café, Paul wandered toward an alcove leading to the men's dressing room, still listening through the parabolic microphone. He opened the door to the room, and Camera 2 captured an unexpected reaction.

EVP: [Female] Hey!

~

I activated the P-SB7 and began a lengthy session.

Peter: Anybody here want to talk to us?

P-SB7: [Young male] Becky.

P-SB7: [Female] Me!

Peter: What is your name, please?

P-SB7: [Male] We're done.

Peter: We're done? Why?

P-SB7: [Male, quiet] You know.

Peter: Why don't you—

P-SB7: [Female, interrupting] I don't!

Peter: I'm sorry?

P-SB7: [Unknown gender; angry] You prick!

P-SB7: [Child] Uh-oh!

Peter: Is Jimmy here?

P-SB7: [Unknown gender; panicked] Hey, hey!

Peter: What's your surname, Jimmy?

P-SB7: [Female] Shut up!

Peter: How many of you are here?

P-SB7: [Male] Bridget.

Peter: [Misinterpreting] Did you just swear?

P-SB7: [Male] No.

P-SB7: [Unknown gender] You know…we just…did it!

P-SB7: [Unknown gender; agreeing] Hm-m!

I halted the session briefly as I reversed the band sweep, which produced a repetitive chugging pattern in the white noise static.

Peter: [Amused] It's a frickin' train!

P-SB7: [Female] Shut up.

Peter: [To the team] There's nothing coming through the box at all.

P-SB7: [Unknown gender] Uh… [As if to say, "Wait a minute, *I'm* here!"]

P-SB7: [Male] Jim.

P-SB7: [Male; urgent whisper] Jim!

P-SB7: [Series of three descending piano notes]

Peter: Is there somebody named Henry who comes up on the stage?

P-SB7: [Female] Shut up.

Peter: Can you say tha—

P-SB7: [Female; screaming] SHUT UP!

Peter: Can you say that name again, please?

P-SB7: [Unknown gender] You…little…prick.

Peter: What's the name of the woman upstairs in the theatre?

P-SB7: [Unknown gender; faint] Don't know.

P-SB7: [Male] Hurt someo[ne].

P-SB7: [Male; shouting] [H]ey!

Peter: I just heard a man's voice. What's your name, sir?

P-SB7: [Male; very faint] Trouble.

P-SB7: [Male] Jim.

P-SB7: [Female; shouting] Hey!

P-SB7: [Male] What'd ya want?

P-SB7: [Male; very faint] You know.

Peter: You know your body's passed away, yes?

P-SB7: [Male] [Th]at's it.

Peter: If you know your body has passed away, can you tell us what it's like on your side?

P-SB7: [Male] A bit.

Peter: Can you describe it for us, please?

P-SB7: [Male] Did on[ce].

P-SB7: [Female] Bob!

Peter: Can you please tell us and help us with that question?

P-SB7: [Female; quiet] Can't.

Peter: Please.

P-SB7: [Male] Can't.

Peter: Who or what is stopping you from telling us what it's like to
live where you are?

P-SB7: [Female; insistent] We can't, though.

Peter: Can you tell us your name?

EVP: [Male] Jimmy.

Peter: We've come an awful long way to speak to you, and our time
is almost finished. Please use this opportunity to speak.

P-SB7: [Male] We're people.

P-SB7: [Male; quiet] Hurting.

⌒

At the time, this session did not seem as fruitful as data
analysis would later reveal, and our investigation was well into
its final hour, so we decided to retreat upstairs to use the P-SB7
device in the theatre. I sat on the edge of the apron, centre stage,
facing the others as they separated and seated themselves observing the open stage behind me.

Over a two-minute period, the voices emanating from the
P-SB7 were generally too vague and speculative to interpret.
However, at one point a male said, "Help…me," followed imme-
diately by a female calling out, "Michael!"

I became aware of a small commotion among my
companions and looked up from the device in my hand.
Richard locked eyes with me before moving his own to stare
over my right shoulder toward stage right. Although there was
no discernible draft or air movement, the heavy black curtains
at the back of the stage had begun to shift slightly and part
down the middle; the bright light from the illuminated stairwell
beyond was growing wider.

Richard raised his camera and began taking photos as we
asked questions.

Peter: Come on up! Is there a young boy here?

P-SB7: [Female or young male] Benny.

P-SB7: [Male; abrupt] Enough!

P-SB7: [Male; quiet] Benny.

Peter: Are you with us?

P-SB7: [Male; creepy whisper] F**k.

Peter: Yeah? What's your name, please?

P-SB7: [Unknown gender] Benny.

P-SB7: [Male; cautioning] Benny!

Paul: Who's behind that black curtain over there?

P-SB7: [Female] Hey!

Richard: Come on out!

Paul: Ya gotta come onstage and show me!

P-SB7: [Unknown gender; indifferent] Eh.

P-SB7: [Male] David.

P-SB7: [Female] Carla?

Peter: Is there a woman named Rhonda here? Rhonda, please tell us your surname. We want to help you if we can. We can't help you if you don't help us.

P-SB7: [Male; calm] Wrong.

Peter: Wrong?

P-SB7: [Male; foreign accent] Stop me.

At this point, Jeannette's footfalls could be heard as she crossed the green room to the theatre.

P-SB7: [Female] Janet.

Pure white noise continued to emanate from the P-SB7 while the team took a moment to discuss finishing the investigation. Jeannette's movement indicated to us we were nearing the end of our time there.

I addressed the air once more: "I'm going to stop this machine if you're not going to speak with us. Do you understand that?"

P-SB7: [Female; quiet] 'Kay.

I deactivated the P-SB7 and placed it on the stage beside me. As I produced my pendulum to begin a new session, my digital recorder caught a distinct wheeze-like sound, resembling the stretching-out of several coiled springs and ending in a creepy male whisper.

EVP: [Male; whispering] Whaaaaa-tay.

Although none of us heard the sound or the voice, James lowered his camera to report he had just spotted a green orb zip upward before banking sharply, followed by a second one that had zoomed along the stage and passed in front of me.

Richard spoke up next; he had just witnessed more movement of the stage-right curtain. He began taking photos of the stage as I attempted to communicate using the pendulum.

After asking a few questions without any replies, Paul became restless and got up from his seat. He paced the floor in front of the stage.

Disappointed with the lack of pendulum activity amid the growing suspicion the team was not alone, I ended the session: "Nobody wants to talk, eh? Okay."

EVP: [Male; whispering] All eyes.

Lowering the pendulum, I looked up and realized the E. Probe 2.0—which had been leaning against a case of bottled water on a small table in the main aisle—was now flat on its back. No one on the team had been near the table the entire evening. Paul re-positioned the meter and confirmed the rubber casing surrounding it should have prevented it from sliding flat onto the table of its own accord.

While the others were taking a final break before closing down the investigation, I decided to try the pendulum downstairs alone in the Loonie Café and called out Jimmy and Dan. When no responses came, I felt exasperated and questioned the existence of any of the spirits. "I'm not afraid of you. Should I be?" I asked. The pendulum began to rotate clockwise; yes.

"I *should* be afraid of you?" I asked. The circles grew; yes.

"Why, because you're a spirit?" The pendulum slowed to neutral/unsure.

"Are you a male?" Neutral/unsure.

"Were you a woman?" The pendulum swung clockwise; yes.

"Thank you, ma'am. Did I frighten you?" Yes.

"I do apologize. Do you understand why I was getting frustrated?" Yes.

"Are you willing to speak with me?" Yes.

"Do you know Jimmy?" Yes.

"Is he here in the room with me?" Yes.

"How about Dan? Is Dan here?" Yes.

"Are Dan and Jimmy friends?" Yes.

Just then Paul entered the basement to shut down Camera 2, and replies via the pendulum abruptly stopped.

The team gathered its equipment, thanked Jeannette for hosting and departed just as a light rain began to fall over Caledon. It was an interesting night, but it was far from over.

⁓

Two hours later I was back home, checking my email before turning in. I discovered three messages from Richard, each with a photo attached. He asked me for my opinion regarding what he had captured.

The first photo was a wide shot of me, sitting at the edge of the stage holding my recorder near the P-SB7. Although there was some unfortunate camera shake evident (the flash had not been activated), it was clear that the stage-right curtain was caught in the midst of opening.

The first photo: note the upper stage-right curtains parting behind Peter at left.

The second photo—a closer view of the curtains taken seconds after the first—was the game-changer. In this photo was a 60-centimetre-tall mass of solid blackness in front of what looked like a long, thick black tail, caught mid-flight. The object appeared to be emerging westward from between the curtains, hovering about 1.5 metres above the surface of the stage. I couldn't help but be reminded of the Dementor characters described in the *Harry Potter* series. It was an incredible—albeit bizarre—catch.

The second photo: the horizontal black mass protruding outward was not seen by the naked eye.

The third photo—another wide shot—depicted Paul near me as I prepared to try the pendulum session. The black mass was no longer visible, but the stage-right curtains were still ajar, and a small number of glowing shapes were present, including a shrouded skeletal face and the right side of an elderly person's face looking toward stage left (exaggerated like a comedy/tragedy mask). There was also a series of shapes resembling the curls and curves found in the pattern of a human brain.

The third photo: several coil-shaped energy "bursts" fill the space around the curtain.

The likelihood of pareidolia with regards to the third image aside, this sequence of photos proved to be an exciting memento of the evening's visit. The EVPs and glowing anomaly Paul discovered emerging from the curtains during his surveillance analysis certainly augmented our efforts to establish contact with things unseen.

Exactly who—or what—had we been dealing with? Was the sound captured on my recorder ("Whaaaa-taay!") produced by the dark entity as it made its appearance through the curtain? Where did it go after the photo was taken? Were we dealing with something much darker than what is normally present during a "standard" haunting?

Afterthoughts

Once the motive behind the team's presence is understood, the spirits will do one of two things: avoid detection in the hope that the investigators will be discouraged by the lack of activity and cease to return, or take advantage of the attention being paid to them and put more effort into conveying messages. In the case of the Old Caledon Township Hall, there was a mix of both reactions. We were clearly not welcomed by the likes of Jimmy and Dan, yet they went as far as to supply us with direct answers to some of our questions.

Perhaps more interesting were the instances of physical manifestation during this visit, such as equipment being touched (Camera 1 deactivated twice; E. Probe 1.0 alarmed; E. Probe 2.0 knocked down) and the motion sensor activated, as well as visible forms caught on camera (white figure on stage by Camera 1; black mass levitating using a still camera).

Communication via Emotion

One of the highlights of the evening was Jeannette's robust reaction to Richard's insight regarding physical and spirit lives. While it is possible Jeannette is either overly emotional or an exceptionally talented actor specializing in spontaneous episodes of upset, we ought to emphasize that even she was completely mystified by her reaction to Richard's comments.

Who is Jenny Frost?

Another exceptional data capture of the evening was the full name spoken in apparent surprise (likely) by Jimmy as he exclaimed, "Jenny Frost?!" at her sudden arrival in the building inquiring after Danny. This exchange raised more questions: who was Jenny Frost? A member of the theatre? A patron? A local celebrity? Was Jenny a contemporary of Jimmy and Danny while physically alive? If not, how did their relationship (even in terms of recognition) develop after death?

Assuming it was Jimmy's voice that was recorded uttering her name, how was he able to sense Jenny's spirit? Visually? Audibly? By detecting a familiar vibration or frequency?

Jenny must have perceived Jimmy first (and recognized he was not Danny) in order to ask him her question. How was she able to sense Jimmy's presence?

Was Jenny Frost really present at all? Could this whole episode have been another spirit's memory recall that manifested on an audible frequency the camera microphone was able to capture?

We attempted to track down the identity of Jenny Frost, but incredibly, no one of this name had any association with the town hall or its resident theatre troupe that we could find. Perhaps a reader will be able to shed further light on this mystery?

Similarly, we were flummoxed by a lack of possible connections to any of the names we obtained at this location. Several hours spent carefully scouring the Caledon Townhall Players' archives yielded a few possibilities, but those names turned out to belong to present-day or past members who are still very much among the physical living.

~

At last communication, The Searcher Group was granted an exclusive, open invitation to further investigate the Old Caledon Township Hall. Perhaps when we do, we will find a few more clues that will aid us in answering these lingering questions.

~

Chapter 9

Orangeville Town Hall: First Investigation

If the living are haunted by the dead, then the dead are haunted by their own mistakes.
                                   —Chuck Palahniuk, *Damned*

~

Searcher Group Team: Joanna, David, Peter
Wellington County P.I. Team: Barb, Tony, Michelle
Guest: Wayne
Hosts: Sheila, Lindsay

Erected in 1875, the Orangeville Town Hall continues to this day to house its municipal council chamber and the mayor's office. The building is also home to a popular theatre space—the Opera House—located on the second floor, last renovated in 2013. In this vibrant community of 28,000, it is rare to find the Opera House not in use, and it's heartening to know that the living, interactive arts are still very much alive for the citizens, guests—and ghosts—of Orangeville to enjoy year-round.

We were about to take advantage of a rare quiet time, ensuring no sound contamination from the theatre would interfere with our investigation. After months of arrangements, it was determined that the Saturday of Labour Day weekend 2015 was the first opportunity in the foreseeable future that we would get to formally investigate the Orangeville Town Hall.

Orangeville Town Hall, present day

So it was that on a bright, warm afternoon in early September, Joanna and I converged on Orangeville at the local Tim Horton's an hour before our work was to begin. We were taken aback when the woman serving us from behind the counter recognized the team name emblazoned on our t-shirts.

"A lot of people have said they've felt stuff at the town hall, like they were being watched," commented the 40-something-year-old woman. She squinted her eyes, raised her chin and jutted her bottom lip confidently. "But I've been inside many times; there's nothin' there."

"Oh?" I asked. "What makes you say that?"

"I'm psychic, you know."

She wished us well as we departed with our refreshments. On the way to joining this evening's team at a nearby table, I shared with Joanna that our arrival had been preceded by a couple of news articles and a local radio report, courtesy of a press release issued by our enthusiastic host.

Waiting for us across the room were Barb, Michelle and Tony—three members of the Wellington County Paranormal Investigators (WCPI) team. Over the last few years, I had heard nothing but positive things about the work of the WCPI and—at my good friend Barb's suggestion—requested some collaborative assistance because Richard, James and Paul were unable to participate this time.

After establishing a game plan, I informed the evening's team that we would be accompanied for the first hour by three members of the media—a reporter from a local newspaper, a photographer for another and a cameraman for a major television news broadcaster. We would also be introduced to a prominent Orangeville historian and assisted by a member of the town hall staff for the duration of our time there.

~

We arrived at the town hall and were immediately greeted by communications manager Sheila Duncan, who was as enthusiastic as her email correspondence reflected. The members of the media had already arrived, so we wasted no time in transferring our equipment inside the building. Moving through a wide stairwell, we found ourselves in the large atrium of an addition that had been made to the original town hall building. Here the press interviewed us and took a number of photographs.

As we geared up for our first tour of the premises, Joanna approached me to share that she had sensed a spirit's presence almost immediately upon entering the atrium. She guessed the spirit was watching us from the balcony of the second floor, directly above.

Beginning our tour, Sheila directed us through a large brick archway into the original town hall. As is The Searcher Group's custom for an inaugural visit with a medium, Joanna led the way and stepped into the present-day council chamber while I followed close by, digital recorder in hand, ready to capture her findings. Sheila, the media members and the remainder of the team settled quietly against one wall of the room to observe.

Joanna paced about the chamber noting aloud that she sensed a lot of energy. Her focus narrowed on a desk to the right of the mayor's seat, and she shivered as we paused beside it. "Whoever used to work here is still working here," she said.

"Male? Female?" I asked.

"Larger male...balding...facial hair. He's a powerful presence."

Although I was leery of leading Joanna on, I felt it was appropriate to log what I was experiencing in the moment: "I don't know why, but my heart is racing. I'm feeling really anxious."

Orangeville Town Hall in the 1980s

"He's right there. He's not intimidated by us, that's why. This is his domain. I think he carried a lot of weight. He was in office, and he had a lot of authority. Even though he's not in the [mayor's] chair, he had a lot of authority. I think he was a big confidante of whoever was in jurisdiction at that time. His opinion mattered. If you wanted something done or passed or forgive[n], you had to go through him. He was a big power in this town."

"His age, approximately?" I asked.

"Early 60s, maybe, late 50s...I'm almost seeing the 1960s or '70s, based on the suit he's wearing."

I turned to the onlookers. Barb agreed she was feeling a similar energy in the room. I looked back at Joanna. "Can he sense us?" I asked.

"Oh yeah," she nodded.

"Is he willing to share with us his name so we can identify him?"

"I was picking up on a George."

"We'd like to address you properly, if we may," I said, eyeing the empty chair.

"He's serious; he doesn't crack a smile or seem jovial, or any of that. He's more of an intense guy. He's more like a, 'So what do you want?' type of guy."

"Well, I'm curious to know your surname, please. And what you do here."

The information came at Joanna in a flash. "Wilson," she said. "I flashed a Wilson."

"Wilson? George Wilson?" A gasp from among the onlookers caught my attention. A quick glance across the room told me that the name Joanna had relayed struck a chord with Sheila, who was murmuring among the media and the rest of the team.

"There's almost an arrogance about him," Joanna contin-
ued. "It's like, 'This is *my* place. You're in *my* jurisdiction, now.'"

"I understand that," I replied to the empty desk. "I am visiting from out of town; [most] of us are. May I ask you—with all
due respect—why you've decided to continue working here?"

"'I never stopped,'" said Joanna, interpreting.

"What kind of work do you do? What do you oversee?"

"His response is just like, 'Everything that goes on here in
this office.'"

"If I were to come to Council and ask for something in
particular, which departments do you look after? Do I come to
you about a zoning issue? A complaint of some kind?"

"I was getting, 'Permissions.'"

"Permissions, okay. I understand you're high up in the hierarchy, but who's over you in a working sense? Can you tell me
their name, please?"

"I got the name Cliff."

"And [his] surname, please?"

Joanna shook her head. "It's not coming."

"[Is he] here right now?"

"'No,'" Joanna relayed.

"It's just you?"

"'It's all there needs to be!'"

"Do you mind that we're here, interviewing you?" I asked.

"'No, not at all.'"

"Can you tell me the year, please?"

"Not clear," frowned Joanna.

"Are you confused?"

Joanna broke into a smile. "He's a bit arrogant. He said,
'No, are you?'"

"Do you have family here in Orangeville?"

"'Of course I do.'"

"Wife and children?" I pressed.

"'Three girls.'"

"What are their ages?"

"Ah, I'm getting quick flashes...a seven, a four and a 14."

EVP: [Male, faint, exaggerated] Wow!

"Is your home near the building here?"

"I feel like he moved; there was one [home] closer and then he moved to a newer one farther away."

"Can you tell me the street name, please?" I asked.

Joanna chuckled. "I can't tune in. It's not clear."

After addressing the empty air and not receiving any further confirmation of George's presence, we thanked him for his time and stepped away from the desk. Joanna scanned the rest of the council chamber, but any other spirits there at the outset were all gone now

~

Michelle and I followed Joanna up a wide staircase to the south lobby on the second floor, just outside the doors to the Opera House. Sheila and the press followed us and stayed behind in the lobby to converse while the three of us entered the darkened 273-seat theatre where staff have claimed to have had unexplainable experiences since its establishment more than one hundred years ago.

Joanna's take was surprising. "It's the kind of place you would definitely think something's here, and yet I'm not feeling anything," she said, shaking her head. "At least not anything as strong as what was in that council chamber."

Meanwhile, Tony and Barb had remained behind in the council chamber to log baseline electromagnetic readings of the environment using a KII meter. Tony noted slight rises in energy as he neared the desk at which Joanna had sensed George.

He and Barb asked several questions, but only one response was captured after Tony asked, "Are you proud of your son?"

EVP: [Female, very faint] He'll be fine.

⌒

Upstairs, Sheila led us up a flight of backstage stairs to a mezzanine where the dressing rooms were located. After examining the attic under the eaves of the town hall roof, Joanna declared this space was also clear of unseen presences.

As Michelle, Joanna and I entered the men's dressing room, my digital recorder picked up some very heavy breathing or panting, that none of us was responsible for. The disembodied gasping disappeared less than three minutes later, after Joanna said that she wasn't sensing anything in the dressing room, either.

A second round of panting began anew but ended quickly as Joanna and Michelle began to rehash the exciting psychic hit downstairs in the council chamber. Perhaps the heavy breather had paused to listen to the women speaking.

We returned to the theatre house and from there walked into the brightly lit north lobby, which overlooked the main-floor atrium. Here Joanna was convinced she would encounter the spirit energy she had sensed upon entering the building and was bewildered when she did not. She asked Sheila if there was a basement we could access. Although the town hall itself did not have a basement, the addition—erected in the mid-1980s—did.

⌒

Rejoined by Barb and Tony, we all descended the main staircase to the basement, where we were shown a long hallway extending the length of the building addition. To our right was a kitchenette, a meeting room and a door to some offices that were inaccessible to us.

Joanna shared that she was picking up on the trail of another presence and followed it along the hallway, stopping before a locked supply room door marked "Janitor." The media crew hung back, observing from the end of the hall as I knocked on the door, asking for a reply.

"Oh, there's pressure all around my head," Joanna shared.

"I feel like there's somebody on the other side," added Barb. "It's a male and he's standing in front of the door to keep it shut, so we can't get in. Do you sense what he looks like?"

"I just get slim build, but older," Joanna replied, concentrating.

"He doesn't wear glasses," added Barb. "He doesn't have a lot of hair."

"No," agreed Joanna, "scruff. [I think] he feels he really shouldn't be here, and if we find him, we're gonna get rid of him, or something."

From our position outside the locked door, we tried to assure the unnerved spirit of our friendly intentions. When no further information surfaced psychically, Sheila left the basement to retrieve the key to the supply room.

I noted a new face among the media people, so I left the team briefly to introduce myself to Wayne Townsend—a local Orangeville historian—and quickly brought him up to speed on the proceedings so far.

"I can tell you about what was here before, which is very interesting," Wayne began. "This basement was never here before. There was an old church here before the [addition], so you're pretty well where the old church is. When we excavated here, what we did was we photographed and recorded stuff and we actually buried it again; we just left it intact."

When I asked what kinds of articles were discovered, Wayne said they were merely broken bottles and pieces of pottery: signs of life with no archaeological significance.

Sheila returned and unlocked the janitor's supply room door. Joanna, Barb, Michelle and I cautiously entered the sizeable space. Tony stepped in and scanned the room carefully using his KII meter, picking up expected fluctuations near electrical power boxes, but also high readings in the very centre of the room among the gathered team where no apparent power sources existed. Immediately after Tony called our attention to this phenomenon, the reading dropped, indicating no electromagnetic field was present.

Joanna shared what she was sensing about the male spirit, who had now allegedly backed himself into a corner of the room farthest from us. "Phil? Phillip? We mean you no harm," she said, trying to sound convincing as once more, a pressure seemed to envelop her head.

She concentrated, then relayed what Phillip was saying to her for our benefit. "'Not supposed to be here,'" she shared before assuring him, "We're not kicking you out."

"We're just here to communicate with you," Barb chimed in warmly.

"He's scared; he's frightened. He's cornered right there; he's shivering," added Joanna.

"We come with all due respect, and we come as friends," I said. "Phillip, can you tell us your last name, please? We mean you no harm."

"He doesn't want to talk," Joanna said, shaking her head. "He wants us to go away."

"Phillip, if we left something here for you to talk into, would you help us out by telling us who you are and what year it is, please?"

"He's like, 'Yeah, if you go, I'll do it,'" Joanna said, underscoring the anxiety Phillip was feeling at our presence.

Tony perched his digital recorder on the edge of a maintenance cart, pointed toward the corner where Phillip was cowering. After explaining the kind of information the team was interested in learning from him, everyone left the room.

Outside in the hallway, Joanna said she felt that Phillip was not tied specifically to the supply room but "scurries about" elsewhere. Tony observed that the LED display on the KII meter in his hand lit up briefly to red (the top-most reading of 20+ milliGauss) as we left the supply room.

I decided to conduct a test for the benefit of the observing media. "Would you like us to leave, Phillip?" I asked, then gestured to the KII device. "Can you make this [light up to] red if you'd like us to leave?"

The row of lights on the KII meter immediately flashed to red, then just as quickly returned to the baseline green colour. Everyone watching was amazed. I was pleased, but I wanted to verify the first test to eliminate the chance of a fluke electromagnetic energy spike. "Thank you, Phillip. Do you *really* want us to leave?"

Again the KII meter flashed red before the eyes of all present. Unfortunately the television cameraman had not filmed this demonstration, but I was grateful that representatives of the media had witnessed tangible, measurable proof of direct spirit interaction.

Meanwhile, Tony's recorder was capturing a flurry of indistinguishable vocal exchanges behind us in the janitor's supply room. Less than two minutes after our departure, a male grunted briefly; seven seconds later, the scream of a woman sounded in the distance. Eight minutes later, another voice came through.

EVP: [Male; urgent] Why can't you leave?

The initial tour complete, everyone congregated once more inside the north atrium on the ground floor. There the team was introduced to Lindsay Bailey, another staff member of the town hall and Sheila's relief for the duration of our investigation. The members of the press also chose this moment to depart for the evening.

We began to unpack the bulk of our equipment in preparation for the investigation ahead as Wayne provided us with more of the history of the premises, including its origins as farmland. It was owned by Mary Ann "Granny" Newton before being transformed into a park and town hall/market. He pointed out the large archway through which wagon traffic once traversed and identified the areas that had originally housed butcher stalls. "There was no basement; there was all rubble down there, and all the blood from the butcher shops would leak down [from] the animals and would drip through there, so it was all contaminated and we took as much of that [out] as we possibly could."

Wayne then led us through the main archway, where he made a point of stopping about midway down the hall. "Along here is quite a historic area," he said, indicating a section of the west wall beside a display case. "Sometimes people talk about feeling things here, and I've always found this interesting because [there] was a low [bench] along here where prisoners would sit before they were taken in [to the courtroom] to be sentenced."

As we continued southward, Wayne shared an additional detail that was appropriately macabre (given our reason for investigating). According to him, when coroner's inquests were conducted at the town hall, the bodies were held in cold storage at a large meat-packing facility next door to the building, only a few metres away.

The team gathered around Wayne inside the ground-floor lobby of the Opera House. Here he shared how emotionally important the town hall was—and remains—to the local people. "Certainly a lot happened on this corner," said Wayne. Apart from the continuous popularity of the beloved Opera House, this building was where Orangeville's able young men came to enlist in both World Wars, for instance. "There was a lot of mixed emotion about that."

Having provided us all the information he could, Wayne decided to depart. I thanked him for his time and walked him outside the building.

⌒

At the same time Wayne had been supplying the team with historical context, downstairs inside the janitor's supply room, Tony's recorder continued to log disembodied conversations and signs of movement.

EVP: [Male; faint, distorted] Hey, Gary!

The sound of running footfalls was followed by a brief silence.

EVP: [Male] Go f**k yourself!
EVP: [Male; deeper voice, growling] But don't, a**hole!
EVP: [Unknown gender] What's he say?

⌒

Tony got to work setting up a multiple-camera DVR system using a corner of the council chamber as his base of operations. There he set up a large monitor that displayed four camera views at once: the main-floor atrium, the council chamber, the west-side lobby outside the mayor's office and the theatre house, pointed toward the stage.

After deploying the theatre camera, Michelle and I made sure that the extension cables leading back outside the theatre and downstairs were not a tripping hazard. As we conversed, my digital recorder captured a disembodied male's voice uttering something indistinguishable. Seconds later the same male spoke again.

EVP: [Male; whispering] Where are we?

Because the DVR cameras were not equipped with microphones, we left a recorder activated on the stage, as well as a pair of motion detectors and the E. Probe 1.0 proximity alarm. Less than two minutes after Michelle and I exited the theatre came the first of four distinct dull taps on the stage, sounding very close to the recorder. Was someone mustering their courage to touch the equipment?

~

Michelle and Lindsay accompanied me as I deployed one of our own surveillance systems midway down the main basement hallway. I aimed the lens westward toward the janitor's supply room where we encountered Phillip and set the DVD to record. The three of us left the basement and closed the door to the stairwell behind us. Six minutes after our departure, Tony's recorder captured more disembodied exchanges inside the supply room.

EVP: [Male A] Don't ever talk to them!
EVP: [Male B] I can't help it!

A swish-like crack noise erupted.

EVP: [Female] Why is he helping out?

The brown noise dominating the room drowned out a male's rather lengthy response, but then came another command.

EVP: [Male A; growling] Do not tell him. Do not betray us! Papa will get him!

EVP: [Female; faint] [Indistinguishable] mind, man!

EVP: [Male A; aggressive] Listen to us!…Think I'm nuts? [Deep growl] Blame me

~

David arrived mid-afternoon, bringing the number of investigators to six. He entered the council chamber, and I introduced him to Tony and Lindsay. My digital recorder captured the following exchange.

Peter: This is Lindsay, and you know Joanna.

David: Hi, Lindsay.

Lindsay: Hi!

David: [To Joanna] Hey, Jo.

EVP: [Male] Lin-zee.

This EVP was unsettling because it resembled someone pronouncing Lindsay's name aloud—for what purpose, we had no clue.

I summoned everyone to the main atrium to split into two teams: Tony, Lindsay (wearing the parabolic microphone) and Barb went off to perform an EVP session in the theatre, while Joanna, Michelle, David and I headed down to the basement armed with a compass, Gauss meter, motion detector and Spirit Box. Each team was outfitted with walkie-talkies.

As our group neared the foot of the staircase, the needle on the Gauss meter David was holding suddenly spiked with an audible chirp, indicating a fleeting electromagnetic presence. He stopped in his tracks and tried to relocate the exact area of energy, but nothing more was detected.

~

Inside the theatre, Tony settled at the back of the house close to the sound and lighting board areas and activated another digital recorder, laying it on a railing. Barb wandered the aisles and took photographs, while Lindsay scanned the room listening through the parabolic microphone.

"Is there anybody here with us?" Tony called out. Less than 30 seconds later, Tony's recorder captured a loud, slow exhale.

"My name's Tony. What is your name?" The recorder captured three rapid knocks that none of the group heard in the moment.

Barb and Lindsay remained quiet as Tony fished out a laptop computer and readied his Spirit Communications Device (SCD-1) software to perform an EVP session. While he was busy preparing the internet radio-sweeping program, his recorder captured an offer he wouldn't have refused—had he heard it in the moment.

EVP: [Male] I will tell you something.

The SCD-1 software activated, Tony, Barb and Lindsay took turns asking questions. For the first five minutes of this session, indecipherable radio blurts dominated the air of the Opera House. What follows are the most interesting results to come from this communication attempt.

Barb: Are you an actress or an actor that played on the stage?
SCD-1: [Male] Actor.
Tony: I thought I heard, 'actor.'
SCD-1: [Male] Bloody actor, yes!
Tony: If you are an actor or actress, please give us your name.
SCD-1: [Female] I don't want…
SCD-1: [Male] Rest, Falstaff.
SCD-1: [Male] You too.

Tony: Do you know that you are no longer with the living? Dead?

A cacophony of radio noise immediately blasted from the laptop speakers, as if several voices expressed outrage at once.

SCD-1: [Female] He asked!

SCD-1: [Male] Did you want ask, uh…our help?

SCD-1: [Male; distorted] Don't be a fool!

SCD-1: [Female] Hey, Benny!

SCD-1: [Male; casual] S'okay.

SCD-1: [Female] Shut up!

SCD-1: [Male; distant] F**k you done talkin' to me.

Tony: Are you okay with us being here?

SCD-1: [Male] Pal, a couple years' life a day.

SCD-1: [Male; distant] We're not talking!

SCD-1: [Male; slowly] Elizabeth…Lyle.

Tony deactivated the SCD-1 software and thanked the spirits for their participation. Taking his laptop with him, he, Lindsay and Barb returned to the main floor, leaving the recorder behind to monitor the theatre.

In the basement, Joanna tried to communicate with Phillip alone inside the supply room. As she settled inside, I placed a motion detector on the hallway floor in view of the surveillance camera. Although Joanna did not pick up on a presence, a loud blast of EMI static sounded on the audio of the digital recorder I gave her to wander with. None of us knew yet of the earlier tensions expressed inside the room that were captured by Tony's recorder.

A second, much shorter burst of static was caught immediately after Joanna took a flash photograph of the room, as if someone objected to the blinding light. Joanna apologized if the flash was disturbing, then exited the supply room, informing the group outside that Phillip was no longer present.

Undeterred, I addressed Phillip directly, asking him to influence the compass I had placed on the hallway floor. The compass needle remained steady, but louder, more intense EMI static and clicking noises were caught on the recorder for six seconds.

The four of us positioned ourselves in view of the camera and attempted an EVP session, asking various questions, hoping to provoke a quantifiable response. Although David reported a single spike of unexplainable energy on the Gauss meter, no other replies were recorded by our other equipment. As the group prepared to move elsewhere, the Gauss meter registered another split-second spike in the same location Phillip had used Tony's KII meter to respond to me during the media tour.

We settled around a long meeting table inside the community room at the opposite end of the basement. After a brief EVP session, I left my digital recorder behind with Joanna, David and Michelle and went to change the surveillance camera DVD in the hallway. Several more instances of EMI static were recorded in seeming response to questions, but none of it was decipherable.

~

It was time for a dinner break. We all ascended the staircase and met with the other group inside the main-floor atrium. Ensuring all recording systems deployed throughout the premises were operational, we left the building shortly after 5:30 PM.

In our absence, much activity was captured by our recorders. In the janitor's supply room, more vague whispers of people conversing intermingled with the ambient sounds natural to the interior space, but one voice was later distinguished during analysis.

EVP: [Female or young male; faint whispering] Nine, eight, three, one, seven…

The voice faded quickly.

At the back of the Opera House, Tony's recorder captured a varied range of activity, from indistinguishable voices carrying on animated conversations to multiple sounds indicating movement in the vicinity of the recorder and as far away as the atrium outside the theatre.

Meanwhile, Barb's recorder on the mayor's desk in the council chamber was also busy capturing a multitude of raps, snaps, clicks and popping sounds. The restless sounds of movement inside the room culminated in a physical tap on the recorder itself, but unfortunately no voices were caught at this time.

———

It was just after 7:00 PM when we returned from dinner and congregated inside the council chamber. Joanna didn't feel the same presences she felt earlier. The team again split into two groups. David, Michelle, Lindsay and I moved up to the theatre while Joanna, Tony and Barb remained inside the council chamber to try an SCD-1 session. The following are notable highlights of this communication attempt.

Tony: My name is Tony. What is your name?

SCD-1: [Male] McTaggart.

Tony: Are you okay with us being here?

SCD-1: [Male] Yeah.

Joanna: Why are you still here?

SCD-1: [Male] There's others too.

Joanna: How many of you are here?

SCD-1: [Male] Uh, the counts are in doubt.

Joanna: What are your names?

SCD-1: [Male] Bill Ch—

SCD-1: [Female] Becky Anum.

Joanna: Do you have a message for us?

SCD-1: [Male] Charles is dead.

SCD-1: [Male; carefully enunciating] Howard...he lied.

Barb: If you're here because you committed a crime, what was that crime?

SCD-1: [Female] We each whore in here!

SCD-1: [Male; calm] We change the subject.

Tony: The question is, why are you still here?

SCD-1: [Male] It's...not departure.

Meanwhile, our group entered the Opera House from the north entrance leading to the second-floor atrium. Lindsay looked about the theatre, frowned and shivered. "It's cold in here!" she remarked.

EVP: [Female; loud whisper] No!

Michelle, David and Lindsay wandered in different directions between the house seats and sat down as I sat on the edge of the stage and began a Spirit Box session. I asked several questions, but the reception was choppy and uneven. Suddenly, a rattling sound emitted from the device.

Spirit Box: [Female or child; clear] Choppy!

Unaware of the voice that just blurted, I tried again. The following are highlights of this session.

Peter: Is there anyone else here besides the four of us? What's your name, please?

Spirit Box: [Female] I-mel-da.

Peter: Do you work here?

Spirit Box: [Male] You won't find me.

Peter: Are you an actor?

Spirit Box: [Male] I will be.

Peter: [Indicating Lindsay] What's the name of the woman sitting closest to me?

Spirit Box: [Male; garbled] It's Li-say.

Peter: [Pointing to David] What's his name, in the middle row?

Spirit Box: [Female; sing-song] Daaa-vid!

Peter: Is George downstairs in the council room?

Spirit Box: [Male; clear, quick] Warning!

Spirit Box: [Female] George!

Peter: Is there somebody named Phillip in the building at this moment?

Spirit Box: [Male; curt] Sure.

Peter: Phillip, we'd like to speak with you.

Spirit Box: [Male; static-filled] Yeah, fine.

Peter: Please don't be afraid of us.

Spirit Box: [Older female] David?

Spirit Box: [Male, distant] Yes.

Peter: Do you have anything to say to us before I turn this off?

Spirit Box: [Female; very distant] No.

Peter: Is this noise driving you crazy?

Spirit Box: [Female] A little.

I deactivated the Spirit Box, plunging the theatre into silence. Our group proceeded onto the stage and ascended the metal staircase toward the dressing rooms.

Behind us, Tony's recorder captured a Class A example of an EVP from the back of the house.

EVP: [Female; agitated] Two-O-one-two Barton Street East. Oh!

A loud, metallic clang noise immediately followed the woman's pained-sounding "Oh!" before all went quiet again.

I attempted a pendulum session in the women's dressing room without success. While David, Michelle and Lindsay moved into the men's dressing room, I went to retrieve the Spirit Box from the stage. As I returned, Joanna radioed me on the walkie-talkie to report that the camera trained on the stage had caught a sizable orb of light moving across it immediately after my departure.

Meanwhile, Tony's recorder caught the following exchange.

EVP: [Female] [Cough-sneeze]
EVP: [Unknown gender; muffled] Bless you.
EVP: [Female; very faint, cautioning] Shut up.

We performed another Spirit Box session inside the men's dressing room; the highlights follow.

Peter: Would you please use this device to say your name?
Spirit Box: [Female or child] Lindsay.
Peter: Is there anybody on the stage right now?
Spirit Box: [Female] No. [A clunk sound]
Peter: Did you just shut a door?
Spirit Box: [Female; very faint] No!
Peter: Can you tell us the names of the people in spirit who reside here at Orangeville Town Hall, please?
Spirit Box: [Unknown gender] Fearful.
Spirit Box: [Male] Francois.
Spirit Box: [Female; faint, clear] Ken.
Michelle: Can you tell us what year it is?
Spirit Box: [Female; faint] Don't know.
Peter: Did you like the last play that was put on here?
Spirit Box: [Unknown gender; faint] No.
Peter: Can you tell me the name of the last play?
Spirit Box: [Male; slightly annoyed] Kid, enough!
Spirit Box: [Female or child] No.

Spirit Box: [Female] No. [Musical notes]
Peter: We're going to go soon. Is that all right with you?
Spirit Box: [Female; sing-song] 'Kay!

The Spirit Box deactivated, our group returned to the main floor. Tony's recorder continued logging activity inside the otherwise empty Opera House.

EVP: [Male; whispering] Okay.
EVP: [Female] Aiden!

Both groups continued; the four of us settled inside the council chamber while Tony, Barb and Joanna descended into the basement. From inside the janitor's supply room, Tony's recorder listened as the trio walked the length of the main hallway, asking questions aloud and discussing the perceived lack of paranormal activity. The group decided to perform an EVP session inside the community room at the opposite end of the basement. Six minutes later, the supply room recorder captured a rather bizarre exchange, sounding as if spoken through a vacuum.

EVP: [Female] Ooh! Damn right!
EVP: [Male; whispering] Seek it; no more body.
EVP: [Female; whispering] Found it. Ehh! F**k! Heh heh!

Then after 90 seconds, a tremendous crash ruptured the silence of the supply room. Astonishingly, this noise went completely unheard by the investigators as well as by the surveillance camera a few metres away.

EVP: [Male; faint] What now?
EVP: [Female; loud whispering] Let me out!

The trio of investigators ascended the staircase to the main floor. Another 90 seconds later, Tony's recorder captured even more subtle conversation inside the supply room.

EVP: [Female; very faint] I love you.

EVP: [Male; deep, raspy voice] When do we begin to begin?

EVP: [Female] I'm here, Stephen!

⁓

I returned to the theatre alone to assess whether the motion detector on the stage had been activated or not. It hadn't been, but the angle of the device in relation to the DVR camera lens reflected a stage light that created the illusion of illumination from the monitor downstairs. I took a moment to speak to the house and anyone watching me, encouraging communication and activation of the proximity sensor onstage. After a couple of minutes, I started to leave, calling out, "See you later."

EVP: [Older male; annoyed] Just...get...out!

⁓

As the hour neared 9:00 PM, everyone showed signs of weariness. I decided to call it an evening, and the process of deactivating the equipment and packing up began. Before anyone stepped foot on the second floor, Tony's recorder captured what resembled several hurried footfalls pounding across a wooden floor. This was most likely someone crossing the stage, as every other walking surface in the town hall and its addition was concrete or carpet.

Michelle, Lindsay and I returned to dismantle the Opera House DVR camera and collect my hand-held gear. As we departed the theatre five minutes later, I thanked our ghostly hosts and wished them goodnight.

EVP: [Female or young male; British accent, whispering] Not over!

Unaware that Tony's recorder remained behind at the back of the house, Lindsay turned the theatre lights off and locked the doors as we left. Ambient silence fell over the Opera House before the recorder captured a parting voice a minute and a half later.

EVP: [Female or young male] Just me!

Six minutes later, Tony's recorder stopped itself—its internal memory card was full. A half-hour later, the team and Lindsay (along with Tony's recorder retrieved from the Opera House) exited the building, said our goodbyes and parted ways.

~

I arrived home to find an email from one of the visiting reporters, who wished to share an audio clip captured by his own digital recorder. It seemed that before Joanna sensed George's presence in the council chamber, a disembodied female had whispered, "Help me," from the opposite side of the room.

Afterthoughts

A lot seemed to happen within a short period of time on this first outing of The Searcher Group and members of WCPI at the Orangeville Town Hall. We were certainly grateful that members of the media had witnessed a paranormal "hit" for themselves: the confirmed presence of a spirit who definitely wanted us to leave him alone. We were unable to determine whether his real name was Phillip or not. This name was never spoken by another spirit.

George Wilson or R.B. Lackey?

The detection of someone claiming to be George Wilson inside the council chamber produced an immediate reaction from Sheila. George Alexander Wilson had passed away just the year before, three weeks shy of his 90th birthday. Although

Mr. Wilson did not work at the town hall, as a local business owner he certainly was familiar with the building and with the council. Another connection is that his son Scott served on the council at the time of the investigation.

However, the accompanying information Joanna got from George is questionable. Her physical description of the spirit did not match that of the man, and the genders of his children did not match what he told her, either. Also, Scott Wilson was adamant that "George Wilson" the spirit behaved nothing like his dad.

Sheila told me that before George's name came up, Joanna's description of the male spirit reminded her of someone else: a former clerk-treasurer named R.B. Lackey, who had long since passed away. In the course of our research, I made the acquaintance of his son John Lackey, manager of operations and development/public works for the Town of Orangeville, and together we reviewed Joanna's reading. According to John, Joanna and I were indeed in the vicinity of the desk R.B. Lackey would have sat at recording minutes of council meetings and that "while heavier in the years to come, he was not large, but definitely bald."

R.B. Lackey

John Lackey continued to go over Joanna's impressions with us:

- On Joanna's revelation the male spirit "carried a lot of weight" and "had a lot of authority": "He would not be intimidating, but more inquisitive about your presence. He did have power in that if anyone needed to know anything or get anything done, Mr. Lackey was the man to see. In later years he was referred to on occasion as 'Mr. Orangeville.' His opinions did matter, and he was often approached for advice."

- On the male spirit being an "intense guy": "I am not sure if 'intense' would describe my father. He was always patient and helpful and courteous."

- On the male spirit seeming arrogant: "My father would not be arrogant, but as noted, interested in terms of helping or finding out what you would be inquiring about."

- On my asking the male spirit why he chooses to remain at the Orangeville Town Hall: "My father worked long hours, working most nights and weekends to prepare for various meetings and to address town issues."

- On the duties the male spirit was asked about doing ("Everything that goes on here in this office"): "This is true; he did everything and knew everything about the town."

- On the name Cliff: "I do not recognize this name."

- On the male spirit claiming to have three daughters: "My father only had two children—a boy and a girl."

- On the proximity of the spirit's home to the town hall: "[He] lived a block from the town hall on Second Avenue for approximately 50 years before moving to the Avalon nursing care home." (A quick check using Google Maps showed the Avalon Care Centre is indeed much farther away from the town hall, just as Joanna had shared.)

Perhaps the most fitting conclusion to this possible psychic connection to Mr. Lackey are his own words, published upon his retirement in 1984: "I will still have the interest of the town at heart. I don't think I will ever lose that. I have always been a great Orangeville booster and always will be."

Cemetery Proximity

Because of a natural tendency to associate a haunting with the disquieted spirits of those whose bodies have been disturbed by exhumation, the team was intrigued by the possibility that where there was once a church, a cemetery had also once existed within the immediate vicinity of the town hall. This idea was quickly put to rest when archivist Laura Camilleri of the Museum of Dufferin told us there was no record of the excavators finding any evidence of a burial ground while laying the foundation of the town hall addition in the mid-1980s.

My own research revealed that Orangeville's first Presbyterian church was indeed established as a log structure circa 1845 (about eight years after a congregation was organized) close to the town hall. It was dismantled, and a second church (built of stone) was erected about 350 metres west in 1859. This location was the one referred to as Old Bethel (or Auld Kirk), but more importantly, it was the location of the original cemetery—about a four-minute walk from the town hall.

~

In all, the data collected by WCPI and The Searcher Group strongly suggested that there were at least four or five male spirits and two female spirits present. The trio recorded inside the theatre seemed to know each other well and collaborated when deciding which questions to answer and the manner with which to reply to them. There seemed to be definite interest shown toward the technology that was used by the team.

Those who we encountered in and about the property were certainly not aggressive toward us by any means. As is a common pattern in this kind of investigation, these people appeared to be going about their business after shedding their physical bodies, yet they also seemed to be well aware of their disembodied condition. Our follow-up visit would result in a significant revelation that would prove exactly *how* aware the spirit people of the Orangeville Town Hall are of their discarnate existence.

~

Chapter 10

Toronto City Hall No. 1: Daytime Tour & First Investigation

It occurred to me that if I were a ghost, this ambiance was what I'd miss most: the ordinary, day-to-day bustle of the living. Ghosts long, I'm sure, for the stupidest, most unremarkable things.

—Banana Yoshimoto, *The Lake*

~

Team: Richard, Paul, Joanna, James, Peter
Guest: Stephanie
Host: Bruce

Our Town Hall Tour would not be complete without investigating at least one from Ontario's capital. Originally established as York, Toronto was a town first before it grew into the thriving, globally renowned metropolis it is today. Not many people are aware that Toronto boasted two former city hall locations before the present-day location was inaugurated in 1965.

Between 1845 and 1899, the original city hall stood as the seat of local government—among other uses—in what is now the St. Lawrence neighbourhood of Toronto. The building survived the Great Fires of 1849 and 1904 and was saved from demolition in 1971, but it has undergone a few modifications; thankfully its "bones" still exist, incorporated into the southern section of the St. Lawrence Market located at Front and Jarvis streets.

St. Lawrence Market

Today visitors are free to visit the Market Gallery on the third floor. It's a wide, open space that once served as council chamber but now provides wall space for art shows and historical photographs depicting the evolution of both the building and Toronto itself. The focal point of the gallery remains the original throne-backed mayor's chair.

The creaking of the 150-year-old floorboards (when no one is standing on them), disembodied footfalls in a stairwell and even malfunctioning lights are attributed to the spirit of Toronto's 13th mayor, John Hutchinson. Plagued by a huge financial scandal during an economic depression, Hutchinson resigned as mayor in 1858 and fled to Montreal, never to be heard from in "Muddy York" again—at least not physically. In recent years, someone among the Market staff suggested that it is Hutchinson's ghost that is to blame for the spooky occurrences. Perhaps he has returned to his former office out of guilt for his part in contributing to those hard times long ago.

On the west side of the second level—where one of a pair of wings on the original structure used to be—is the Market Kitchen, an open-concept space where cooking classes and social gatherings take place. From here can be seen the bricked-in arched windows and doorways that once led to the mayor's office.

In its heyday, the first city hall building also housed a courthouse, police headquarters and—in the perpetually damp, dark sub-basement—jail cells. At that time, crimes from petty theft to murder were punishable by hanging. A magistrate could easily order a married woman locked up among dozens of York's "unfortunates" for days—even weeks—for the crime of having had an argument with her husband. An overhead grate allowed the public to gawk at and abuse the throng of shamed women being held below the street.

Because the original city hall was built so near the shore of Lake Ontario, its basement was subject to frequent flooding. Through landfill efforts, this same shoreline is now 600 metres away. Until the early-to-mid 1850s, the inmates shackled to the brick walls often found themselves stranded knee- (sometimes waist-) deep in a disgusting brew consisting of ice-cold lake water from the south mixed with raw sewage and animal waste trickling downhill from households located directly to the north.

Toronto City Hall No. 1

For several years a rumour persisted of a particularly severe flood that resulted in the gruesome drowning deaths of hundreds of hapless inmates. Try as I might, I could not locate a single historical reference to any such tragedy online; the scant mentions I did come across continued to perpetuate whisperings of this alleged event without a credible source, month or year. More thorough research was definitely required. Still, the slightest possibility of such an unfortunate event was one more question I wished to put to the spirits of the former city hall, given the chance.

One glorious Saturday morning in April 2015, I was privileged to be taken on a private walk-through of the St. Lawrence neighbourhood by amiable historian and tour guide extraordinaire, Bruce Bell. Since 1999, Bruce has written monthly columns for *The Bulletin*, orated at the Winter Garden theatre, conducted hundreds of walking tours for the public, celebrities and dignitaries alike and been named Honorary Historian for the St. Lawrence Hall, King Edward Hotel, Hockey Hall of Fame Heritage Building, Dominion Bank, Fairmont Royal York Hotel, 51 Division Heritage Building and, of course, the St. Lawrence Market.

Upon meeting just inside the main entrance, Bruce wasted no time in showing me the visual remnants of the former mayors' offices from the floor of the Market Kitchen; then he led me to the Market Gallery, where I was introduced to a city staff member posted there. The gallery guard reinforced the suggestion that paranormal activity was quite common inside the former city hall and reiterated the same tales of disembodied footfalls and sensations of being watched that are commonly reported (and likely embellished) online.

I was anxious to visit the notorious sub-basement and what remained of the jail cells. Bruce led me down the east staircase. We then stepped into a brightly lit aisle comprised of the infamous jail cell wall and several walk-in freezers lined parallel to it. The din of the market crowds behind us and the degree of luminosity detracted greatly from what must have once been an extremely somber environment, more than 100 years previous. The only evidence suggesting this area served a more dour purpose were a half-dozen faux chains and shackles adorning the length of the brick wall—leftover decorations from Bruce's last Hallowe'en tour.

"If those walls could talk, they'd scream," Bruce declared.

I was thrilled to think that we might confirm (or debunk) decades of paranormal prattle when no other investigative team had been granted an opportunity to try.

⌒

Soon after my tour with Bruce, The Searcher Group established contact with representatives of the City of Toronto. Over the course of several months, we carefully explained our intentions to conduct formal investigations of City Hall No. 1. Finally, it seemed like we would be permitted to proceed but for one costly caveat—the team would be required to pay for after-hours security, to the tune of several hundreds of dollars per investigation.

This stipulation by City Council marked an abrupt end to our plans to explore the former city hall after-hours; as dedicated volunteers, we were already spending out-of-pocket for equipment, batteries and travel expenses. But fate—in the form of Bruce—intervened and proposed an alternate idea: how would the team feel about co-hosting his annual Hallowe'en after-hours tour of the St. Lawrence Market and incorporate an investigation for the guests?

Bruce's 2015 event would mark the team's first interactive public speaking appearance during All Hallows' Eve, itself. We eagerly accepted his intriguing offer.

⌒

The very nature of this particular outing precluded any chance of conducting a formal, controlled investigation of the former city hall. With upwards of 30 (presumably inexpert) guests at any one time wandering near our cameras and recorders, the odds of capturing viable EVP or photographic evidence were not good. Still, we brought several pieces of equipment along, ready to use and demonstrate over the course of the evening.

I asked Joanna to perform a walk-through of the premises before the guests arrived so that we could record any preliminary findings. She arrived 90 minutes ahead of Bruce's event accompanied by her cousin Stephanie. Starting in the Market Kitchen, Stephanie followed with a digital camera as I accompanied Joanna with a digital recorder. Bruce observed from a short distance away.

We had not even left the Market Kitchen when Joanna stopped to concentrate on the open space above a bar counter in a corner of the room. "It's pretty intense here," she muttered. "Usually when I encounter Spirit, it's very neutral for me, like a person. Once in a while, I get something pretty nasty. And I'm very surprised by this right now because this is not the location I would expect something like that to be."

Bruce was immediately intrigued. "But you don't know what was here?" he asked.

"I've never been to this building before, but this seemed like a very neutral place," Joanna said. "It's not anything we can't handle, but there's that tinge of nausea." She established that this spirit energy belonged to a male.

"Does he perceive us at the moment?" I asked.

"Oh, yeah," she nodded. "I keep getting butcher. Tall gentleman, big man; has an apron; butcher. He's not a nice fellow."

"What's your Christian name, please?" I asked the empty air over the counter.

"At first I heard a Bill, then a William," Joanna replied after a brief pause. "My connection isn't as clear to get a last name on this one. He doesn't like that we're aware of him. He's very stone-faced."

"Do you have family here, Bill?"

"He's not responsive. He doesn't want to speak to us. He has a lot of loathing; [he] never expected to interact with us."

I asked a series of questions designed to probe deeper but was met with the same lack of reaction.

Well aware that our time to privately tour the premises was short, Joanna, Stephanie, Bruce and I proceeded upstairs to the Market Gallery. Joanna walked around the spacious room, sensing a feeling of heaviness that for her that meant she was picking up on multiple spirits. "Nothing negative like in the Market Kitchen, but oh, heavy," she said. "It's hard to breathe!"

We stopped before the mayor's chair, where Joanna composed herself and concentrated. "I've got another gentleman here," she stated, then paused and grinned. "This is weird; I know you said it was the mayor's chair, but I feel someone who is not entitled to sit in this chair."

"He shouldn't be there, but he uses it?" I asked.

"I don't think he liked that comment, but yeah, he likes to think that he commands and oversees from this chair and has some type of power. I'm getting like a Terry or a Tom. I'm not getting a strong enough connection."

"Can you describe him?"

"White, salt and pepper hair, small-framed; a small person, but [he] feels big in the chair. It could be one of the ones that dwell here and this is [his] favourite spot." Joanna touched the left arm of the chair absentmindedly before pulling her hand back, conscious of the nearby sign requesting people refrain from doing so.

As Joanna giggled at her faux pas, my digital recorder captured a curious EVP.

EVP: [Child or female; whispering] Ready…pa!

"I'd be interested if you could tell us what year it is and your name, please?" I inquired.

EVP: [Child or female; breathy] Yaaahh!

"Terence, perhaps?" Joanna said tentatively.

"Terence? Is that correct?" I asked.

"He's acting regal; he likes to think he's like a king."

"May I trouble you for your surname, Terence?"

"Henley? Terence Henley?" Joanna said.

"Your full name is Terence Henley?" I asked.

EVP: [Male; breathy, deep voice] Mah chee-air!

"You're Mayor Henley?" I asked, humouring this unseen spirit.

Joanna giggled and nodded.

"Are there others here that would like to speak with us, Terence? Sir?"

"He just said, 'Look around. They may, if they want to.' I don't think he's giving us much here."

We thanked Terence for his time, then stepped away from the mayor's chair to walk westward, where Joanna sensed the atmosphere was much lighter.

She summed up her impression of Terence. "He's a harmless character. He just enjoys living [here] like this is his kingdom, when really he's delusional," she said with a laugh. "Quite delusional, but harmless."

Back on the ground floor, Stephanie and Bruce held back while Joanna and I settled by the main entrance of the original city hall, where two sets of large glass doors separated us from Front Street.

Joanna paced back and forth, trying to focus. "Did they have security here before, that patrolled? Like a security guard?" she asked.

"Probably," I answered, unsure about the security protocols of the former city hall.

"I feel like he's still working. He's like a patrolman; they looked more like police officers....This guy looks like he's [from] way back. And he's very proud of his job. He's here because he was happy here; he felt he had a duty here." Joanna paused to concentrate some more. "I want to say his name is also Bill. Another tall [male]...moustache...quite a lovely gentleman."

"I know I keep asking this, but is he aware of us?"

"See, technically, they're all aware of us, but he is not intruded upon [or] bothered by us by any means. He's just a lovely gentleman. He feels he's still working here; he's still doing his job. He loves the whole environment here."

"Bill? My name is Peter Roe. Would you share with us your family name, please?"

"Something Smith. It's a compound word," Joanna shared, pausing again. "I think it's Goldsmith."

Peter and Joanna meet security guard William Goldsmith inside the north entranceway.

"What part of being here at the market do you like the most, Bill?" I asked.

"'Greeting everyone that comes in here,'" shared Joanna.

"And you still do that to this day?"

"He's like, 'Never missed a day!'"

"Bill, are you aware of a rather nasty character up on the second floor?"

"I think he is. Such different dimensions."

"Can you tell me what year it is, Bill, please?"

"I don't know how old this building is, but I get late 1800s. I don't know if it existed back then."

"Bill, in your time, did Lake Ontario reach this building?" I asked. "Did it come right up against this building, or was it farther out?"

"I heard, 'It came close but did not reach here,' is what he's saying."

We still had much more ground to cover before the guests arrived for Bruce's event, so we thanked Bill and walked down the main aisle of the market. We stopped just outside a cheese vendor's stall, where Joanna indicated her chest. "There's some pressure here. This is weird, but the impression is [that] someone [was] stabbed here. Like, right in the chest."

As Joanna was describing the feeling she was experiencing, I too believed I felt a split-second poke in my own chest. I wondered if it was a result of trying to relate subconsciously to Joanna's words.

Joanna doubled back along a narrow aisle and stopped near some cafe tables and chairs. "I'm getting a long way back; it was in this spot, a gentleman was stabbed right in the chest. He was a small-framed gentleman, with suspenders..."

EVP: [Male; objecting] Hey!

Unaware of the phantom protest, Joanna continued: "It's going way back again…maybe early 1900s. There were gangs here. I'm getting that people kept territories and trade and there were all kinds of deals going on. He didn't pay, I guess, and they got him right here. I don't think the guy was expecting it."

"Any name for him?"

"No, it's more the action. I'm not even getting him that much. It's like an imprint of the trauma."

We returned to the main aisle of the market. Joanna was drawn to a fish vendor's stall and indicated pressure above her left ear. "I guess there was a lot of violence in this place. Another gentleman was struck in the side of the head—died almost instantly. This gentleman was an older man. He's wearing an apron, so he must've had a stall. He feels he was wrongly accused of something and paid the price."

The south side of City Hall No. 1 beyond the main aisle of the market.

"Can you tell us what you were accused of?" I asked.

"He said, 'Stealing.'"

"Stealing from the market here?"

"No, money [that] I guess belongs to someone else. I don't know if it has something to do with what they're selling..." Joanna was unable to pinpoint the details of the conflict that led to this man's death.

"Can you tell us your full name, sir? So we can help clear it?" I offered.

"I get a Stephen. I see him, he's got short brown hair; he's a shorter man; bit of a belly; weathered kind of skin..."

"How old are you, sir?"

"He says he's in his 40s, but he looks much older than that."

"Do you have family here, Stephen?" I asked.

"Yes. They work at the business."

"Was your family with you when you were struck, Stephen?"

"I think they were."

"Did they witness it?"

"Yeah. But it was so sudden. He didn't see it coming, either."

"I'm really sorry to hear that, Stephen. Could you share with me your surname please so I can help you?"

"Like, McLaren or something like that?" Joanna squinted, trying to psychically interpret.

"Stephen McLaren? Are you from Scotland, originally? I asked.

"Not him. A generation earlier."

"Your parents were from Scotland?"

"Yeah."

"Do you have any family here in York?" I asked, referencing the city's founding name.

"He had daughters."

"Can you tell me your daughters' names, please, so I can verify?"

"I get Elizabeth, a Lucy…" Joanna's voice trailed off.

"And your wife, sir?"

"I think Miriam."

"Was your death gang-related?"

"I think it was from a rival competitor. Man, it was cut-throat back then!"

"And they were never caught, were they?"

"I don't think he knows."

Unfortunately, no EVPs were recorded during this encounter. We wished Stephen well, and all four of us headed down a staircase into the bowels of the lower marketplace. As she stepped into the basement level, Joanna said she felt like she was underwater.

Bruce led us to a common area where a dozen tables were set up next to a large mural depicting various views and landmarks of Toronto. We were a few metres away from the base of the former city hall, standing opposite a vendor specializing in French pastries, when a loud pop erupted from the floor behind Joanna and Bruce. I moved to investigate but found nothing that could have caused this unexpected sound.

Upon later analysis of my recording, a clear footfall echoing from the concrete floor could be heard at the same time the popping sound occurred, as if someone nearby had just stumbled over a paper cup lying on the floor. None of our party had moved at this point, and we were all wearing soft-soled shoes. The floor was also clear of any litter or refuse.

Realizing the time, Bruce excused himself and returned upstairs to greet the guests arriving for the tour event.

On the way toward the remaining jail wall, Joanna felt compelled to share another psychic sensation. "I feel like cattle walked through here. But I don't know if that's possible because we're downstairs, below ground…why'd they come down here?" She shook her head at the seeming nonsense of this impression. "I keep seeing cattle, and I don't know why."

The infamous jail cell wall today. No screaming was captured by the team in this area.

We turned the corner and stepped into the aisle next to the jail cell wall. Neither Joanna nor Stephanie reacted to anything unusual, even after I encouraged them to touch the "screaming" wall.

"Nothing in here?" I tried not to appear discouraged.

The women looked along the length of the wall and about the aisle we were standing in. Each pursed her lips and shook her head.

The three of us retreated and returned to the marketplace. As we walked, Joanna reported that she felt nothing but traces of nondescript residual energy, which was not surprising for such a historically active location still in heavy use to this day.

Shortly after 8:00 PM, Bruce introduced himself and the team to the tour guests. Several people were dressed to celebrate the occasion, and the general mood was jovial; we were eager to get started.

The procedure established was that Bruce would lead everyone to certain stations throughout the former city hall and the marketplace, enthralling all with his panache for storytelling. Then Joanna would share her findings, including new ones if more surfaced en route. If time allowed, we would then perform a demonstration of some of our equipment.

Paul donned the large parabolic microphone, Richard carried his EMF and ion frequency counter devices, and James walked among the guests with a camera at the ready. I was carrying my digital recorder, a digital thermometer, a camera and an EMF meter.

The first stop of the tour was the Market Kitchen, where Joanna shared her encounter with the butcher, Bill. Our new acquaintance was apparently still watching us sternly, just as unhappy that he had been discovered.

The crowd filed upstairs to the Market Gallery and gathered around the former mayor's chair to listen to Bruce regale everyone with the history of the council chamber. Then while Joanna shared her earlier meeting with Terence (who was apparently no longer in the chair or the room), Paul, who had been walking quietly around the periphery of the crowd listening through the parabolic mic, caught my attention and signalled me to come over; he had heard an indistinguishable male voice.

The tour moved downstairs to the marketplace, where Paul took several shots of the exterior of the original city hall. Bruce led us along the main aisle of the market, speaking of a former railway station that once existed not far from where we were standing.

Paul listens intently through the parabolic microphone.

As everyone listened to Bruce's commentary, the EMF meter in my left hand suddenly rose to 2 milliGauss (mG). I noted the device was directly above a small puddle of water that had formed in the centre of the concrete aisle, near a meat vendor's stall. Presumably this water was leftover from the rinsing-off of the butcher's tools and implements earlier that day, as were the periodic wafts of decomposing garbage and the unmistakable aroma of blood. Although the small rise of the meter needle was interesting to note, it was not significant enough to interrupt Bruce as he and Joanna led the crowd eastward toward the site of the alleged stabbing.

I remained behind and carefully waved the meter over the puddle on the floor. A woman named Donna broke away from the tour and approached to observe. As she watched, the meter needle began to alternate between 3 and 4 mG, its readings high enough that the device began to emit its familiar ticking sounds, increasing to a scratchy groan. I moved the meter away from the puddle and the needle dropped back to zero. Remarkably, when I returned it to the exact area, no readings came through.

Richard approached with his EMF meter and ion frequency counter, and as he neared, my device spiked back up to 3 mG while his registered 2 mG.

The putrid smell from the floor returned, filling our nostrils. "It smells like guts!" I commented, wincing. Just then my meter needle rose to 5 mG and remained there while I held the device absolutely stationary.

Donna grinned and revealed that she had experience as a spirit channeller. No sooner had she spoken than the Gauss meter needle rose to 6 mG for a number of seconds before slowly dropping back to 5, then 4 mG, where it held steady. "It's a drowning," Donna said candidly.

The Gauss meter needle dropped to 3 mG as I inquired about the spirit's gender, then spiked loudly for two seconds before returning to 3.

I marvelled aloud at the impossibility of this phenomenon being caused by a human-made electromagnetic source—we were standing on solid concrete, nowhere near a machine or electric device of any kind. I'd just finished uttering this observation when the Gauss meter needle jumped to 5 mG, as if someone unseen was acknowledging what I'd said and had figured out that its proximity affected the meter.

Richard and Peter note unexplainable ion and electromagnetic readings in the centre of the St. Lawrence Market.

Another waft of rotting-garbage scent drifted up from the damp floor, causing Richard, Donna and I to react in disgust. It too disappeared as quickly as it had arrived, and once again the meter reading dropped and held steady at 3 mG.

Bruce, Joanna, Paul and James returned to the main aisle followed closely by the tour group and gathered around as I explained the various phenomena that were occurring in the moment. In the midst of my spiel, the Gauss meter slowly climbed to 4 mG before squealing loudly as the needle shot up to 10 mG and back down again, startling several people standing nearby and drawing murmurs of appreciation from the onlookers.

I was among the impressed. "If there's somebody with us right now," I began as the meter needle rose slowly and the buzzing grew louder, "would you please let us know your name?" The meter remained at a steady buzz, registering 4 mG, but no EVPs came through.

"Did you drown here? Can you make this go back up to 10 if you drowned? Are you a male? Are you a female? Are you a child?" The meter dropped to 3.5 mG, and a new gust of putrid air seemed to burst from the floor under it. "Now it's at five," I reported. The meter buzz grew louder. "Six!"

Although these ongoing readings were extremely fascinating, I was aware that this display of unexplainable activity was eating into the limited time Bruce had for his tour. "Whoever you are, please follow us, all right? Bruce has a tour going on right now, so let's hear what he has to say."

"Never work with kids, animals or ghosts!" said Bruce as he rolled his eyes and shook his head.

Everyone chuckled at Bruce's variation of the old show biz adage and resumed following him along the main aisle. Donna stayed back with Richard and me as I continued monitoring the EMF meter over the puddle. The needle began to climb again to 4 mG.

"Did you drown?" Donna asked. The needle rose slightly in seeming response.

"Are you male?" I asked. The meter continued holding steady just above 4 mG.

"I think it's an adolescent male," said Donna. "He said it was. Did you fall off a—" Her question was cut short by an EVP coming through.

EVP: [Male] Wha-umm.

"Did somebody kill you?" I asked. The buzz from the meter grew slightly louder as the needle climbed to 6 mG, then dropped back to zero.

Richard, Donna and I thanked whoever had put in an appearance and moved to rejoin the group, now gathered at the southernmost end of the marketplace. Richard walked ahead and spotted Paul gesturing for his attention.

Keeping the Gauss meter activated, I walked slowly. Stepping into a junction where one aisle crossed the main one, the needle rose to 3 mG with a steady buzz before dropping back to zero. Subsequent sweeps of the same area resulted in no further spikes of electromagnetic energy.

While the crowd assembled and listened to Joanna describe her earlier conference with Stephen, Paul joined me and we moved aside to converse. A short time earlier, Paul had detected the sound of a loud commotion originating from the wide, empty archway at the centre of the former city hall.

"Did it sound like a riot of some sort?" I asked.

"Yeah. Bruce was the only one talking, but over him—even with the sound of the HVAC system booming over the market-place—there were multiple voices of people screaming." Paul hesitated and looked around to ensure we weren't disturbing the tour before he turned back to me, pointing to the area we were standing in. "And," he added, "there was something here, too. It was a male yelling something, but I couldn't make out what he was saying."

Paul donned the headphones connected to the parabolic mic and disappeared deep into the marketplace. My attention turned back to Joanna concluding her findings concerning Stephen, and I began to think on the challenge of researching gang activity in early Toronto. How much would I find? Were incidents of violence in this part of town even reported back then? If so, where? Would copies of this publication be stored in a library archive?

Bruce spoke loudly enough to be heard over the constant drone of the marketplace HVAC system. "Up until 1977, this [market] was strictly wholesale, and for the public it was only [open] Friday nights and Saturdays. So a lot of stuff could've happened that we'd not know about."

He led the tour group down a nearby staircase, warning people that the lower level was a very dark place before retail vendors began to ply their trades there.

Bruce asked Joanna for her impressions of the lower level, and she shared her earlier feeling of being underwater and of seeing cattle wandering along this floor. Bruce seemed impressed but not surprised. "Well, this *was* underwater up until about 1858 when they started to fill in the harbour," he stated. "Cattle would have been brought through here. At Front and Jarvis, right on the corner, there used to be a weigh station. All the cattle would be brought right along Front Street and into the market."

The tour resumed and Bruce led the crowd to what remained of the former jail cell. Although his commentary on the deplorable prison conditions for both male and female inmates was colourful and gruesomely detailed, Joanna maintained she did not sense any spirit energies in the immediate area. Neither were there any EMF spikes or EVPs captured.

The group made its way back up to the ground floor. "This is the old foyer of the city hall," Bruce informed the guests as they settled around the last tour station of the evening. "[The building] was very opulent—winding staircases, chandeliers, oil paintings, all lit with gas. And it was also shared space, just below us; next to the jail was a courthouse downstairs and the police station. Everything was here."

Richard tries to take ion and EMF readings of the former jail cell wall.

He pointed out some early photographs mounted on the foyer walls, depicting the building's structural metamorphosis through the years, before turning back to Joanna for her readings of Bill, the ghostly security guard.

"He's still here," Joanna acknowledged. "Bill or William— security guard, turn-of-the-century; he has a goatee; tall gentleman; lovely man, he loved his job and he's still here and has a baton, but he doesn't use it. He greets people."

Bruce seemed taken aback. "Really, still?"

He pointed to an object in a small alcove inside the wall of one of the arches. "You see the old night bell? That's from 1900. Before we had electricity and electronic surveillance, all public buildings had someone living on-site. Families would live in public buildings." Bruce pointed northward. "The family would have had an apartment there at St. Lawrence Hall, and [the guard] would come to work here at night. If you wanted to get a hold of him, you'd press the night bell. We've asked them to keep that there, too. We've implored the City, 'Don't move that!' because it's history and that's his bell and this is where he is."

I asked Bruce if there were any staff records from the early 1900s that we could use to connect Bill's name to, but he wasn't sure; record-keeping was very haphazard back then.

The tour officially concluded, and the assembly was invited to return to the Market Kitchen for refreshments and a Searcher Group slide show presentation conducted by Richard and me. After a brief Q&A session, the evening's event concluded. The team exited the former city hall shortly after 10:00 PM.

Afterthoughts

The Hallowe'en after-hours tour event at City Hall No. 1 and the St. Lawrence Market was very successful; the guests seemed pleased (as were we) that they had witnessed some unexplainable activity for themselves.

Unfortunately, no tangible evidence was recorded in the form of EVPs in the case of the phantom shouting that Paul detected using the parabolic microphone during the public tour. But neither was there evidence to discount what Paul heard; had there been living Hallowe'en revellers shouting from outside the building, the digital recorder I was holding nearby would most definitely have captured those sounds.

History Hunting

Naturally, you might think that having three full names would be an easy starting point in terms of research. Certainly the inclusion of surnames helps to narrow down historical hits, and if someone from the past fits the bill completely, it is very satisfying validation for both psychic medium and investigator.

The primary challenge is the names themselves and how accurately they are translated through Joanna. She receives information in flashes, and there is undeniably room for error: even if a spirit communicates his/her name earnestly, we must consider if the name was transmitted to Joanna successfully and without interference from other spirits present. Are there instances when Joanna's brain fills in missing or inaccurate information?

After contacting St. Lawrence Market Complex Real Estate Services and the Toronto Police Museum, we were ultimately led to the Humanities and Social Sciences department of the Toronto Reference Library. Researching the names and scenarios that Joanna had come up with posed quite a challenge. Several people shared identical names throughout the history of Toronto, as well as having similar-sounding names with various spellings. I asked James to help pore through millions of archived entries with me; this was what we found:

- William Goldsmith: the William Goldsmiths we found ranged from confectioners and organ key makers to bricklayers, labourers, barbers and carpenters. Although one was listed as a fireman in 1913, none appeared to be in the security or law-enforcement fields.

- Terence/Terrence Henley (also Hanley, Hanly, Henly, Henry): I personally didn't have high hopes for finding this fellow, as Joanna had sensed he was a bit of a wild card who seemed to exhibit delusions of grandeur and was calling the city hall home. The closest match to a registered Torontonian was a gentleman named Edward T. Hanly, whose occupation was listed as "helper" at J&J Taylor in the 1918 City Directory. J&J Taylor was a safe-making company that had relocated their warehouse in 1871 to Front and Frederick streets—just two blocks east of city hall and the St. Lawrence Market. We will not outright claim this is our present-day gallery ghost, but then, who is to say he isn't?

- Stephen/Steven McClaren (also MacClaren, McClaurin, Maclaurin): with so much personal detail provided by the spirit of this alleged former market vendor, it was particularly exciting to imagine finding an exact hit. Alas, the few matches that were found revealed men whose occupations included stone mason, watch-maker, machinist and "dentelmaness" (dentist?).

Disappointingly, nothing came of researching rampant gang-related murders and acts of violence involving the St. Lawrence district, let alone the market itself. Certainly there were articles describing petty theft of vendors' stalls, or drunk and disorderly citizens roaming the aisles, but nothing as significant as a murder was officially reported.

As for the child who may have drowned off the pier that used to exist where the marketplace is now, it is, of course, a possibility, but any record has been lost to history.

Lastly, let this be the final word that completely debunks the rumour that the jail cells below City Hall No. 1 ever flooded to such a depth that hundreds of inmates drowned at any point in its existence. While the physical condition of the cells was deplorable and the prison system itself across Upper Canada was in dire need of restructuring, the sole jail-related death in this location involved a 90-year-old vagrant named Patrick Harold, who had been imprisoned for two years before he passed away of natural causes in the fall of 1899.

～

Being inside the former city hall and the market after-hours was enough to tell us that as much as we would love to try to conduct formal investigations there, we would have an extremely challenging time differentiating between audible paranormal evidence and the continuous roar of the giant HVAC system operating from the ceiling above the marketplace.

As for the comparatively quiet Market Gallery, an employee of the City of Toronto informed us that we would not be permitted to take photographs or surveillance footage of any kind inside the gallery, due to the presence of framed photographs and art hanging on every wall. The policy is a standard precaution against possible copyright infringement of the respective artists whose work is on display.

Obtaining permission to use cameras in the former council chamber was a matter separate from obtaining permission to be on the premises after-hours and needed to be taken up with the City long in advance of an investigation. Further compounding the proverbial red tape was the matter of somehow raising hundreds of dollars to pay for after-hours security to cover at least two separate eight-hour visits.

As dedicated researchers and investigators, we love what we do, but the amount of time, money and effort required to arrange a proper investigation within a controlled environment—with no guarantee we'd capture any evidence of paranormal activity—was much more than we could handle alone. We were extremely grateful therefore for the opportunity we were given and for the interesting phenomena that occurred within the space of four hours. Perhaps because we were the first party to show an interest in communicating with the spirits of City Hall No. 1, they likewise showed an interest in us.

Chapter 11

Orangeville Town Hall: Second Investigation

"We have our own version of the telephone," Fletcher reported. "Word somehow gets around to discarnates who may be interested in the sitters at a given séance that the occasion is pending."

—Arthur Ford, *Unknown But Known*

Team: Richard, Paul, Joanna, James, Peter
Guests: Dawn, Hannah, Mary
Host: Alison

A second opportunity to investigate the Orangeville Town Hall presented itself five months after our initial visit. Although it was an afternoon in early February 2016 when the team—today consisting of Richard, Paul, James and myself—converged north of Halton Hills and Brampton, the roads were dry and the sun shone brightly. We had an eight-hour window of which to take advantage.

Joanna arrived with a surprise guest for this outing: her friend and mentor, Dawn Mark. Dawn is a practicing psychic medium who accompanied the team on a few investigations three years previous, but she had to stop for personal reasons—one being that she needed to rid herself of a particularly nasty spiritual assailant that had attached itself to her.

We were therefore pleasantly surprised to see her again and welcomed the idea of the pair of psychic comrades working together to tune in to the spirits of the Orangeville Town Hall. Perhaps their combined efforts would produce stronger, verifiable information over the course of this investigation. Joanna assured us that she had told Dawn nothing of the results of our first visit, nor had she divulged the specific location in Orangeville we were investigating.

We were greeted at the entrance by the town hall's administrative assistant Alison Woodside, who would be with us the entire afternoon and evening observing, participating and ready with keys to admit us into areas we were authorized to investigate. Alison had never had an eerie experience at the town hall to report before this evening, but she remained open-minded to the possibility that we weren't the only occupants of the building.

Once inside the north atrium of the building addition, Dawn filled us in on the readings she received from home the night before. She felt that a tunnel-like structure used to exist under the building, specifically a waterway of some sort that might have run through the property at one time. Dawn also claimed to have sensed a death by asphyxiation in the attic or bell tower. Lastly, she shared that a male spirit we had encountered during the first visit was no longer present because—according to her—he had departed with one of the investigators.

We moved our equipment inside, the atrium of the addition once again serving as our base camp, away from the surveillance cameras. Joanna and Dawn began their walk-through in the basement, feeling drawn there. Everyone followed. Upon settling in the main hallway, both mediums reacted to an intense feeling of pressure owing to hundreds of spirit energies clambering over each other in an effort to communicate with them.

While Joanna and Dawn worked to distinguish these sensations, Paul heard no disembodied voices through the parabolic microphone, and Richard detected no readings of electromagnetic energy from the Natural Tri-Field meter he was using.

Fully aware that the sole intent of our visit was to gather data and that it is not Searcher Group policy to cleanse a space of its resident spirits, Joanna and Dawn felt moved enough by the plight of the unseen hordes to request an attempt to clear them toward the conclusion of the investigation. Both added that a negative presence was apparently "ruling the roost," thereby contributing to the dire situation.

As the leader of this outing, I promised to consider their request but reminded them that first we needed to learn all we could from any spirits who might be present.

We began inside the janitor's supply room. While Dawn was speaking, my digital recorder captured an obscure word that had no context with what was being discussed.

EVP: [Female; whispering] How…?

James spotted a small, faint source of light move rapidly behind Dawn, elevated about 45 centimetres higher than her head.

Outside the supply room, Joanna and Dawn shared with Alison their desire to perform a crossing-over/cleansing ritual.

They explained the spiritual bombardment they were feeling—Dawn described one female spirit as "hysterical."

I suggested that individual ought to step forward and become the spokesperson for the others. It was determined that this spirit's name was Mary, that she was 43 years of age and had been present at this site for 85 years. According to Dawn, Mary claimed that she was being held there against her will.

At that point, James' recorder captured a disembodied male's voice.

EVP: [Male] They don't really get [me.]

Dawn then shared she was being shown an image of an infirmary and said that a disease may have plagued Orangeville in the past. She felt Mary acted as a nurse in this case and added that she felt that the layers of spirit energies went back as far as 200 years.

While Joanna and Dawn began to explore the nearby storage room, Paul and Richard suggested we deploy the surveillance cameras about the building. I asked James to accompany and log the findings of the mediums with his recorder as they toured the premises. Before parting ways with us, James realized that the fresh batteries inside his infrared and full-spectrum cameras had completely drained; he asked if any of us had some spare batteries with us. None of us did. My digital recorder captured a disembodied reply.

EVP: [Male; low] F**k.

Was there a spirit present who was perhaps intending to appear in a photo? Was this person wanting to sap more battery energy to "feed" himself? He would be disappointed. Paul, Richard and I left the basement for the ground-floor atrium while James headed to the storage room.

Inside the storage room, both Joanna and Dawn shared sensations of suffocating. James felt woozy and a tightness in his chest. He moved to a corner of the room and stopped short when he detected a cold, tingling sensation that seemed to ebb, as if someone unseen had just realized they were sharing the same space and stepped away

Stepping into the main-floor council chamber, Richard, Paul and I discussed where to place a surveillance camera. As I agreed with one of Paul's suggestions, my recorder caught a near-indistinguishable comment.

EVP: [Male] Keep it low, Rick.

Next finding the doors to the second-floor Opera House locked, the three of us backtracked to the atrium in search of Alison. Once she had unlocked the doors, Paul and I headed back upstairs with Camera 1 while Richard headed back down the hall to the council chamber with Camera 2.

As Paul set the camera onstage with the lens aimed toward the house, I set a recorder atop a short wall dividing a group of seats from a sound control board at the back of the house, then rejoined Paul on the stage.

EVP: [Male; thick accent] Oh dear.

Paul commented on the colder temperature of the theatre in relation to the rest of the premises. As soon as he voiced his observation, a loud thud erupted from centre stage. Naturally we stopped to encourage communication, but our invitation seemed to go unheeded, and we resumed assembling the surveillance camera. At that point, the recorder at the back of the house caught an interesting comment.

EVP: [Male] One's bad.

Whether this statement was directed toward Paul, me or shared between two or more spirits remains undetermined, but there was no doubt we were being watched from a safe distance.

Meanwhile, directly below the stage, Richard finished deploying Camera 2 in the council chamber and left the room. Almost immediately, the surveillance system caught its first EVP of the investigation.

EVP: [Older male] I'll get you for this!...Damn!

Richard entered the theatre shortly afterward to tell Paul and I that Camera 2 was operational. Thinking perhaps Camera 3 ought to be deployed in the basement, we all headed downstairs to explore that possibility.

As soon as we were gone, the digital recorder at the back of the house captured several instances of movement close to and in the direct vicinity of the device, while the stage camera caught the following exchange.

EVP: [Male] Barbara.
EVP: [Male] Peter.
EVP: [Female] Jimmy.
EVP: [Male] Believe me.

Continuing their tour, Joanna, Dawn, James and Alison entered the theatre and stepped onto the stage, where Dawn shared that she was being shown an image of a dance hall. She said that the dance floor was where the stage is now and the band played on a stage where the house is at present.

EVP: [Male] Hot diggity.

As the foursome toured the dressing rooms backstage, a single chirp emitted from somewhere in the house that no one heard or acknowledged in the moment. James and the women soon returned and spread themselves out among the seats of the house to listen quietly for replies to James' questions. Camera 1 captured a few responses.

James: My name is James. Can you tell me yours?
EVP: [Male] Pat.

After several more questions went unanswered…

James: Thank you for your time.
EVP: [Male] Yep.
James: I'd like to come back for a visit again, sometime.
EVP: [Male] Could do that.

Dawn shared she was sensing an older female spirit with a youthful face named Dolores Stillman who did not reside in the building full time, but who visited frequently to watch the plays performed there. According to Dawn, Dolores gave off "the air of being an esteemed actress" and had performed onstage herself. Apparently she had come from England by boat and wasn't in Canada for very long before dying of pneumonia. "She said it's been a long time since she's been able to communicate with anybody," said Dawn. "Her family's not from this area. She's missing her son. She said he left. I'm getting a sense that he was sent to war and never came back. He was in the First World War."

At this point I entered the theatre, but stopped short as Dawn spoke up from her seat in the middle of the house. "When Peter walked in, [Dolores] felt like she needed to leave and she rushed out," said Dawn, indicating the door I had just come through. "It's related to her son and it upset her. I'll see if I can get her back. She's kind of timid and she's staying in the corner. She's really missing her son, Peter. Actually, she wants to be reunited with her son; she really wants to be crossed over. You remind her of her son."

"What was your son's name, please?" I asked, beginning another EVP session.

"Timothy," said Dawn, interpreting.

"What was Timothy's father's name?"

"Lawrence."

"Do you have any more family here in Orangeville?" I asked.

"Her son was only 19 when he left."

James took over the line of questioning. "So, was her husband's name Lawrence Stillman?" he asked for confirmation.

"Yes," said Dawn, immediately. "He died in 1909."

"What year did you pass over?" James asked of Dolores.

"1937," relayed Dawn.

"Ah, so you were missing your husband for a long time—and your son."

"Yes. He died in 1911, the son."

James tactfully pointed out that World War I did not begin until 1914.

"Oh, sorry. Maybe he left home in 1911," frowned Dawn, quickly reinterpreting.

"Can you tell me what your maiden name was?" asked James.

"I'm hearing the name Moira. That's not a maiden name, but I think that's her mother's name, Moira."

The recorder I was holding captured a disembodied response that was not caught by the recorder at the back of the house, nor by Camera 1.

EVP: [Female; agreeing] Mmm…

"What was your father's name?" James persisted.

"Charles," said Dawn.

"Full name?" I asked.

"It starts with a 'T,'" said Dawn, frowning. "I'm not getting anything."

Further questions about Dolores's intent on visiting the theatre, the cause of death of her son and his age at the time of his death went unanswered. When I asked for the name of the Orangeville mayor during Dolores's lifetime, Dawn paused, then advised that Dolores was getting tired and that she'd left.

Camera 1 captured one more EVP in response to one of my questions.

Peter: Could you tell us how many spirits are here?
EVP: [Male] I can't.

Approximately the same time the EVP session was taking place in the theatre, Camera 2 captured a number of voices inside the otherwise empty council chamber.

EVP: [Male A] Patrick?
EVP: [Male B] Ask a lot.
EVP: [Male A] Benny! Benny, come!
EVP: [Male B] What?
EVP: [Older male; shouting, upset] Get out! Get out! Get out now!
EVP: [Female; calling] [Indeterminable name]
EVP: [Male B] Barbara!…Barbara, get over here. Barbara!
EVP: [Another male] Mitchell, don't you…
EVP: [Male A] They have to have the time on it.
EVP: [Male B] Yes.

By this time Richard and Paul had joined us in the theatre. Still armed with the parabolic microphone, Paul went out to the mezzanine overlooking the open-air atrium. He settled midway along the railing and directed the dish down toward to the main floor, listening intently. Moments passed with no sound but that of the invariable drone of the HVAC system.

Then, outside of the ear-covering headphones he was wearing, the voice of a child addressed Paul from over his left shoulder, inquiring, "Sir?"

Paul straightened immediately and turned to look behind him to find he was still alone on the mezzanine.

Just then, Alison, Joanna, Dawn, James and I walked out from inside the theatre. Paul took me aside to report what he'd just experienced and recommended that the mediums scan the area without being told what to expect. Unbidden, Dawn shared that she was picking up on a giggling little girl named Jessica who was playing hide-and-seek with us.

Alone for the moment inside the theatre, Richard sat quietly. Unbeknownst to him at the time, the recorder at the back of the house captured a rebuke.

EVP: [Male; accusatory] You know!

Paul re-entered the theatre and shared his experience with Richard before asking some EVP-provoking questions.

Paul: Anybody here tonight with us? Tell me what year it is? What year is it? Who's on the stage tonight? What's your name?
EVP: [Unknown gender; faint] Back a bit.
Paul: Are there any females here tonight?
EVP: [Female; faint] [Indistinguishable] thing.

After a few more questions with no responses, Paul and Richard left the Opera House to take a break outside.

The rest of the team and Alison gathered around the upright piano outside the Opera House and asked Jessica to play a note on it.

I commented on the comparatively warm temperature and asked Alison if the theatre is normally maintained as cold as the team was finding it.

"Typically, they keep the theatre cool," she replied.

EVP: [Child; whispering] Why?

⌒

Everyone present retreated to the main-floor atrium. Returning from his break, Paul joined James and I as we moved to the basement to perform more EVP sessions and an audio sweep using the parabolic microphone. Aside from shuffling sounds and an EVP of a male whistling, this visit to the basement was fruitless.

Meanwhile, inside the Opera House, after eight minutes of movement noise and a hollow thump originating from somewhere deeper in the theatre, I returned alone to deploy the E. Probe 1.0 proximity alarm and placed it among the centre of the house seats. Tagging the time as 4:36 PM, I left to rejoin the team and Alison on the main floor and we prepared to exit the building for dinner.

⌒

The amount and sheer variety of noise that was recorded inside the "empty" Opera House over the course of the dinner hour was such that to detail it all would make for a very long book. Suffice it to say there was much evidence to support some manner of disembodied presence, including the following highlights:

- four instances of loud crashes resembling push-bar doors opening and closing somewhere outside the Opera House
- a snap resembling a sheaf of papers (a script?) being slammed on a solid surface

- an incredibly loud impact close to the recorder (notable especially for the amount of energy it would take to make such a noise)
- seven hollow banging sounds that seemed to recede from the stage, possibly ending in the dressing rooms
- a female-like voice close to the recorder grunting, then very faintly saying, "Whose is it?" (a reference to the recorder?)
- a loud chirp from somewhere deeper in the house—possibly a split-second activation of the E. Probe 1.0 alarm
- rustling fabric, small clicks, a possible footfall followed by a series of snaps that seemed to retreat from the recorder over a 15-minute period
- a sudden sharp rap that resounded loudly throughout the house followed by more sounds of movement, then a second loud, hollow pounding followed by a hard, metallic impact—not unlike something solid striking a chain link fence
- a short shuffle sound, then the sound of a small object bouncing from something metallic (an auditorium flood-light?) as if whatever "it" was was flung with force. Almost three minutes later, the sound of a toggle switch (possibly part of the nearby lighting/sound control board) clicked on or off.

If these were common noises, I had to wonder if an audience could fully enjoy a theatrical performance with such jarring distractions. I was later assured by Opera House management that what we captured was not typical.

Meanwhile, in the basement, approximately 75 minutes into the dinner break, another recorder captured a loud bang erupting from behind one of the closed doors off the main hallway. The sound resembled someone kicking a large refuse bin.

Less than two minutes later, the recorder monitoring the passageway caught what sounded like a finger snap.

Just before 6:00 PM, Alison re-entered the building with Hannah and Mary, local historians who were curious about our work and had asked to participate in this investigation for a short time. The team and Dawn arrived next and were introduced to our temporary para-explorers.

Similar to other field experiences, the banging noises and sounds of movement inside the theatre stopped once (physical) people entered the building. However, as introductions between the team and guest historians were being made downstairs, one more loud, hollow bang erupted from somewhere inside the theatre, to which no one reacted

~

James entered the council chamber to retrieve the recorder he left over the dinner break, then he took several photos of the room using his full-spectrum and infrared cameras. Most of the resulting images showed nothing anomalous, but one— once brightened significantly using photo-editing software—revealed what appeared to be a tall person wearing a brimmed hat sitting on one of the benches, their right arm resting along the top of the bench back.

Simultaneously, Richard had changed recordable DVDs of the camera system and left it to continue recording the council chamber while he headed up to the theatre. Seven minutes of silence later…

EVP: [Male] Anna.
EVP: [Female] Yes?

Paul and I had gone up to the theatre to relocate Camera 1. We wished to film the stage from the back of the house. Within six minutes, the transfer was accomplished and surveillance recording was re-established.

As Richard joined us, I retrieved the recorder from the back of the house and moved the E. Probe 1.0 device from among the seats to the stage apron. I then left Richard and Paul to quietly observe the environment while I went downstairs to join the others.

Back inside the main-floor atrium, I asked James to lead Joanna, Dawn and Mary in an EVP session inside the council chamber while I took Hannah and Alison to the basement to do the same.

~

Inside the council chamber, James opened the session with a standard line of introductory statements and questions, but he got no responses until Dawn began to converse with someone unseen.

"Can you tell us what era you are from or what year you passed over?" asked James.

"No, he's not giving us a date," replied Dawn. "He seems shy. He came up from the basement."

"Are you waiting for us to come back down?" Joanna asked.

"Yes," interpreted Dawn.

"Is there someone in the basement who is negative?" inquired James.

"He's cowering, so, yes."

"Should we be concerned about them?"

"Yes. His wife is downstairs, too. Anne."

"Do you have any children?"

"Yes, two boys, but they are not here," said Dawn.

"They have passed over?"

"Yes, but they are buried somewhere else."

"If we can get rid of the negative energy and open the light, can you cross?" asked Joanna.

EVP: [Unknown gender; very light whisper] Yeah...

"He's not sure," said Dawn. "Would you like to go to heaven?" she asked the unnamed spirit. After a pause, she got his reply: "Yes."

Joanna attempted to explain the clearing procedure to the male spirit and encouraged him to relay the message to the other ghost occupants of the basement.

"How many are there?" asked James.

"Two hundred and seventy-five," responded Dawn almost immediately.

"Is your heritage English?"

"No, it's Scottish."

"Mine is [too], and my father was born here in Orangeville," shared James. "Did you know any McCullochs?"

"He is smiling, yes," nodded Dawn.

After Joanna reinforced the humanitarian nature of their offer to open a portal for those spirits who wished to complete their crossing over, the session ended.

Unbeknownst to all as they left the council chamber, the discussion of the proposed clearing did not sit well with at least two other spirits. Camera 2 captured the unmistakable panic of a female and a protective male companion. Their initial shouts were likely directed toward Joanna and Dawn.

EVP: [Female] Damn you for scaring me!
EVP: [Male] Damn you!
EVP: [Female] Damn you!

There was a brief pause before the conversation resumed in a more subdued, but no less upsetting tone.

EVP: [Male] It's okay.

EVP: [Female] What if they free me?

A few minutes later, emotions peaked between the male and female couple. Camera 2 captured the female spirit screaming in utter distress. Her anguish seemed to rile the male.

EVP: [Male] Damn you!

EVP: [Female] [Sobbing hysterically]

EVP: [Same male] DAMN YOU!

Then, recomposing himself, the male spoke calmly to the sobbing female.

EVP: [Same male] Stand over here with me.

No further EVPs were captured by Camera 2 after this episode.

Meanwhile in the basement, we conducted an EVP session in the main hallway but got no responses. Alison, Hannah (using the parabolic microphone) and I moved into the board-room to attempt a Spirit Box session. Surprisingly, for such an allegedly crowded area, we obtained no responses to any questions nor captured any anomalous sounds during this period.

All the team members and guests reunited in the main-floor atrium. Richard shared that as he stood on the stage of the Opera House, his cell phone battery (fully charged at the outset of the visit) had lost close to all its power. James shared the events of the council chamber session, then took a short break outside with Richard and Paul.

Feeling their own energy draining as the investigation continued, Dawn and Joanna requested permission to try clearing the basement of the 275 souls they believed were occupying it before they became too tired to do so. I consented. Alison, Hannah, Mary and James agreed to assist in the clearing procedure while Paul, Richard and I returned to the theatre to continue communication attempts.

~

In the basement, Alison unlocked the storage room where Dawn and Joanna sensed the negative spirit had retreated. James, Mary, Alison and Hannah were asked to occupy the aisles between the shelves and to begin projecting thoughts of pure love and joy while Dawn called upon the archangels Michael and Metatron to lovingly coax the negative entity to accompany them to a more positive state.

The clearing party was next directed eastward down the hallway to flank the elevator near the stairwell. Once more all six participants were asked to project feelings of pure love and to collectively visualize pure white light forming a portal in place of the closed elevator door. Dawn claimed to be in touch with the archangels as they ushered the remaining spirits seeking release from the basement into the waiting portal.

Although he did not feel any particular changes to the environment throughout this process, James thought he detected a brief, waist-high rush of coldness brush past him, at which time the onlookers were informed a little girl had sped into the portal.

Hannah and Mary were visibly moved by the procedure, as was Joanna, who reported feeling a surge of love-filled energy swoop back from inside the portal to envelop her briefly before re-entering it again. She interpreted it as a grateful hug—a parting gesture of gratitude

~

Meanwhile upstairs in the Opera House, amid several EVP-provoking questions, the camera microphone captured one disembodied comment that, timing-wise, roughly coincided with the negative entity being assisted in the basement.

EVP: [Male] What's happening?

We asked several more questions over the course of two or three minutes, followed by silence, when the now-familiar hollow bang once again erupted from the direction of the stage. This sound prompted friendly invitations from all three of us to an open dialogue, but as before, no responses were recorded.

I held out a pendulum and explained that a clockwise turn symbolized "yes," while counter-clockwise meant "no." Initially the chain of the pendulum only quivered as the weight remained plumb, which may have been indicative of fear or nervousness on the part of a reluctant unseen communicator.

"Are the women and James helping the people in the basement right now?" I asked. The pendulum swung counter-clockwise. "No?" I was surprised.

"Is what they're doing in the basement scaring you?" Richard asked. The pendulum continued swinging counter-clockwise.

I decided to try a test question to ensure the rotation of the pendulum was deliberate. "You realize you're saying 'no,' right?" I asked.

The pendulum immediately slowed its counter-clockwise arc on its way to changing direction. Suddenly another loud, hollow bang emitted from the stage.

"Is that a 'yes' or 'no'?" asked Paul. The pendulum swung clockwise; yes.

"So you *do* understand us?" I confirmed. The clockwise circle grew; yes.

"Are you a male?" It slowed to neutral/unsure.

"You're a woman?" Neutral/unsure.

"Are you a young girl?" It swung a small yes.

"Are you afraid of us?" The pendulum slowed to a complete stop, and subsequent questions received no perceivable responses, save a loud snap from the direction of the stage. All went silent in the Opera House.

The three of us exited the theatre and moved to a water cooler outside. The atrium lobby remained silent, but my recorder captured a distant, dual-note whistle (resembling the universal "Yoo-hoo!") that none of us heard in the moment.

And inside the theatre, Camera 1 recorded more banging coming from the direction of the stage, unheard by the three of us relaxing quietly just outside the door on the atrium mezzanine

~

With the clearing ritual complete, Dawn and Joanna took their leave. They were followed shortly afterward by Mary and Hannah. James filled the team in on the details of the events in the basement, and Alison shared she now felt the atmosphere seemed lighter. Paul, Richard and James left the building for a break (and to send James for caffeinated refreshments), leaving Alison and me to chat in the atrium.

About this time, Camera 1 captured another disembodied voice inside the theatre.

EVP: [Female] Jimmy!...Jimmy!

Richard and Paul rejoined Alison and me. Upstairs in the theatre, Camera 1 recorded what sounded like a warning from one spirit to another.

EVP: [Male] They are coming back.

As I began mentioning other town halls we would like to investigate, everyone present heard a loud chirp erupt from the theatre above us. I asked for the noise to be repeated but was not obliged. Interestingly, this same sound was not captured by the house camera.

James returned with refreshments as Paul and I reviewed photographic examples of Searcher Group evidence with Alison using my laptop. As Paul shared his belief that some ghosts have the ability to invite others into their space, I put my coffee down abruptly so I could use my left hand to feel the air around my right hand.

"What's the matter?" Richard and James asked at once.

"Something cold touched the top of my hand," I replied.

"Sometimes when you start talking about [paranormal-related] stuff, they get interested," said Richard.

"Yeah, that's happened before," nodded Paul.

Trust the Brothers Palmisano to have had similar encounters on several occasions throughout their investigative tenure.

Despite the caffeine fix, general exhaustion was beginning to set in, so we agreed to separate once more and conduct some final EVP sessions before calling it a night.

I entered the council chamber and placed a digital recorder on a dais before joining Alison and James in the basement for one last tour. Paul and Richard went to monitor the Opera House.

Apart from the inevitable sounds of car traffic outside the building and the HVAC system drone inside, all was quiet in the council chamber for several minutes when suddenly an incredibly loud snap erupted from somewhere inside the room.

Two seconds later, heavy footfalls were recorded walking away. These were followed by a pair of loud, dull thuds 10 seconds apart (the second one louder than the first), then a sharp click. It seemed someone was restless.

Meanwhile in the basement, I used a compass to test for anomalous needle readings, but none occurred. We conducted a pendulum session in the boardroom but experienced nothing extraordinary nor recorded anything of a paranormal nature. Just as I finished asking if someone had tried touching the proximity alarm set up in the basement hallway, all three of us heard a dual-note whine emanate from the east end of the hallway. The noise resembled a faint, attention-seeking whistle (as in, "Over here!").

As our party of three ascended the east stairwell and continued past the main floor, we noticed that the light that had illuminated the steps between the main and second floors all afternoon and evening was now off, throwing the upper stairwell into gloomy darkness. We next discovered that the second-floor mezzanine also sported deactivated lights as we walked through it to join Richard and Paul in the Opera House. They confirmed that neither of them had touched any electrical switches; they weren't even aware the lights were out.

Richard shared that from their vantage point among the house seats, he and Paul had heard several more impact sounds erupting from the stage, but nothing else in terms of intelligent communication.

I settled in a seat and called out, "Hello!"

EVP: [Older female or male] Good day.

No further responses were recorded. Perhaps the last one captured was a final parting salutation.

〜

On the main floor, the recorder in the council chamber captured several more marching footfalls over a 12-minute period, pacing back and forth overhead. These noises were peppered by three thumps, as if something very heavy was being dropped on the stage above.

Concurrently, the team and Alison were spread out and seated around the theatre listening to the silence that greeted our questions. No one moved, let alone dropped heavy objects on the floor or the stage.

～

Shortly before 9:00 PM, we decided to call it a night. Richard, Paul and Alison returned to the main floor to deactivate and pack up the council chamber camera. After doing the same with the Opera House camera, James and I thanked any listening spirits for their participation then rejoined the others on the main floor. By 9:17 PM, all of the gear, investigators and host were outside the building as Alison locked up. We thanked her for accommodating us and departed for home.

Afterthoughts

Second Floor: Phantoms of the Opera House

During this second visit, the theatre continued to exhibit signs of otherworldly occupation. From several unexplainable indications of movement to a variety of EVPs of male and female voices, true to form, the draw of the odeum is irresistible even after physical death.

I contacted local historian Wayne Townsend about Dawn's assertion that the Opera House stage was once located on the opposite side of the room; he confirmed that at one time it was.

Interestingly, while none of the names associated with the Stillman family—Dolores, Lawrence or Timothy—that Dawn shared with us turned up as she had interpreted, one local Orangeville obituary revealed a pair of similar names: one of the surviving sisters of Mr. Arthur Joseph Williams was named Nora, and she was married to a Clarence Stillman.

Main Floor: Council's in Session 24/7

Again, similar to the amount of evidence gleaned from the initial investigation, the council chamber proved to be quite active. Names referenced and captured as EVPs here include, Rick (although this may have been someone addressing Richard), Barbara, Patrick, Benny (who acknowledged being called), Mitchell and Anna (who also acknowledged being called). Interestingly, the name George did not come up at all over the course of this investigation. Was he the spirit who—according to Dawn—attached himself to one of us at the conclusion of the first visit and departed the property?

It would appear that the older gentleman knew precisely why the team was there, based on the first EVP captured by Camera 2 ("I'll get you for this! Damn!"). This male resented the presence of our equipment, likely knowing what it was capable of doing—and why we were visiting.

Another comment I found fascinating was that of a younger male saying, "They have to have the time on it." This explanation was likely delivered to another spirit regarding the team's practice of periodically logging the time of day as we investigate for the benefit of our recording devices.

The sheer amount of emotion exuded by the council chamber spirits—particularly the female, presumably Anna—was easily the most significant discovery during this investigation.

She became hysterical at the height of Joanna and Dawn's discussion on clearing the basement, sobbing, "What if they free me?" What could possibly be meant by that?

Most people consider freedom as a positive ideal, something to strive for and celebrate. Why did this woman become so upset at the idea of being free? How does this woman's definition of being free differ from ours? Has she been influenced somehow by outside persuasion? Have the other two males convinced her that freedom equates to something undesirable? If so, what?

A long-held theory in paranormal research speaks to the reason some spirits choose to remain "stuck" between the physical and ethereal planes, and that is that they fear repercussions for some kind of sin they believe they committed during their physical lifetime. Could this be true for this woman? If so, what did she do that she considers a punishable offence?

What about freedom of choice in this woman's case? Most psychic mediums we've worked with over the years have insisted that spirit people have the choice to move on or not. After this incident, we might now ask ourselves whether that's true. Although it was the spirits of the basement that were being discussed, the woman in the council chamber reacted as if she might not have a choice to stay on at the Orangeville Town Hall. Did she believe that the opening of a cross-over portal on any level of the building had the ability to pull every spirit into it (like a vacuum), willing or not? Was or is this the case? And if so, how far can a portal expand to accomplish such a feat?

It was this woman's outburst, as well as the male spirits cursing ("Damn you!") our party of investigators and psychic mediums, that cemented the conviction of The Searcher Group that clearings—for all their good intentions—are not necessarily considered helpful or appreciated by everyone in the spirit realm. Spirits are where they are for their own reasons, and it is not our right to evict them from their homes, especially if the people in the physical world sharing the same space are not being harmed.

Basement: Phantoms in the Footing?

No psychic medium—no matter how talented—is perfect. Some of the claims made on this occasion, particularly involving the basement, seemed too extreme to be taken seriously. As was noted, though there were a few stray EVP responses to the investigators' presence ("They don't really get me"; brief whistling), no disembodied voices were heard, no anomalous EMF readings were observed, the proximity alarm was never tripped and no sensible responses came through the Spirit Box.

Recalling our single, validated encounter with Phillip during the first investigation, I doubt most of us present five months later accepted that suddenly there were 275 more souls (including an oppressor figure) seeking release.

Sharing my doubts about what was picked up on in the basement is *not* to dismiss the abilities of Dawn, Joanna or anyone with psychic talents; however, it is important that readers and clients alike understand that The Searcher Group is not in the habit of claiming complete proof of paranormal activity solely based on the claims of a clairvoyant.

I granted permission for the clearing ritual firstly because Alison, our client representative authorized it, and secondly because there was no overwhelming proof at the time that multitudes of desperate souls were actually present. Obviously no paranormal investigator is perfect as well, as it wasn't until after the investigation that data analysis revealed the extraordinarily high degree of upset expressed by the council chamber spirits over this clearing decision of mine. I must chalk this incident up to experience and share it here with fellow investigators and mediums alike for serious consideration.

No doubt the experience of participating in the ritual itself was likely one that Alison, Mary, Hannah and James will not soon forget.

⁓

The most gratifying facet of our line of work as paranormal investigators is that every investigation—short or long-term—yields something of particular interest. Whether it is a location that would likely house a spirit or two due to its historic relevance but does not, or another where no one has experienced any indication of anything supernatural and yet is quite haunted, all venues hold intrigue.

It was quite remarkable to think that of the 140 years the Orangeville Town Hall has remained standing and operational, it took less than 14 hours to determine it is definitely *not* empty when the last corporeal employee secures the door behind them for the night.

⁓

Chapter 12

Waterford Old Town Hall: Third Investigation

We are eternal beings. We lived as intelligent spirits before this mortal life. We are now living part of eternity. Our mortal birth was not the beginning; death, which faces all of us, is not the end.

–Ezra Taft Benson

$\sim$

Team: James, David, Peter
Host: Jennifer

The team had a standing invitation to return to the Waterford Old Town Hall in order to dig deeper into the mysteries involving its (mostly) unseen residents. Although I had committed to documenting a maximum of two visits per town hall, the lure of this location was difficult to resist—especially given the encouraging results of our second investigation the previous year. We simply had to try reaching the girl who identified herself as Mary Ferrin, at least one more time. An opening in the team's schedule in the summer of 2016 was too great an opportunity to pass up.

$\sim$

David, James and I were admitted into the Old Town Hall by Jennifer, who entrusted us with the care and security of the building for the next six hours. The street traffic was minimal but steady, and although a few townspeople strolled past the historic edifice every once in a while, exterior noise pollution was not a concern.

Within minutes of our base camp being established inside the boardroom on the ground floor, an overwhelming bang resounded through the south end of the building, instantly stopping the three of us in our tracks. Whereas James' first thought was that a heavy door (possibly that of the ground floor vault) had been slammed, I likened the sound to that of a powerful impact originating from directly above, as if someone had struck the vertical pipe that ran down from the theatre above to the front vestibule, a few metres outside the boardroom.

David and James finish unpacking equipment inside base camp minutes after a loud metallic bang greeted the team.

Fortunately James had already activated one of his recorders and had captured the rather violent-sounding greeting (or was it protest?). A friendly hello was in order, so I called out. James' recorder captured a cryptic response.

EVP: [Young male or female] I know you didn't!

We posed several more introductory questions in reply to the jarring noise, but no further responses were recorded, nor did the noise reoccur.

We resumed unpacking and readied our gear. The equipment at our disposal for this visit was quite extensive; however, two pieces in particular were sorely missing: the surveillance cameras. We reminded ourselves that decades ago, the Palmisano brothers began their quest to capture evidence of ghosts using a simple cassette tape recorder and some baby powder and were quite successful. We would be just fine.

We reviewed the long list of names we had accumulated at the Old Town Hall so far, including those of spirit people we hoped to confirm were present and willing to communicate with us. "During my visit with Joanna, she picked up on a Harold Fitzgerald," I reminded the group. One of our recorders captured an anonymous comment just then.

EVP: [Older male; breathy] Yup.

Following a briefing of the evening's goals, we moved to the kitchen to attempt contact with Lindsay. When no responses from her seemed forthcoming, we opened up questions to anyone else who might be present. Although we did not hear anything with the naked ear, the recorder captured a series of distant-sounding knocks erupting between our questions, followed by a pair of dull thuds like a brief set of footfalls moving among us as we remained stationary.

We continued to the main lobby, where I called out for Henry and then addressed Danny. Next we asked after Benny and his place in the pecking order of the spirits.

Peter: Benny, are you the boss of the town hall?

EVP: [Unknown gender] No.

Peter: Barbara? If you're here, can you give us your surname, please? Mine is Roe.

EVP: [Female; breathy, faint] Why?

Peter: Barbara, who's in charge here?

EVP: [Same female] Benny is.

A tour of the second-floor auditorium turned up some occasional sounds that resembled disembodied voices or dull thumps in seeming response to questioning, but we attributed all of these to natural settling noises of the building and slamming of car doors outside.

We went back to the ground floor via the emergency stairwell, where we had experienced a pair of incidents during the last visit. I thought I heard the jingle of a small chain as we descended, so the team stood still to listen. "Can you do that again, please?" I asked.

EVP: [Male] Hi.

~

Before stepping outside for a break, James left a digital recorder inside the front vestibule. David activated an HD GoPro camera and aimed it across the lobby while I positioned a recorder on a chair near the staircase and paired it with an activated Gauss meter.

Within minutes of the team's absence and throughout the duration of the break, a series of knocks, thuds, snaps and taps erupted from the south-end of the lobby. As was the case with so many other town hall visits on our tour, none of this same activity ever occurred while an investigator was present.

～

After the break, I placed the E. Probe 2.0 alarm next to my recorder in the lobby and James moved his recorder into the former council chamber. As the team descended the steps to the basement and our footfalls receded, the lobby recorder captured the telltale sound of rustling fabric, followed by a distinct impact nearby. A few minutes after the team had entered the bookstore at the north end of the building, this same device captured the following exchange.

EVP: [Male] Henry!
EVP: [Male; annoyed] What do you want?

During our time in the bookstore, more wooden-sounding knocks, raps and taps—even distant stumbling footfalls—were recorded. No sooner did the stumbling cease than a light impact accompanied by a single (almost cautious-sounding) knock occurred very close to the recorder. Then a noise from downstairs indicating the approach of James and David seemed to inspire two more rapid-fire knocks, as if someone wanted to get some more playful drumming in before the team returned to the main floor.

As I conducted a solo communication session inside the bookstore and James and David stepped outside for a break, the lobby recorder caught a question.

EVP: [Unknown gender; extremely faint] [How] 'bout this?

The very next second, the recorder picked up a huge crash—resembling a set of doors being slammed together or a heavy object falling on the floor—that must have resounded throughout the lobby. None of us heard it from our respective positions in the basement and outside.

I returned upstairs from an unsuccessful EVP session, then volunteered to remain behind while James and David left to pick up dinner.

~

I activated the E. Probe 1.0 and placed it on the floor of the front vestibule, then returned briefly to the basement with a digital recorder and a second proximity alarm. I left them running in tandem inside the room believed to have been a holding cell. Then I returned upstairs and continued to the auditorium.

I sat quietly in a chair in the middle of the auditorium to conduct a pendulum session. I had placed a digital recorder on the newel post of the staircase leading up to the seats, pointing toward the stage and me.

A series of standard questions received no responses of any kind through the pendulum. The need to reach the spirit named Mary was essential to this visit, and time was running out. "Is there someone named Mary here?" I asked, trying again.

A loud rap erupted from the stage area. "Come on in," I offered, congenially.

Another rap sounding even farther away was caught by the recorder, but I did not hear it in the moment. I continued to use the pendulum for several minutes, calling upon Mary in particular, but received no responses.

I closed my eyes and relaxed, trying to clear my mind and induce meditation in an attempt to be receptive to any activity around me. A vehicle passed by outside. Then the nearby recorder captured a voice…

EVP: [Female; vague, sing-song lilt] All here!

…followed first by a distinct, sharp snap from somewhere in the auditorium, then a short nasal exhale in the vicinity of the recorder. From downstairs came the sound of four faint, unmistakable footfalls.

Finally, I broke my silence and the recorder caught the results. "Henry?" I asked. The muffled sounds of a howling dog outside replied.

"Dan?" I continued, "When you were in the physical…" I paused to formulate my question but also to let the words I'd just spoken register with whoever was listening to me. Instead the recorder picked up the female again.

EVP: [Female] [Nondescript singing, lasting four seconds]

I asked several more questions addressing Mary, Barbara and Danny, inquiring into their interrelationships and surnames, and I even asked Mary to sing part of her favourite song—unaware that my recorder had captured singing a minute or two beforehand. Disappointed that no one seemed to be trying to communicate, I offered another opportunity to use the pendulum and asked after Reginald and Emily. Again, no response.

I left the auditorium for the main floor and settled on the bottom landing to try another pendulum session, asking after Henry. I stopped the pendulum session short when no movement seemed forthcoming, but I continued asking questions aloud until James and David arrived with take-out dinner. At that point I moved back to base camp to join them

Over the dinner hour, some subtle ticks and natural settling sounds were captured on the recorder in the basement cell, as well as a single soft tap on the box surface under it. A sharp snap suggested movement in the vicinity of the recorder, but the proximity alarm was never tripped.

Around the same time inside the council chamber, one of James' digital recorders captured a whisper.

EVP: [Male; whispering] James.

Upstairs in the auditorium, another of James' recorders captured another obscure disembodied voice.

EVP: [Male; slight echo] Hey, ball hamer. [Phonetic interpretation]

Approximately three minutes later, the familiar rhythm of a heartbeat was captured, lasting just short of two minutes. [This sound was later analyzed by a qualified paramedic who confirmed it was an irregular heartbeat belonging to someone experiencing a Type 1 blockage.]

Meanwhile, I had invited Lindsay to speak into a digital recorder in the kitchen before I sat down with the others for dinner in the adjacent boardroom. About 40 minutes later, the recorder captured a brief response to a snippet of our conversation.

"Yeah, it's not the speed that kills—it's the sudden stop," I joked.

"That's right," smiled David.

EVP: [Female; immediate, amused] Mm.

It was subtle, but it sounded very close to the recorder.

Then as we were discussing the nature of ectoplasm, a loud impact and bounce erupted from somewhere in the kitchen (resembling a package of paper towels being thrown hard against a wall, then dropping), but none of us at the nearby table heard it in the moment.

A few minutes later, during a lull in the conversation, a loud knock rang out from inside the kitchen, but again, no one heard it in the moment.

Shortly after 8:00 PM, David and James stepped outside while I went to the restroom. As the kitchen recorder caught the last of my footfalls fading away in the distance, a male voice (resembling David's in timbre) spoke up.

EVP: [Youthful-sounding male; distant] Boo!
EVP: [Female; extremely faint] I'm having a grand [entrance].
EVP: [Same male; louder] Hoo!

After a couple of seconds of ambient silence, there was a short, distinct tap very close to the recorder, followed by a louder, "thicker" rap—again, very close to the recorder. Minutes later, James and David returned, and we resumed investigating the main floor.

James retired to the council chamber to try to reconnect with Reginald, the alleged Scottish-born military man who Michele claimed to contact during our first investigation.

Placing a chair inside the front vestibule, David took a seat in view of his GoPro camera and attempted to establish communication using a pendulum. He appeared to be receiving some confused responses as the pendulum bobbed about in aimless directions, so he suggested that I retrieve some EM pumps to provide a source of electromagnetic energy that the spirit(s) might draw from in order to make their manifestation stronger. After 10 minutes, still no sense could be made of the pendulum movements David received.

I joined James inside the former council chamber and commented on the recently purchased ultraviolet/infrared camera system he was using. "This is set for low light, right?" I asked.

James nodded.

EVP: [Female] Nae.

After I left to rejoin David, James also activated an EM pump and proceeded to ask questions. He received but one response; when he asked, "Who is here with me right now?" someone answered.

EVP: [Male] Tony.

While the stronger, louder of the EM pumps (nicknamed Taz) was in full swing in the lobby, a sudden knock sounded very near the recorder inside the kitchen, followed soon after by a secondary/settling knock, not as loud as the first.

Unaware of the percussive activity, I retrieved the recorder from the kitchen, and as I opened the door leading to the basement stairs, it captured a disembodied voice that sounded as if it was spoken in a vacuum.

EVP: [Male; shouting] Yup!

Down in the basement, David and James conducted an EVP session in the bookstore while I activated the Spirit Box in the small room rumoured to have been used as a holding cell at the opposite end of the building.

Peter: Who's with me right now?
Spirit Box: [Male; clear] That's Jackson!
Peter: Jackson?

Some choppy, loud gibberish continued for several seconds, so I changed the sweep band to FM and found pure white noise. I began again.

Peter: Hello, is anybody with me right now?
Spirit Box: [Older female] Go ahead, hon.
Peter: Hello, ma'am. I think I heard your voice. What's your name, please?
Spirit Box: [Younger female] Enid Cleff.

Peter: Is Emily down here somewhere?

Spirit Box: [Male; extremely deep voice] Could be.

Peter: Is there somebody named Annie here? Annie?

Spirit Box: [Unknown gender] Careful.

Peter: Would you like us to leave?

Spirit Box: [Young female; faint] Papa!

Peter: Is there a little girl named Emily here in the basement?

Spirit Box: [Female; tentative-sounding] Yeah.

Peter: Yes?

Spirit Box: [Unknown gender] Uh-huh.

Peter: What's Emily's surname, please? Please use as much energy as you can muster.…Please be truthful; are you afraid of going into the light?

Spirit Box: [Female] Well…

Peter: Mary, are you here? Mary Ferrin, please speak to me.

Spirit Box: [Female; quickly] Spare bed.

Peter: Hi Mary! Is someone trying to stop you from speaking?

Spirit Box: [Male; super-fast] Go.

Spirit Box: [Female; clear] Michael?

Without warning I deactivated the Spirit Box, plunging the room into complete silence. I didn't observe any reactions, so I proceeded to ask more questions: of Mary, for Henry's surname, of Harold Fitzgerald and whoever might be in the bookstore. No EVP responses were recorded.

David and James, having had no luck with their bookstore EVP session, proceeded to the auditorium. I entered the bookstore alone to continue communication attempts using the Spirit Box.

Peter: Hello?

Spirit Box: [Female] Hi!

Peter: Hi! How are you?

Spirit Box: [Female] Fine.

Peter: You're fine? Do you remember me?

Spirit Box: [Female] Yes, we...see.

Spirit Box: [Female; quiet, fast] We need help.

Spirit Box: [Female] We need help?

Peter: Emily, are you here? Who's here with me right now? Please say your name clearly.

Spirit Box: [Female; distant] Talk! They'll hear talk!

Spirit Box: [Male] Embarrassing.

Peter: Who am I speaking with?

Spirit Box: [Female] Debbie.

Peter: I thought I heard a woman's voice. Can you say your name again, please? Ma'am?

Spirit Box: [Unknown gender] Close the do[or].

Spirit Box: [Male] Help me.

Peter: Do you have any questions for me?

EVP: [Female] Huh. I don't have one.

Peter: What's Henry's last name, please?

Spirit Box: [Female] Tell them.

Spirit Box: [Female] No, you!

Spirit Box: [Male; whispering] Jameson.

Peter: What's Danny's last name?

Spirit Box: [Female; deep under static] Stop it.

Spirit Box: [Female] Go away.

Peter: Is Mary Ferrin here with me? Am I all alone down here? Nobody wants to speak with me? Wow. I was hoping to speak to Emily.

Spirit Box: [Male] Uh-huh.

Peter: Yes, Emily. I'm sorry, I don't know Emily's last name. Can somebody tell me what her last name is, please?

Spirit Box: [Young male] Infidel.

Peter: Does Emily live here or just visit?

Spirit Box: [Unknown gender] Good bye.

Again I deactivated the Spirit Box abruptly, in case a stray EVP might be caught as the room became silent again. Hearing no responses to my presence, I turned the store lights off and exited.

～

Meanwhile, in the auditorium, David and James had taken up a position on the stairs leading to the upper seats. "So, is there anyone up here with us?" James asked.

EVP: [Female or child] Me.

They asked several more questions over a 30-minute period, but apart from the occasional tick coming from the stage area, they detected no discernible responses.

As James and David stepped outside for a break, I returned to the auditorium to perform another solo Spirit Box session in an attempt contact Mary. Simply activating the device seemed to result in a reaction.

Spirit Box: [Female] Ahhh!

Peter: Hello!

Spirit Box: [Same female] Please…stop!

Spirit Box: [Male] [Radio blurt that resembled agreement]

Spirit Box: [Same female] Um…

Spirit Box: [Male] He's the [indistinguishable].

Peter: Is Mary Ferrin with me right now?

Spirit Box: [Male; matter-of-fact] Yup.

Spirit Box: [Male; British accent, warning] Watch it!

Peter: I heard a man say yes. Who are you, sir?

Spirit Box: [Female; jovial] That's Sentally!

Spirit Box: [Unknown gender] You're the one…Henry.

Spirit Box: [Female voice composed of overlapping sounds] You're a sh*t!

Peter: I want to speak with Mary; is she here, please?

An indiscernible cacophony of radio voices overlapped each other.

Peter: Do you remember me from about a year ago?
Spirit Box: [Female] Hello!
Peter: Who's here with me right now?
Spirit Box: [Female; deep under other voices] This is silly. Stop it.
Peter: Who's here with me right now?
Spirit Box: [Female] Whatever!
Peter: I want to speak with Mary Ferrin only.
Spirit Box: [Female; cheerful] She's here!
Peter: Mary, are you from Waterford?
Spirit Box: [Female] Michael?
Spirit Box: [Unknown gender; amiable] Peter!
Peter: Mary? How old are you, please?
Spirit Box: [Female; distant] -nine. [The first word was cut off]
Spirit Box: [Female] Stop it!
Spirit Box: [Older female] You're helping.
Spirit Box: [Young female] Stop…him!
Peter: Mary? How old were you when your body died? Who else is in the room with me right now? What's your name, please? Full name.
Spirit Box: [Female] I a[m].
Spirit Box: [Male] Raym— [Name was cut short]
Spirit Box: [Female; panicked] Raymond!
Spirit Box: [Female; static-filled] Raymond.
Spirit Box: [Female; loud] Hello!
Spirit Box: [Male; quiet but clear] Raymond.
Spirit Box: [Unknown gender] That's your name.

Although I did not consciously hear the many references to Raymond coming from the Spirit Box in the moment—the voices come in so fast—I did recall that his name came up during analysis of the last investigation's data, so I decided to inquire about him.

Peter: Raymond! Is there somebody named Raymond here?

Spirit Box: [Female] Can't get it.

Peter: Raymond, can you tell me Henry's last name, please? Quickly?

Spirit Box: [Electronic-sounding; teasing] I know!

Spirit Box: [Older female] Why?

Peter: Why? I want to know who Henry is and I need his full name, please.

Spirit Box: [Male; casual] Hang on… [This was akin to, "Gimme a sec and I'll tell you."]

Peter: What is it, please?

Spirit Box: [Male; faint] Uh.

Spirit Box: [Female] [Want] a full name.

Spirit Box: [Female] Forget it.

Spirit Box: [Female] You're aaallll a joke.

Spirit Box: [Unknown gender] Who are you?

Peter: Is Henry the one in charge of the guys downstairs?

Spirit Box: [Male; deep voice, gruff] Wha[t]?

Spirit Box: [Male; angry, very deep audio level] Bridget! I'm gonna beat you!

Spirit Box: [Female; British accent, sing-song, taunting] That's your father!

Peter: What's the name of the dark-haired girl in the lobby?

Spirit Box: [Unknown gender] Bridget!

Spirit Box: [Unknown gender; gravelly-voiced] Talia.

Spirit Box: [Unknown genders; mix of voices] …wants the girl!

Spirit Box: [Male; clear] Four-year-old.

Spirit Box: [Female; faint] Dave!

I deactivated the Spirit Box and proceeded to ask EVP-provoking questions using the pendulum one final time, but I received no responses.

I then asked about the nature of death. "What is death like? Do you feel free outside of the body?"

Two seconds later, a single wooden knock resonated from far away—likely from the safety of the very back of the stage.

"Is that a yes?" I asked, though silence seemed to be my reply. "Are you able to move anywhere you wish, outside of the body?"

EVP: [Female; extremely faint] Some of us!
EVP: [Male] Luke…

I did not perceive these voices in the moment, but I proceeded to ask more questions. After waiting a few more seconds in silence, I walked toward the light switch panel for the auditorium.

EVP: [Male; whispering] Man!

I turned the lights off and continued the session. "Are you afraid of the light? Are you afraid I won't be able to see you manifest with the light on? You don't have that much power, do you? Would you like to use some of my energy to play the piano? Can you touch one of my hands, please? Take some energy and use that to play the piano? [Silence] Wow, I'm amazed. I really am."

EVP: [Male; faint, casual] F**k you.

Turning the auditorium lights on again, I offered to play a game using a rubber ball. I tossed it up the stairs, where it disappeared among the seats. When no one rolled it back (a la *The Changeling*), I retrieved it myself. As I returned to the floor of the auditorium, the shrill alarm of the E. Probe 1.0 began blaring from inside the front vestibule, downstairs.

I left the auditorium to investigate and found David and James standing frozen several metres away from the vestibule, nowhere close to the alarm.

Approximately 45 seconds after I stopped the alarm, the recorder left behind upstairs in the auditorium captured a quiet rubber-like squeak or water-drip sound that erupted from somewhere in the room. Twelve seconds later, a second squeak was caught. Four seconds after that...

EVP: [Male; whispering, slightly raspy] A**hole!

Meanwhile in the main lobby, David and James shared with me that while they were outside on break, both had spotted a shadowy figure cross the length of the lobby southward toward the boardroom.

Our time was up. I returned to the auditorium to collect the equipment, thanked the spirits who participated and left the second floor after turning the lights off.

Jennifer arrived to make sure all was well before arming and securing the building behind us. We exited the Waterford Old Town Hall shortly after 10:00 PM without further incident.

Afterthoughts

The primary goal for this third visit to the Waterford Old Town Hall was to try to tie up loose ends and accumulate as many surnames as we could to help identify those who repeatedly made it clear they are choosing to occupy the premises for undetermined personal reasons. Just as importantly, we wished to re-establish contact with the female spirit who identified herself as Mary Ferrin the previous year. It seemed she was eager to begin speaking just as the team was winding up the last investigation, so this time we wanted to glean as much information as possible from her.

One of the many things we have learned over the course of our work is that the concept of time differs between our side of the veil and the dimension(s) ghosts occupy. For one thing, our studies have not indicated at this point if the length of time between investigations factors significantly into communication opportunities (or clarity). We cannot say whether the faint responses by the female identifying herself as Mary on this trip had anything to do with her personal energy levels (do they weaken over time?) or whether her responses were purposely being suppressed by other spirit people trying to throw us off the scent. We have encountered "alpha" ghosts several times over the years, and some of the conversations overheard using the Spirit Box confirmed the presence of a social hierarchy at this historic location.

Unfortunately, thorough research on Mary Ferrin turned up only someone who passed away in Quebec in 1878. At least 53 other people named Mary Ferrin have been interred through-out the United States between 1827 and 2009. It is possible our Mary could be one of these people, but lack of time (on *our* side of the veil) and resources stymied further mining for information.

Similarly, nine people named Raymond are interred at Waterford's Greenwood cemetery out of 91 people named Raymond buried throughout Norfolk County. Without our Raymond's surname, finding a connection in history to the male speaking to us in the auditorium is next to impossible.

We also researched Henry Jameson and Enid Cleff, but no one by those names is interred anywhere in all of Norfolk County, let alone within Waterford town limits.

Sometimes we are fortunate and receive desired answers, but this time, we simply amassed still more confirmation that we were not alone inside the Waterford Old Town Hall.

At Tour's End:
Reflecting on the Experience

There are things that I said and did that I could regret,
but, on this side, we soon learn to have no regrets. Life
would be meaningless if we did not all make mistakes, and
eternity intolerable if we spent it regretting them.
    –William Lyon Mackenzie King's ghost (as reported by
            Percy J. Philip), *Fate Magazine*, October 1955

W e arrive now at the conclusion of this two-and-a-
half-year-long chapter in The Searcher Group's
after-hours adventures. We meet a lot of wonderful
people (on both sides of the veil) doing this kind of work, and
I hope those who have crossed our path have enjoyed experiencing even a modicum of what we do in our efforts to find answers
to ongoing living after physical death.

We tend to leave any location we investigate with more
questions than answers. However, very rarely, we do glimpse or
obtain some shred of information that aids us in our quest, and
this is why we persist—we never know where or when the clues
will surface next.

The Searcher Group reaches many people and shares many
of its unpublished findings while hosting special presentations,

often giving back to the community by raising money for charities. After each presentation, we open the floor to questions from our supporters, and believe me, there have been many. But one question has never been posed, though it's one I have asked myself: what should I take away from all this information?

This query is subjective, but if I am ever asked, based on what we have learned so far, my answer would be this: no matter what your belief system is in this world, life energy survives past the expiration of the body, and that energy—commonly called the Soul—maintains emotion and all of the memories it has gained from one physical lifetime experience to the next, regardless of the length of stay. Once outside of the physical body, we are faced with choice. That choice is either to move forward and continue the cycle of learning-by-experience, or to stay behind, straddling realities/frequencies.

Ninety-eight percent of the spirits paranormal investigators encounter are souls that have made the latter choice. Whatever their reason—whether they feel they have unfinished business, something to hide or simply do not realize that they're living outside of their body—these souls vibrate at a frequency closest to our own range of perception, and this is why we perceive them the most.

So at the risk of sounding like a spacey, philosophical, New Age inspirational love guru, perhaps the ultimate take-away is this: to avoid becoming a miserable, fearful, misunderstood ghost of your former physical self, try to live your physical life with as much warmth, laughter, compassion and love as possible; appreciate every gift of knowledge (good and bad) this reality has to offer, and above all, regret nothing (good or bad).

Otherwise, prepare for a visit by The Searcher Group.

Yours in great spirits,

Peter

Notes on Sources

~

Listed here are various resource materials that aided with "fleshing out" some of the mysteries behind those who are no longer "of the flesh." I am sincerely indebted to the historians and librarians who pointed the way to many of these discoveries.

Acton
Acton Free Press. "Acton Contingent Entrained on Monday."
August 20, 1914.
———. "Obituary: Robertson." October 27, 1960.
———. "Robertson, Riley and Douglas." May 6, 1915.
———. "Town Hall Here Damaged in Early Morning Fire."
December 20, 1945.
———. "Twenty Years Ago." August 16, 1934.
———. "Volunteers Enlisting Here." August 13, 1914.
Acton Town Hall Centre: http://www.actontownhallcentre.ca/.
Rowe, John Mark Benbow. *Acton: The History of Leathertown*.
Acton: Esquesing Historical Society, 2002.
Toronto Star. "Toronto-area paranormal investigators seek ghost hunter." August 29, 2012.

Waterford
Brown, Sarah, David Judd and Christopher Blythe. *Townsend and Waterford: A Double Portrait*. Waterford & Townsend Historical Society, 1977.
Old Town Hall Association: http://oldtownhall.org/.
Waterford Star. "Old Boys' Reunion." June 28, 1906.

Stouffville

Stouffville Tribune. "Auditorium Theatre CLOSED." July 2, 1931.

———. "Bowling Alley Robbery Solved." January 8, 1931.

———. "Council Buys Park Theatre Will Convert to Mun. Office." May 7, 1959.

———. "Ends Long Career as Theatre Projectionist at Local Cinema." May 21, 1959.

———. "If Stouffville is to be denied the amusement…" December 3, 1931.

———. "Messrs Green & Co. Are opening up an up-to-date garage…" March 30, 1922.

———. "New 'Talkie' Theatre Opens This Thursday." July 13, 1933.

———. "Park Theatre Opens Saturday." December 5, 1957.

———. "Sunday Service In Theatre." May 14, 1959.

———. "Sidney Schmidt Theatre Owner Thirty Years." February 10, 1966.

———. "Theatre Building is Making Headway." May 4, 1933.

———. "Theatre Building Sold to Two Local Businessmen." February 28, 1957.

———. "Theatre Mgr. Marks 17th Year Here." October 10, 1940.

———. "The old picture theatre over the bowling alley…" November 19, 1931.

———. "Work Started on Talkie Theatre." March 16, 1933.

———. "Work Starts On Municipal Building." October 22, 1959.

Caledon

Allengame, Diane. *Criteria for Preservation: Caledon Village (Township Hall)*. Town of Caledon Heritage Committee, 1981.

Caledon Townhall Players: www.caledontownhallplayers.com.

Orangeville

Citizen Canada. "Orangeville Town Hall A Spooky Place?" March 19, 2009.

Museum of Dufferin: https://dufferinmuseum.com/.

Orangeville Banner. "Obituary: Arthur Joseph Williams." November 6, 1969.

————. "Orangeville booster retires from heart of town affairs." March 30, 1984.

Toronto

Ancestry.ca: http://search.ancestrylibrary.com/search/group/canadiancensus.

Bell, Bruce. *Amazing Tales of St. Lawrence Neighbourhood,* Toronto: Community Bulletin Newspaper Group Inc., 2001.

Globe (Toronto). "Gaol Inspection." April 22, 1852.

————. "Police Court: Robbery in St. Lawrence Market." November 8, 1882.

————. "The Gaol." March 3, 1853.

Globe and Mail. "Coroner Johnson yesterday held an inquest at the jail…" September 16, 1899.

Toronto Daily Star. "Stephen McClaren of 107 Bolton Avenue…" April 18, 1921.

About the Author

~

Peter has maintained a keen interest in life-after-death research since he was knee-high to an orb, reading every book his local library had to offer on ghosts and daydreaming of visiting the locations described within. Inspired by his first ghost tour, the advent of paranormal-based television and the real-life investigations published by Richard Palmisano, he was welcomed into The Searcher Group in 2010. Peter's passion and dedication to the team earned him the appointment of Assistant Director shortly thereafter, and he now leads the volunteer company's inaugural subdivision, Mortal Coil Paranormal, serving the Greater Toronto Area and southwestern Ontario. *Haunted Town Halls* is his first book on the paranormal.

Peter can be reached at mortalcoilparanormal@gmail.com.

~